The
Green
Felt
Jungle

The Green Felt Jungle

Ed Reid/Ovid Demaris

TRIDENT PRESS • NEW YORK • 1963

TO THE POLICE OFFICIALS, CRIME REPORTERS, AND
SYMPATHETIC INFORMANTS WHO LEVELED WITH US,
AND IN MEMORY OF UNITED STATES SENATOR
ESTES KEFAUVER, WHO HAD THE COURAGE AND
THE CONVICTION TO PROBE THE DEPTHS OF CRIME
AND CORRUPTION IN OUR SOCIETY.

AUTHORS' NOTE

This book is the result of two years of exhaustive research during which we talked to officials and reporters and informants in Seattle, San Francisco, Los Angeles, San Diego, Tucson, Phoenix, Dallas, Houston, New Orleans, Minneapolis, Cleveland, Reno, Carson City, Detroit, Chicago, New York, Newark, and Miami.

It might seem odd that we should have had to range so far afield for material for a book on Las Vegas, which, after all, is more than 2,000 miles from New York and almost as far from Miami and Detroit. What, you may wonder, ties Las Vegas to these distant cities, besides airline connections?

That is a question of reverberating implications—a question which is answered for the first time in the following pages.

ED REID
OVID DEMARIS
August, 1963

CONTENTS

CONTENTS

CHAPTER ONE

Where's the Action?

Las Vegas is a city in statistics only. In every other respect, it is a jungle—a jungle of green-felt crap tables, roulette layouts, and slot machines in which the entire population, directly or indirectly, is devoted to fleecing tourists. There were twelve million of these in 1962 (seventeen million in the state), and the number has been increasing each year. They come to gamble or to have a fling or out of curiosity, and Las Vegas embraces them all, eager to satisfy their craving for gambling—or any vice—with a flourish not seen since Cecil B. De Mille's last Roman spectacle.

The city itself looks like a grotesque Disneyland. Its growth has been horizontal, along the lines of Florida and southern California, especially Los Angeles (which provides 80 per cent of its sucker trade). An aerial view would reveal an accumulation of shopping centers, tract houses, garish casinos downtown on Fremont Street (known as Glitter Gulch), and sprawling hotel–casinos along the Strip, where the architecture follows two popular styles: "Ranch Rococo" or "Miami Baroque."

There are eleven Strip luxury hotel–casinos, or "carpet joints" —Tropicana, Flamingo, Sands, Desert Inn, Riviera, Thunderbird, Sahara, Stardust, New Frontier, Dunes, and Hacienda. Each one is subtly constructed to keep the player's attention on the business at hand: gambling. Within the casino, the gambler is protected from secular distractions. There are no clocks on the walls to point out the time, no windows or doors in the vast, brightly lighted room to inadvertently reveal the position of the sun or moon. There is only the cacophony of the *action* which imbues the gambler with a sense of eternal life. In the casino there is no place to rest, no chair or couch to relieve the fatigue —except before the various green felt tables.

Status in the jungle is determined by the size of a player's bankroll. A high roller achieves the ultimate station. He may possess anything—or anyone—he covets. Most high rollers are known to the fraternity, and each new one arrives with introductions from impeccable sources. During his stay, hieroglyphics are secretly appended to his name on the hotel register, which catalogue him as a "dropper" (businessman and heavy loser), "producer" (businessman), or "nonproducer" (professional gambler). The hieroglyphics increase as pit bosses, bellhops, maids, cocktail waitresses, deputies, and plain-clothes dicks add their own observations—"generous when drunk or in a winning streak," "whorer," "lush," "grind," and other enlightening data —an analysis of which determines his status.

As comedians will tell you, there are only three things a visitor can do in Las Vegas, and two of them are drinking and gambling. In the daytime on hot summer days you can lie on blistering tiles beside a turquoise pool, or you can cavort in the pool with a couple of busty movie stars. But the management knows that sooner or later you must pick up your cigarettes, slip your feet into thongs, and paddle into the sanctuary for a little action. Damp bathing trunks are quite proper if you have money to risk.

At night, except for a brief (from an hour to an hour and a quarter) floor show, there is no place to go but the casino. You can, of course, wander from casino to casino, but unless you use a cab, the parking problem will soon discourage that idea. If you like to dance, there's a postage-size spot called the Starlight Room upstairs in the Desert Inn. Otherwise, you will have to confine your dancing to your own room. There are the lounge shows adjoining the casino in every hotel, but they are noisy and crude, and the drinks are watery and the cocktail waitresses keep them coming (at standard prices). The chuck-wagon dinners are reasonably priced, and you can eat all you want, but the chefs have a way of scowling at ravenous guests who come for second helpings.

Unless you are addicted to gambling, drinking, or fornication, the Las Vegas action soon becomes a bore, and most sensible guests find themselves getting restless after two or three days and are ready to call it quits and go home. The gamblers stay until they go broke.

The go-brokes instantly become lepers. There is no place for them in Las Vegas. Even permanent residents (many who were there before the hoodlums) are told to move on, to get out of town; and when they refuse to leave, they may, after endless red tape, receive a few dollars for food, never more than twenty a month. Nonresidents are summarily banished on sight—threatened with incarceration if they are not out by a certain time. Where families are involved, the law will provide a bus ticket that deposits the indigents just over the state line—or if they have a car, just enough gas to get them out of the state. Tears are never shed by the hardheaded casino owners over a loser; tears are reserved for the rare winners.

The commercial center of Las Vegas is Glitter Gulch, the two blocks of Fremont Street which comprise the most concentrated gambling complex in the world. The casinos here are sawdust joints—loud and gaudy but without the fancy trappings of the Strip hotels. (Both are alike in that once you see one, you've seen them all.) Besides the usual Strip games of craps, roulette and blackjack, there is poker, chuck-a-luck, faro, bingo, keno, and literally thousands of slot machines (the Mint has six hundred one-armed bandits and handles a daily bankroll of over $600,000).

The action is fast and dedicated here. The floors are hard, the whiskey is straight, the cigar smoke is thick, and the players are tight-lipped. This is where most Nevadans gamble: cowboys, sheepherders, miners, store clerks, factory workers, cab drivers, brassy show girls, pensioners, and little old ladies who play four machines at once for hours on end, wear a workman's glove, and look like they have just eaten their young.

Some of the names of the sawdust joints are as direct as their actions: Golden Nugget, Horseshoe, Golden Gate, Monte Carlo, Lucky Strike, Pioneer, Mint, and, of course, Jackpot. Sandwiched in with the clubs in Glitter Gulch is a Western Union office, which like everything else in Las Vegas is open around the clock, and does the largest money-order business in the world.

A century ago, Mark Twain journeyed through Nevada, which he described as "the most rocky, wintry, repulsive wastes that our country or any other can exhibit." "In Nevada," he wrote, in his book *Roughing It,* "the lawyer, the editor, the banker, the chief desperado, the chief gambler, and the saloon-

4

keeper occupied the same level of society, and it was the highest. The cheapest and easiest way to become an influential man, and be looked up to by the community at large, was to stand behind a bar, wear a cluster-diamond stickpin, and sell whiskey. . . . [The saloonkeeper's] opinion had weight. It was his privilege to say how the elections should go. No great movement could succeed without the countenance and direction of the saloonkeepers. . . . To be a saloonkeeper and kill a man was to be illustrious."

Not much has changed since Mark Twain's sojourn. The structure of Nevadan society has remained intact—only the characters and décor have changed. The barrel-chested saloonkeeper with the handle-bar mustache has been replaced by the silk-suited, pock-marked, thick-lipped hoodlum from the East, the South, the Midwest and the Far West; diamond stickpins have been supplanted by sparkling pinkie rings. As for murder, there's a lot of desert between here and Los Angeles, and not all of it is completely barren. In the words of one Las Vegas wag: "That's the old elephant burial grounds, buddy, where all good little torpedoes come to die."

There are eighty-one places of worship in Las Vegas, but there is only one true god—*money.* In Las Vegas, money *is* at the root of all evil, legal or illegal. You name it, and if you can pay for it, you can have it—pronto.

Nevada Governor Grant Sawyer puts it differently. Reclining on a chaise longue beside the turquoise waters of the Flamingo swimming pool, his youthful face creased by a pleasant grin, he says: "Our attitude toward life, save under the most urgent provocation, is relaxed, tolerant, and mindful that if others are allowed to go on their way unmolested, a man stands a chance of getting through the world himself with a minimum of irritation."

The Governor is (as the saying goes in Las Vegas) a thousand per cent correct. It is a live-and-let-live society. That is, you let the hoods live the way they want to live and maybe they'll let you live. There is no question about it. The town belongs to the Mob. They have nearly $250 million invested in Vegas alone (estimated to reach $300 million by the end of 1963—skyscraper additions will provide five thousand more rooms). Nobody is about to take it away from them.

The hoods are careful to maintain a respectable front. Today's saloonkeeper is a businessman, a sports fan, a civic leader, a pillar of the church; he surrounds himself with lawyers, tax accountants, and public-relations experts. Carl Cohen, an old Cleveland gambler and now a vice-president at the Sands, has been in Las Vegas for twenty years. One of his sons graduated from UCLA and now works as a producer–director–actor in his own theater in Los Angeles, and the other graduated *cum laude* from Brandeis and is presently studying medicine in New York. "I came to Vegas with all I had to my name," Cohen says, "a thorough background in gambling. I don't mind saying I was one of the best dice dealers in America." Smiling now, Cohen uses a couple of carefully prepared ad libs. "We're carrying on a tradition of the old West. Bret Harte, Tex Rickard, all the pioneers were gamblers, you know. Read Mark Twain."

Everybody in Las Vegas talks this way.

Sheriff Ralph Lamb, a Mormon, says: "As far as I know, everyone in the gambling business out here always has been a gentleman. Maybe they got caught elsewhere doing the same thing they do here legitimately, but that don't make them wrong, just the laws where they come from."

Rev. Welles Miller, pastor of the Las Vegas Community Church, believes that "a man or woman who gets into trouble through gambling in Las Vegas would also be getting into trouble through gambling in some form anywhere in this world. Basically these individuals are compulsive gamblers led by a strong desire to get something for nothing." Rev. Miller's religio-psychological viewpoint on moral issues is very popular with the Mob.

Very few ministers are hardy enough for an all-out war against organized sin. "What can I do about it?" asked Rev. Dr. Donald O'Connor, former pastor of the First Methodist Church of Las Vegas. "I'll tell you: nothing."

Some Catholic priests have important connections inside the casinos who flash them tips on big winners so they can make their pitch for donations ahead of the other churches.

For three years, the Rev. Richard Anthony Crowley conducted a 4:30 A.M. mass for show people, croupiers, and baggy-eyed tourists in the Crown Room of the Stardust Auditorium (formerly Royal Nevada Hotel), within the shadow of a marquee advertising a nude Parisienne review. "After all," said the broad-minded priest, "there was gambling for the Robe at the foot of the Cross."

Father Crowley recently was reassigned by his superiors. An ad in the Las Vegas *Review–Journal* read:

FATHER CROWLEY'S LOSS IS YOUR GAIN
1961 Mercedes-Benz 190 SL, air-conditioned. This car is only 3 months old. Save $1,350.

The $6,850 white sports car with green leather upholstery had been a gift from an anonymous benefactor. Chagrined at his leaving, the gambling fraternity threw Father Crowley a farewell party in the new Convention Center. It was attended by nine thousand guests, who were entertained by sixty-four acts, including acrobats, show girls, and comics. Father Crowley shook hands all around, soft-shoed with a bowler hat and sang "Harrigan, That's Me." The bash began at 9 P.M. and ended at 3:30 A.M., with the crowd singing "God Bless America."

To the twelve million tourists who flung more than $3 billion across the gaming tables in 1962, Las Vegas is an air-conditioned oasis shimmering in the desert heat. But what are a tourist's real chances of hitting it big? Old-timers have a number of wry answers to this question, such as "The surest way to beat Las Vegas is to get off the plane that has taken you there and walk straight into the propeller."

There are plenty of stories about men who made fortunes, but few ever leave town with more money than they brought in. More typical are the tourists who find themselves broke and stranded, the players who arrive in an $8,000 automobile and leave in one worth about $55,000—a Greyhound bus. The pawnshops do a lively business. It is not unusual to see a man walk into a pawnshop and try to hock his eyeglasses. Fortunately, there is a limit even in Las Vegas. A state law prevents pawnshops from loaning money on devices essential to health, such as glasses, hearing aids, and false teeth.

And if a player has a system, a *foolproof* system—they will send a limousine to meet him at the airport! Las Vegas gamblers have a tender spot in their hard-case hearts for brainy people with systems.

But assuming a player is very lucky and he really cleans up, what then? He becomes the most pampered tourist in town. If he's half as smart as he's lucky, he'll pack his winnings and his clothes and take the next plane out, because from the moment he grabs that brass ring, the merry-go-round never stops. He will be moved bodily, compliments of the house, into a plush suite with king-size bed and balcony overlooking the pool area. (The odds are five to eight that there will be a one-way mirror and a half-dozen well planted microphones to record his every word.) If the lucky winner is alone, a king-size kewpie doll will be added to the house's tab. Most likely she will be a show girl, and the lucky winner can watch her prance alfresco across the footlights from his ringside table. Later he can lay her down on his king-size bed and playfully undress her while she bats her false eyelashes.

A motor cruiser on Lake Mead will be placed at his disposal, but chances are he'll never see Boulder Dam. Kewpie doll will lead him back to the gaming tables, where a common fate awaits him. No matter how lucky a player is, there is a mathematics governing gambling that is as irrefutable as the law of gravity. The house takes a percentage of every dollar that is put down on a gambling table. The percentage may vary from hour to hour, but in the long run it averages out to 1.41 per cent on craps, 5.9 per cent on blackjack, 5.19 to 7 17/19 per cent on roulette, and anywhere from 17 per cent and up on slot machines, depending on how tightly the screw has been set. Therefore, the longer a player remains at the tables, the better are the house's chances of taking his money. Given enough time, any player will have to borrow money to get out of town.

A local psychologist, Dr. Sidney Saltzman, has made a study of the tourist. "A tourist who comes to Las Vegas is fulfilling the wish to regress. He allows himself to do the things his superego will not permit him to do in his own community. He leaves his responsibilities and his conscience at home and ventures into a taboo area—where, interestingly enough, those indulgences are not taboo because of local custom: 'When in Rome'—and attempts to recapture many of his infantile feelings of omnipotence. Actually one might say that the city (as far as the tourist is concerned) is sexually sterile. Money has replaced sexuality. The wad in a man's pants is a roll of bills."

"It's the money," says Dean Shendal, casino assistant at the

Sands, "the presence of it, the obviousness of it, that distorts all other values. It's the only thing that matters in this town. A man with $10,000 to lose gets a ringside table. A man with only $5,000 gets the table in back of him."

One wise hotel executive said: "The tourist gets confused and feels out of step when he first gets here. But in no time he's right in the middle of it, swinging like a big shot. If he wins, he's a big winner. If he loses, he's a big loser. There's free drinks and food everywhere and plenty of sex, and it's all casual and relaxed. Makes a guy feel like he's getting something for nothing. This town swings around the clock. You might say all systems are 'Go' all the time."

Most Vegans are very defensive about their town. When needled by the authors about the hoodlums in the casinos, Sheriff Ralph Lamb replied vigorously: "Now, now—wait just a minute. Don't forget this town owes something to these people. Without them there wouldn't be a Las Vegas. Listen, we can't forget that. . . ."

Governor Sawyer, whose frantic Twist with Mrs. Allard Roen (at the time her husband was in New York awaiting trial on a $5 million stock swindle) made the front page of the Soviet's *Izvestia,* insists that "people who live and settle in Nevada don't gamble." And he adds: "A man who is unstable in Nevada will be unstable in New York, Atlanta, Los Angeles, Chicago, or anywhere else."

Pancho Aliatti, maître d'hôtel at the Desert Inn, expresses a different viewpoint. "Some of my men have come to me and begged me to fire them because they cannot make any money in their jobs. It is all taken away from them by the crap tables or the slot machines."

Sherlock Feldman, pit boss at the Dunes, said: "People in the rest of the world merely go broke and die broke. In Vegas, you live broke."

Gambling is such a part of Nevada life that even the State Prison at Carson City operates a gambling casino for its inmates. The prisoners deposit their money with Warden Jack Fogliani, who in turn issues brass checks—circular pieces of shiny brass cut to the size of the various coins of the realm and stamped with the denomination of the coins they represent. The casino is a low structure just off the exercise yard and is known as the "bull pen." Besides card games and craps, there is a complete racing service, with entries and odds posted before each race. Chief bookie is one John Clary, a convicted murderer who is serving a life term for the fatal stabbing of a Reno woman with a screw driver. The cons can cash in their brass checks when they are released from prison. If they go broke they must get money from family or friends on the outside. Warden Fogliani is proud of this enlightened penal policy but less proud of the psychotic Indian who has been in solitary confinement for ten years. There is no light in his cell and no other place to send him since there are no facilities for criminally insane persons in the state of Nevada.

In recent months, Governor Sawyer has been meeting with representatives of major church groups who feel it is incongruous for the prison to have wide-open gambling on Sunday but no room for church services. Two years ago the state legislature appropriated $12,500 for a prison chapel but it has not been built as of this date.

The tourists foot 70 to 80 per cent of Nevada's tax bill. Here is an economy—the very survival of the state—which depends entirely on the roll of the dice, the turn of a card, the ping of a plastic ball, and the clatter of a one-armed bandit.

"We don't apologize for gambling," Governor Sawyer says. "To us, it is simply another industry, differing from others only in that its operation is rigidly policed and controlled by a state agency."

The sad truth is that without gambling, Nevada wouldn't need a governor—just a night watchman. In 1940, six years before Bugsy Siegel carved out an empire in the desert for the Mob, the entire population of Clark County, which includes Las Vegas, North Las Vegas, Henderson, Boulder City, and the four-and-a-half-mile highway stretch of U.S. 91 known as the Strip, was a mere 16,000. Today Clark County totals 200,000, nearly twice the population of the entire state in 1940. (Since the 1960 census, it has been growing at seven times the national rate.) The annual tax return from gambling between 1931 and 1945 averaged $30,000. Last year, Nevada's tax revenue from the state's 17,880 slot machines and 1,363 games in its 288 casinos (which provided 35,000 jobs) was a whopping $15 million—$11 million to the state, $3 million to the counties and $1 million to the cities. Sales taxes, collected mostly from tourists, added another $15 million to the state coffers.

Never have so few done so much for so few.

It has been said that a picture is worth a thousand words. Today, statistics speak even more boldly. Here are a few to the point. Nevada has the highest crime rate in the country. Both Reno and Las Vegas have police forces three times larger than other communities their size. The ratio of suicides in Las Vegas is the highest of any city in the world (30.1 per 100,000 as opposed to the national average of 1.9); the state's rate is frequently double the average for the rest of the nation. Divorce is a $6 million annual business and quickie marriages take in $9 million. (The most lucrative office in the state is that of Justice of the Peace of Las Vegas Township, bestowed by voters as a reward for outstanding public service. A J.P. is allowed only one term but can pick up $100,000 in that period.) Prostitution, the world's oldest profession, is second in income only to the world's oldest business, gambling. Prostitution has never been specifically outlawed by the state. It operates in the counties on a purely local option; its sole restriction makes it a misdemeanor to conduct business "within 400 yards of a school, church, or public thoroughfare." (A few years back a house was found to be within the 400-yard limit of a school. It was suggested, seriously, that the school be moved.)

Narcotics and juvenile delinquency have become the most pressing police problems. In the last six months of 1961 there was a 400 per cent increase in narcotics arrests over the same period for the previous years. The juvenile delinquency rate (mostly locals who have reached their teens since the Mob took over in 1946) is more than twice the national average (72 per thousand in Nevada as against 31 per thousand in the nation) and accounts for a major portion of the fantastic crime figures— 13,133 reported crimes and 7,627 arrests in a single year. All of this in a city of 64,405 population.

Vegans are quick to blame their crime rate on transients. It is true that the amoral atmosphere attracts a wide variety of criminals and psychopaths. For example, in June, 1962, a total of forty-four ex-felons registered with the police and forty-one of them intended to live permanently in Las Vegas. But, after all, these people are the true citizens of Las Vegas; they find asylum there. To them it is a home, a place in the sun, a niche where they can prosper and be respected.

Behind these shocking facts is the true story of Las Vegas, a story now told for the first time.

CHAPTER TWO

Dawn of a Golden Age

Before the advent of Benjamin "Bugsy" Siegel, Las Vegas served principally as a comfort station for tourists fleeing across the desert heat, escaping from one focus of civilization to another. Gambling was legal even then, but except for a few ancient one-armed bandits and a couple of homemade crap tables, the action was mainly around a poker table. In the decade after Siegel, Las Vegas multiplied tenfold, which was ten times more than it had done in the preceding century.

In 1776, while a handful of revolutionaries were plucking the thirteen American colonies from the diadem of George III, Padre Escalante and a small band of soldiers bearing the flag of Charles III of Spain discovered Las Vegas. Seventy-nine years later, in 1855, Brigham Young sent a mission from Salt

14

Lake City to Las Vegas—the town's first white settlers—to cultivate the land and convert Indians to the Mormon faith. But the Paiutes, a lazy, ignorant desert tribe, were not the converting type. They idled the hours away rolling bones and colored sticks in the brown sand—the true ancestors of the modern Vegans. In 1858 the mission returned to Salt Lake City a failure.

Years later, fortune-hunting miners wrested great treasures in gold and silver from the mountains that ring the arid valley of Las Vegas. The San Pedro, Los Angeles and Salt Lake Railroad (now the Union Pacific) extended its lines to the city in 1905, laying hundreds of miles of tracks to the various mines. In ten years it was all gone, the gold, the silver, the railroad; only ghost towns and grizzly old prospectors remained.

In the Thirties, Boulder Dam, thirty miles away, stirred up a little action on weekends. Then the war came and thousands of soldiers found themselves training in a mock-up Sahara. Later the Atomic Energy Commission tested its bombs at Yucca Flats. Meanwhile, movie stars, seeking quickie marriages, shuttled back and forth between Las Vegas and Hollywood. When it came time for the not-so-quickie divorce (six weeks residence), they went north to Reno and the plush dude ranches.

Then, in the summer of 1941, Bugsy Siegel sent a trusted disciple, Moe Sedway, to scout the territory. Sedway, a Jewish Sancho Panza, was a tiny guy with a large nose and moist, close-set eyes, who talked freely from both sides of his mouth and liked to play both ends against the middle. His job was to establish the Trans-America wire service in Nevada. This wire service was controlled by the Capone Mob in Chicago and had been set up to compete with James M. Ragen's Continental Press Service, which up to then had enjoyed a virtual monopoly with bookmakers west of Chicago. The Capone Mob was deadly serious and so was Siegel, their West Coast representative. Gus

15

Greenbaum had already established Trans-America in Arizona and Siegel, with the assistance of Jack Dragna and Mickey Cohen, was forging ahead in California. Now it was up to Little Moey.

Up to then Sedway, a boyhood pal of Siegel, had been a dismal failure in every enterprise Bugsy had generously handed him. His most recent fiascoes had been as bookmaker in Los Angeles and San Diego.

Sedway had lived in the midst of crime and violence all his life. As a young punk on New York City's Lower East Side, Little Moey had trotted faithfully behind the much younger Bugsy. For years he had been a nobody, just the guy who went out for the sandwiches when the big boys got together. In a way it had been an advantage. Little Moey had kept his ears open and had learned much with a minimum of exposure. The big boys never thought of asking him to do anything dangerous. He definitely was not the torpedo type; and besides, he was Bugsy's personal flunky.

In Las Vegas, for the first time in his life, Little Moey Sedway achieved success. Three major factors contributed to his change of luck. First, Continental Press needed all its guns in California and didn't think the meager pickings in Nevada worth the struggle. Second, the operation was legal and the subscribers to the service were the state-licensed gambling casinos. Third, the casinos depended heavily on their books to attract daytime patronage. The action they were pushing was the one-armed bandits lined up against the walls, the crap tables, blackjack, and poker. It was a long drink between races and bangtail bettors are not usually averse to other forms of gambling.

Once Little Moey realized this he moved quickly. The unrestricted access to the wire service which had been available to anyone willing to pay the fee was suddenly cut off early in 1942. Little Moey wanted more than a fee. What he wanted was a piece of the action and he wanted it gratis. Now, to operate a book without a reliable wire service is about as feasible as flying without an engine. You may stay up there awhile, but sooner than later you're going to drop. Any unethical (as if it could ever be otherwise) wire service can pastpost a bookmaker into bankruptcy in a week's time. So the bookies in Las Vegas had only two choices: Come up with an interest or close the book. A few of the big casinos on Fremont Street came across and Little Moey was on his way to a legitimate business career.

That same year, 1942, Siegel made a brief personal appearance in the gambling town and let it be known that the wire service could be obtained in the casinos upon the condition that he would receive in some cases all, and in other cases as much as two-thirds of the income from the favored casinos' bookmaking operations. There was no argument from anyone. From then on Siegel's income from Las Vegas' bookmaking alone totaled at least $25,000 a month. At the same time Siegel managed to acquire an interest in the Golden Nugget and the Frontier Club, two of Las Vegas' busier joints.

Siegel went back to Los Angeles and Little Moey settled down to the good life of a gentleman of leisure. He became publicly civic-minded and poured money into many community enterprises, including two different church building projects (still the number-one philanthropic dodge of the underworld). Overnight, Sedway donned a mask of respectability that radiated warmth and aging benevolence. He socialized with the city fathers and talked politics with the state's most influential politicians. And from time to time, he sneaked into the FBI office to talk to Leo Kuykendall, who to this day regards Little Moey as the most important informer in his twenty-one years as the head of the Las Vegas FBI bureau (Kuykendall is presently Chief of Police in Las Vegas).

For the first time in his life, Sedway had achieved recognition on his own. He was not a flunky any longer, but a man respected by the community. He drove around in a big black car and smoked the longest coronas he could buy. The next step was inevitable. Little Moey decided to run for political office—but without consulting his mentor. Siegel heard about it and that was the end of Sedway. "We don't run for office," Siegel bellowed in a characteristic fit of temper. "We own the politicians." Sedway was summarily banished from social and business contact with the boss. The word went out that if Bugsy should ever run into him on the street, Little Moey would be hit in the head. Sedway had been around Siegel long enough to know that he meant every word of it. It was three years before Little Moey was returned into the good graces of his boyhood pal. Meanwhile, his visits to Kuykendall's office became more frequent and more revealing. Like a rejected lover, Sedway became a bitter man. Nevertheless, he was cagey enough to keep quiet about important things. His stooling was restricted to the Las Vegas scene. Nothing of Bugsy's past was ever revealed. But if he had wanted to, Little Moey could have told a hair-curling story.

There have been few hoodlums of Bugsy Siegel's ilk. By the age of twenty-one, Siegel had committed every heinous crime in the gangster's handbook: mayhem, white slavery, dope pushing, bootlegging, hijacking, robbery, rape, burglary, bookmaking, numbers racket, extortion, and numerous vicious murders. Bugsy was precocious in crime as some boys are precocious in music, art, or science. His reckless disregard of danger, his wild antics, his ruthless contempt for the rights of others, his psychopathic temper—all these weaknesses became his greatest strength. He was feared and admired by every punk who knew him. Bugsy was never a flunky. From the age of fourteen he had his own gang. By the age of twenty he was a formidable power on the Lower East Side. It was then that he joined forces with Meyer Lansky. The two formed a gang of executioners known as the Bug and Meyer mob, which executed contracts (murders) for all the gangs then operating in New York and New Jersey. They predated Murder, Inc., by seven years.

Siegel and Lansky were friendly with Lepke Buchalter, Gurrah Shapiro, Longie Zwillman, Lucky Luciano, Frank Costello, Joey Adonis, Arnold Rothstein, Willie Moretti, Lil Augie Pisano, Albert Anastasia, Dutch Schultz, Joe Profaci, Vito Genovese, Waxey Gordon, Owney Madden, Legs Diamond, Johnny Torrio, Al Capone, Jake Guzik, Frank Nitti, Charlie Fischetti, Phil Kastel, and Tony Accardo.

They traveled all over the country on contracts. For a while the Bug and Meyer mob transferred its activity to Philadelphia to open the territory for the Combination. Siegel and Lansky sat as equal members on the board of directors with Costello, Luciano, Schultz, Lepke, Gurrah, Adonis, Pisano, Genovese, Torrio, Capone, Moretti, and Zwillman.

Bugsy had one advantage over his hoodlum pals. He was as handsome as a movie star. He liked sharp clothes: broad snap-brimmed hats (a hard-shell derby in the early days); pin-striped suits with high-waisted trousers and narrow pegged cuffs; rakishly tailored overcoats with fur-lined collars; hand-crafted shoes with pointed toes, and handmade silk shirts with six-inch collar points. Everything was monogrammed, right down to his tailored silk shorts. Bugsy wanted class and he tried to buy it at every opportunity. He was one of the first hoodlums to move into the Waldorf Astoria Towers in the early Thirties. His suite of rooms was two floors above Lucky Luciano's. He rode around in a bulletproof limousine with a chauffeur and two bodyguards flanking him (just like George Raft in the movies). He ate in the finest restaurants and spent his evenings cavorting in swank speaks and night clubs.

No one who valued his life ever called him Bugsy to his face.

19

"My friends call me Ben," he once admonished a reporter. "Everybody else calls me Mr. Siegel. Why not? That's my name, ain't it?" "Everybody else" included anyone who was an inch below him on the power scale, except the closest personal flunkies.

Bugsy enjoyed traveling. He made numerous pleasure trips to Mexico, especially Acapulco. Capone entertained him at his Palm Island estate in Florida, and Siegel played golf and took the baths at Hot Springs with other members of the board. There were frequent visits to Hollywood, where he socialized with the crust of the movie set. His sponsors were Jean Harlow and George Raft. In those days Harlow was having a torrid romance with Longie Zwillman, the underworld czar of New Jersey. And Raft, like Little Moey, had always idolized Bugsy. In later years, Raft bragged of his school days with Siegel in Hell's Kitchen. There are two things wrong with that boast. Raft went to school just long enough to learn to spell his own name, and Bugsy never lived in Hell's Kitchen; he was born in the Williamsburg section of Brooklyn in 1905 and lived there until he left home and fled to the Lower East Side.

Actually, Raft, like other child–adults in Hollywood, got a vicarious thrill from associating with real live murderers. Bugsy was shrewd enough to take advantage of such obvious weaknesses. (He once conned Raft into lending him $100,000, which he never repaid.) According to Raft, Siegel "was a frustrated actor and secretly wanted a movie career, but he never quite had nerve enough to ask for a part in one of my pictures."

In 1937, when Siegel was at the zenith of his power in New York, he was voted by the board of directors as the hoodlum most likely to succeed in California. Bugsy was more than happy to oblige. By that time he was married and had two daughters, Barbara and Millicent (whose godmother was Jean Harlow). His wife, Estelle Krakower, was a large-boned blonde with blue eyes and a florid complexion, a product of the Lower East Side.

When they arrived in Los Angeles, Bugsy headed straight for Beverly Hills. Commenting on Siegel's arrival, Raft noted that Bugsy "used Lawrence Tibbett's former home as a starting point and in short order he became one of the darlings of Hollywood. Benny Siegel, in short, was a movieland fad. He browsed around with Jack Warner, Cary Grant, Barbara Hutton, Countess Dorothy di Frasso, and other Hollywood bluebook names, and in public he looked and acted about as tough as a cocker spaniel.

"I had known Benny intimately in earlier days, and so he came often to my Beverly Hills home. There he could be himself, and he wasn't always charming. He was terribly vain about his hair, for instance. He combed it every five minutes, and when it began to fall out, he tried every known lotion, medicine, and treatment without success. . . . I seriously underestimated Benny's vanity on this point one year, and sent him a toupee on his birthday.

"He drove to my house in a fury, stormed in, and snarled, 'I oughta shoot you, you ————'

" 'You want to plug me?' I said. 'Now look here, baby blue eyes, just take it easy.'

"He hesitated and lowered the rod with a sheepish grin. That 'baby blue eyes' line pleased him somehow, and whenever I used it in critical situations Benny would soften up. But I avoided kidding him on personal matters thereafter, and never mentioned that I knew he was using face creams, eye shades, and other things in an attempt to keep his youthful looks."

Bugsy's mission in California was not the conquest of Hollywood but of the underworld. The Mafia had been operating in California since the turn of the century. In thirty-seven years there had been forty-one gangland slayings in Los Angeles alone —thirty-four Sicilians and Italians, four Jews, and three Irishmen, all criminals mixed up in bootlegging, narcotics, prostitution, bookmaking, and other rackets. Though crime was nothing new to California, there had been no organization, no working arrangements between the mobs, no pooling of efforts as in the big eastern and midwestern cities.

Bugsy's first job was to form a coalition of the top mobs. Jack I. Dragna, the most powerful *capo mafioso* (or Mafia leader) on the West Coast, became Siegel's number-one lieutenant. A meeting of top mobsters was held in the banquet room of a downtown restaurant and Bugsy laid down the rules in no uncertain terms. Les Brunemann, a Redondo Beach gambler, was the only hood to stand up and voice an objection. Less than a month later, Brunemann was trapped by two torpedoes in the Roost Café in Redondo Beach. He was shot three times but rushed to a hospital and recovered. Two months later, while visiting the same café with his nurse, Brunemann was cornered by four hoods, who emptied their .45-caliber automatics at him. Brunemann and a bystander were killed instantly and the nurse was wounded in both legs.

Meanwhile, goon squads, armed with tire chains and lead pipes, were raiding reluctant bookmakers and small-time racketeers. Siegel's name soon became anathema in the underworld. He took over the gambling at Redondo Beach, took a cut of the profits at the Agua Caliente race track, muscled in on the numbers racket, cut himself a slice of the offshore gambling fleet and the Culver City dog track. He got a 15 per cent interest in Tony Cornero's S.S. "Rex," a gambling ship in Santa Monica Bay, and also an interest in the Clover Club, a plush gambling casino on Sunset Boulevard.

But these were just the trimmings. The big jobs were narcotics, prostitution, and bookmaking. With the assistance of Dragna, he set up a narcotics pipeline through Mexico to import dope from all over the world. A brigade of smugglers was organized, with Joe Sica at the receiving end. A rotation system was set up to handle prostitutes from Seattle to San Diego. Pimps kept the girls moving so the customers wouldn't get bored nor the cops wise.

Bugsy never stopped working on the cops and politicians. He had learned early in life that it was better to buy a cop than to fight one. Thousands of dollars were spent on bribes—"juice" —blanketing the police force from top to bottom; it spread to the D.A.'s office and the Attorney General's. And then finally to Arthur Samish and the legislature. Samish, a powerful lobbyist, once remarked: "To hell with being governor. I am the governor of the legislature." And he wasn't a man who spoke loosely.

By the end of 1945, Siegel had the crime situation in California pretty well in hand. Money was rolling in and the Combination was satisfied. Siegel turned his thoughts to Las Vegas.

For a long time now, a dream had been forming at the back of his mind. He would become the greatest impresario of gambling in America. He would erect the largest and most luxurious gambling casino in the world. It would not be just a casino, but a plush hotel as well, with a night club, restaurant, bars, swimming pool, exotically landscaped grounds, and the finest service imaginable. He would, above all else, become legitimate. So legitimate that "no FBI man can ever as much as lay a finger on my shoulder."

So, early in 1946, Bugsy packed his money in several suitcases and headed for Las Vegas while his wife, Estelle, journeyed north to Reno and the divorce court.

Thus began the Golden Age of Las Vegas.

Ensconced in Las Vegas when Siegel arrived were a number of gamblers who had fled Los Angeles in the late Thirties to escape Bugsy's wrath. These gamblers, Tutor Scherer, Guy McAfee, Chuck Addison, Farmer Page, Bill Curland, and Jake

Katleman, had no ties with the Combination and didn't want any. Now Siegel's arrival signified just one thing to them, organization. Bugsy had to be the advance man for the Combination, for Frank Costello and Meyer Lansky in New York; Joe Adonis and Joe Profaci in Brooklyn; Longie Zwillman, Willie Moretti, and Joe Stacher in New Jersey; Lil Augie Pisano in Florida; Phil Kastel and Carlos Marcello in Louisiana; Charlie Fischetti, Jake Guzik, and Tony Accardo in Illinois; Moe Dalitz in Cleveland; Kid Cann in Minneapolis; the Licavolis and Toccos in Detroit; Charlie Binaggio and Tony Gizzo in Kansas City; and hundreds of lesser but no less tough hoodlums. It wasn't long before their worst fears materialized.

At the beginning, Bugsy seemed to be operating alone. He hired the Del E. Webb Construction Company of Phoenix to turn his dream into a reality. It would be called, he said, the Flamingo Hotel. Later he changed it to the "fabulous Flamingo Hotel." And fabulous it was. The cost was originally estimated at $1.5 million, but it ballooned to $6 million. The plumbing bill alone was $1 million. Every bathroom had its own private sewer line. Bugsy thought this was class. The hotel walls were of solid concrete in a climate where chicken wire and plaster would have been sufficient. He ordered imported woods and marble. He stalked the architects and designers, berating them at every turn, demanding things newer and rarer; and when they balked, he frightened them into compliance with his rages and threats.

Those were the days of postwar priorities. But it didn't mean a thing to Siegel. When Webb couldn't produce the necessary steel, copper, tile, fixtures, or piping, Bugsy went into the black market and paid dearly to get it. Black marketeers would deliver a truckload of supplies in the morning and return at night to steal it. The next morning they were back to sell it again.

He had over a million dollars of his own money when he

started out but soon he was broke. It wasn't long before he was scrounging for more money. He made fourteen trips to the Midwest and the East Coast to raise money. He sold blocks of stock at $50,000 each and raised over $3 million from his hoodlum friends. But he was still in the hole for $2 million to Webb. His racket pals refused to invest another nickel in what they already considered a ridiculous investment.

In June of that year, while the hotel was beginning to take shape, James M. Ragen, the owner of Continental Press Service, was strafed by bullets in Chicago. He lingered in the hospital for six weeks and was well on his way to recovery when suddenly he died. It took months for the story of his death to leak out, but Bugsy and the Mob knew about it before the coroner. The autopsy report indicated enough mercury in Ragen's body to kill him twice. Despite a round-the-clock police guard, they had managed to spike Ragen's Cokes with mercury, which is a cumulative poison. Through a couple of front men, the Capone Mob moved in and took over Continental from the Ragen heirs.

Once the Capone Mob possessed Continental, the need for Trans-America ceased to exist. They decided to scrap it. But Bugsy had other ideas. He had worked hard setting it up in California and Nevada, and Gus Greenbaum, who had become a close friend, had also worked hard in Arizona. Besides the vast profits, Bugsy enjoyed the power it gave him. It paid the wages of hundreds of thugs he couldn't afford to hire (or need) without the service. Also he needed more money for the Flamingo. He flew to New York and a meeting of the board of directors of the Combination was called. By this time Bugsy's ego had completely outgrown his common sense.

Standing before the assembled members, he laid down his terms. It would cost the Combination exactly $2 million to get Trans-America back. Take it or leave it. And with that Siegel

25

left. It goes without saying that the members did more than just gape after Bugsy departed.

Back in Las Vegas, Bugsy became a driven man. He ordered overtime for everybody, demanding a twelve-hour day and a seven-day week. Plasterers were flown in from Los Angeles, San Francisco, Denver, and Salt Lake City and were paid fifty dollars a day to get the place ready. Everything went wrong. The solid-concrete structure built to house the furnace turned out to be too small when the equipment arrived and it had to be blasted out and rebuilt. The air-conditioning system was incorrectly installed with intakes but no outlets. And to top it all, his own penthouse was spoiled by a heavy concrete beam down the middle of the spacious living room, resting so low that a man of average height had to lower his head to walk under it. The only solution was to divide the room in half, depriving Bugsy of the romping space he had grown accustomed to since leaving the Lower East Side.

In Los Angeles there was another kind of trouble. The bookies were screaming for help. They had to pay $150 a week for each telephone to both Bugsy's Trans-America and Capone's new Continental. Siegel told them to go to hell. Dragna and Cohen were on the spot. They couldn't let go of Bugsy and they didn't want to antagonize the Combination. The situation was slowly working up to a crisis.

On the evening of December 26, 1946, Siegel donned a white tie and swallowtail coat, and with Virginia Hill on his arm, flung open the doors to his "fabulous Flamingo Hotel." The hotel was not yet finished, but the theater, casino, lounge, and restaurant were sparkling new and ready for action. Jimmy Durante led off the entertainment with Tommy Wonder, Baby Rosemarie, the Tunetoppers, Eddie Jackson, and Xavier Cugat's band.

It was a flop from the beginning. Bugsy's specially chartered

Constellations were grounded by weather in Los Angeles, and only a few of the invited movie celebrities showed up. Nevertheless, a few stalwarts—George Raft, Sonny Tufts, Charles Coburn, George Sanders, Vivian Blaine, Lon McAllister, and some minor producers and directors—made an appearance. But then, the casino went into the red the very first night. Siegel was fit to be tied.

Just as he was storming through the lobby after the Durante show with the celebrities clustered about him, a small man with his wife and two teen-age daughters approached Bugsy. The man was beaming happily.

"Bugsy," he cried. "This is fabulous. God, what a beautiful place. You are to be congratulated."

Bugsy's blue eyes turned to ice. His hair bristled as he slapped his hands on his hips and leaned forward. "Who are you?" he demanded. "Have we been introduced?"

The man's smile became uncertain as he shook his head. "No, but I just had to tell you how nice this place is. It's just fabulous. My wife and daughters—"

"We ain't been introduced," Bugsy shouted, his blue eyes now black with rage. "So how come you get so intimate?"

The smile froze on the man's face and he turned nervously toward his wife and daughters, shaking his head in confusion.

"Get out of here," Bugsy screamed. "Get the hell out of here, you bum, and don't come back."

There are scores of such anecdotes about Bugsy during those hectic days in Las Vegas. It seems his publicity director, Abe Schiller, antagonized Bugsy one day while out in the pool area. Turning on him angrily, Siegel whipped out a .38 automatic from his waistband and aimed it directly at Schiller's head.

"On your hands and knees, you son of a bitch," Bugsy growled. Schiller dropped as directed. Cursing a blue streak, Bugsy forced him to crawl around the olympic-size swimming pool while he angrily potted shots over his head, the slugs splashing into the water. The guests stood around stupefied.

And Marie "The Body" McDonald made the mistake of telling Siegel that Sanford Adler at the El Rancho had warned her about the Flamingo, saying that it was operated by gangsters. Siegel immediately jumped into his car and sped to the El Rancho in search of Adler. He found the manager by the pool with a group of guests. Without saying a word, Bugsy rushed up and slapped him on the head with the automatic and then mercilessly pistol-whipped him amid the shouts and screams of the horrified guests.

But Bugsy did not always use violence to get his way. Once during a banquet dinner, the chef, who was French and excitable, suddenly threw a tantrum and stalked out of the kitchen after blowing pepper all over the food. Notified of the chef's behavior, Bugsy rushed to his quarters. The chef was still in the throes of the tantrum and Bugsy waited as assorted articles flew dangerously across the room. His blue eyes grew contemplative as he studied the chef. Finally, he dug into his pocket, extracted a C-note, and pushed it into the chef's hand. "Here," he said, smiling. "Come on back to work. Those guys are going nuts down there." The chef pocketed the bill and returned to his pepper-strewn kitchen.

Bugsy was most fastidious about the help's appearance at the Flamingo. Everyone, and that included even janitors, had to wear a tuxedo. It was a very classy place. One morning on his way across the patio, Siegel spotted a tuxedo-clad man stretched out on a chaise longue. Bugsy ran over and kicked viciously at the chair. "What the hell are you doing?" he demanded. "Get back to work, you bum, before I boot your ass."

The man sat up, his eyes popping out of his head. "But—but," he stammered, "I'm a g-g-guest."

Bugsy wanted a nice place, but unless the guests were movie

stars, he couldn't work up too much enthusiasm over their welfare. He had cauliflower-eared gorillas dressed up in tuxes watching the action from every possible angle. If a guest as much as stopped before a slot machine without depositing a coin, the pug would shove him away, "Keep moving, buddy, don't block up the action." Or if a guest dropped a cigarette on the lawn, a pug would jump up from behind a bush and snarl, "Pick up that goddamn butt, you jerk. What the hell d'ya think this is?"

Bugsy carried a rod at all times in those days. For years in Hollywood he had been without one, but now he felt the need for it. He also carried a swagger stick whenever he made his regular inspection of the grounds and buildings. Dick Chappell, the hotel manager (now with the Riviera), recalls the morning Siegel found Mrs. Chappell sun-bathing on the sand in front of their cottage, which was situated at the end of the thirty-five acre tract, a long way from the landscaped grounds of the hotel. Siegel stopped abruptly and pointed the swagger stick at Mrs. Chappell. "What the hell is she doing?" he demanded. Chappell swallowed. "Taking a sun bath." "This ain't no goddamn place for a sun bath," Siegel growled, whirling about and stalking off. Chappell ran after him to explain that it wouldn't happen again, when Bugsy turned and looked back at Mrs. Chappell.

"Tell her to use the pool," he said gently.

"But that's for guests," Chappell protested.

"Guests, my ass," he snapped. "I want to see her there every day. You understand?"

To liven up the action, Siegel, who drank very sparingly, mixed his women instead of his liquor. At one time, he had four favorite beauties ensconced in plush suites at the Flamingo. They were actresses Wendy Barrie and Marie McDonald; Countess Dorothy di Frasso (worth $15 million and once engaged to Gary Cooper), and Virginia Hill, the barefoot kid from

29

Bessemer, Alabama, who has out-conned the biggest con men in the rackets. At one time or another, Virginia has been between the sheets with about every top hoodlum in the country. While so engaged, she has kept her mouth shut and her eyes wide open. The reward has been startling. Her endless source of ready cash has made her an international playgirl. The newspapers called her an "heiress," which is somewhat better than "model." Actually, Virginia Hill was the "bagman" for the syndicate. She carried vast sums of money from mob to mob across the country, and she worked as a decoy for some of the most sinister punks that ever slinked out of a sewer.

A couple of years before the Flamingo was built, Wendy Barrie had announced her engagement to Bugsy. She never gave up hoping. Her presence at the Flamingo would throw Virginia Hill into a cataleptic fit. One night Virginia swung a haymaker at the British actress and nearly dislocated her jaw. Bugsy then swung on Virginia. "You ain't no lady," he shouted. Virginia ran up to the penthouse and promptly took a handful of sleeping tablets. Later in the evening, Dick Chappell found Bugsy leaning out the window of his bedroom, screaming for help. "She's killed herself," he cried. Chappell rushed up and the two of them carried her to Siegel's car. "Goddamn stupid bitch, why did she have to do that. Bitch, bastard, go on, hurry. Step on it." Chappell was doing eighty down the Strip with Bugsy pounding him on the back, swearing and crying. From the rear-view mirror, Chappell saw a police car drawing up on them. "Screw the cops," Siegel cried. "Give 'em a C-note when we get to the hospital and tell 'em to forget it." Virginia recovered to go on to bigger and better suicide attempts. She has not as yet succeeded.

The "fabulous Flamingo" stayed open only two weeks after its dismal opening night. The casino lost over $100,000 in that period. Worried sick, Bugsy closed the doors and waited for the hotel part to be finished before reopening. The small-time Las Vegas gamblers were delirious with joy.

Bugsy had other, more pressing problems. He received word that Lucky Luciano, who had been released from prison and deported to Sicily, was in Havana, Cuba. Lucky, it appeared, had held a meeting of the Combination without inviting Bugsy. Eighteen members, all associates of Siegel, had attended. They were Frank Costello, Joey Adonis, Albert Anastasia, Willie Moretti, Charlie Fischetti, Vito Genovese, Tony Accardo, Joe Profaci, Phil Kastel, Meyer Lansky, Vince Mangano, Lil Augie Pisano, Mike Miranda, Joe Bonanno, Joe Magliocco, Tommy Luchese, Carlo Marcello, and the big boss himself, Charlie "Lucky."

Siegel brooded about it a few days and then picked up the telephone. Lucky was not available. Siegel spent a week trying to reach him, his anger mounting and his fear deepening. Something was definitely wrong. In the old days, Lucky had been like a brother to him. All those guys were his friends. Meyer and he had grown up together, as close as two buddies could be. And Costello and Adonis and he had played golf together for years. There was only one answer. He would have to go to Havana and see Lucky personally; seeing Costello or Lansky or Adonis wouldn't help. Lucky was the only one who could really give the word and smooth things out. He could do it with one word. They all listened to Lucky. Even after all those years behind prison walls and the deportation, Lucky was still the number-one boy in the Combination.

Surrounding himself with six of his toughest torpedoes, Siegel flew down to Havana in the early part of February. Once in the Latin capital, Siegel did not have too much trouble finding Lucky. They met formally in Luciano's suite of rooms in one of Havana's finest luxury hotels. Lucky smiled and shook hands, but there was a hard, fixed look in his dark, opaque eyes. The

31

thick eyelids drooped almost closed. There was some small talk at first, mostly about the "lousy wops" (as Lucky termed it) in Sicily and Italy, and the difference between Europe and America. Gradually the talk turned to the Flamingo and Lucky indicated that he had heard all about it, but he didn't seem overly impressed by its splendor. Bugsy got excited and started to describe it, his eyes shining, his face flushed. "O.K., O.K.," Lucky said. "So it's got class. So where's the three million skins the boys gave you? Class is for suckers if there's no dough in it." Siegel protested, asking for more time. "Look here, Ben," Lucky said, "you go back there and start behaving. You give the Chicago boys the wire and no more bullshit. Those boys are fed up. This has gone far enough. You understand?" "I need more time," Bugsy pleaded. "Give me a year. That's all I ask. One lousy year." Luciano shook his head and stood up. "No more time. You do it right now." Suddenly Bugsy leaped up and began screaming at Lucky. "What do you think you're doing," he bellowed. "Dismissing me? You bastard, nobody dismisses me. And no son of a bitch tells me what to do. Go to hell and take the rest of those bastards along with you. I'll keep the goddamn wire as long as I want." Once again Bugsy had lived up to his cognomen. The psychopathic temper had drowned the fear.

A few weeks later in Las Vegas, Bugsy revealed a part of himself to Del Webb. "He was a remarkable character," Webb informs friends today. "Tough, cold, and terrifying when he wanted to be—but at other times a very easy fellow to be around.

"He told me one night, when I was waiting for my money"— Webb waited in Siegel's office every night to be paid a portion of the day's receipts—"that he had personally killed twelve men, but then he must have noted my face, or something, because he laughed and said that I had nothing to worry about.

32

" 'There's no chance that you'll get killed,' he said. 'We only kill each other.' "

On March 27, 1947, the "fabulous Flamingo Hotel" had reopened its doors to the public. For the first three weeks it continued to run in the red. After returning from Cuba, Siegel had been nervous and apprehensive, but with the daily struggle of operating the hotel, he began to calm down, especially when the money started to roll in. In May the casino cleared over $300,000. Siegel was happy again.

The battles with Virginia Hill continued in private and in public. It got so bad at the end that no one would approach Bugsy when he was with her. They knew that at any moment they would be cursing each other at the top of their lungs. It wasn't a healthy atmosphere to invade. Then one night after a violent argument, Virginia packed her two hundred pairs of shoes and took off for Paris and the Champs Élysées.

A week later (June 20, 1947) Siegel was dead. The police found him slumped on a chintz-covered sofa in the living room of Virginia Hill's pink Moorish mansion in Beverly Hills, California. His handsome face had been torn apart by two steel-jacketed slugs. One had crushed the bridge of his nose and ripped into his left eye. The other had entered his right cheek and passed through the back of his neck, shattering a vertebra. His right eye was found fifteen feet away on the tiled floor of the dining room. Blood had soaked the front of his gray plaid suit and his hands rested limply in his lap. On the floor between his sprawled legs was a copy of the Los Angeles *Times*. Clipped to the top of the paper was a card with an ironic message. It read: "Good night. Sleep peacefully with compliments of Jack's."

According to the police, the killer had waited for Bugsy in the shadow of a rose-covered pergola with a .30-caliber Army carbine. He had rested the barrel of the carbine on a crossbar of the latticework, sighted, and carefully squeezed off the entire clip. Nine slugs slammed through a fourteen-inch pane of glass. Siegel, who had been sitting directly in front of an undraped window, his head illuminated by a table lamp behind the sofa, had taken four of the slugs—two in the head and two in the chest. Five went wild, shattering a marble statue of Bacchus on the grand piano and puncturing a painting of a nude holding a wineglass.

Allen Smiley, one of Bugsy's closest pals in those days, was seated at the other end of the sofa when it happened. "We had just got back from dinner at Ocean Park, that new place, Jack's-at-the-Beach," Smiley told the police. "Ben had just settled down on the sofa to read the early edition of the morning paper when all of a sudden there was a hell of a racket, shots and everything, and glass breaking. I ducked to the floor when I heard the shots and shattering glass. I don't know how many shots were fired, but when I looked up at Siegel, I could see he had taken most of them."

Siegel had the distinction of being the first member of the board of directors to draw the death sentence. Since then there have been many others, including Willie Moretti, Lil Augie Pisano, and Albert Anastasia.

Twenty minutes after Siegel was hit in the head in Beverly Hills, Little Moey Sedway and Morris Rosen walked into the "fabulous Flamingo Hotel" and took over the operation. Gus Greenbaum came in a few minutes later and shook hands all around. In Beverly Hills, the police cars were just growling to a stop in front of 810 Linden Drive; they had yet to find out who was dead.

Siegel was dead but Las Vegas was just coming to life. When the sun broke across the horizon that morning, the whole town was bathed in gold.

CHAPTER THREE
Mayor of Paradise

Less than twenty-four hours after Siegel's death, a stockholders' meeting was called at the Flamingo. Representing Bugsy's interest was Joseph Ross, a prominent Beverly Hills attorney. Meyer Lansky and Morris Rosen represented the Mob. Gus Greenbaum and Moe Sedway were there to assist Rosen and Lansky. Joe Epstein, Virginia Hill's hoodlum "banker" from Chicago, was on hand with his own set of books. The leaders of the group of buyers were Sanford Adler and Charlie Resnick, co-owners of El Rancho; the group included Israel "Icepick Willie" Alderman, a Minneapolis gangster with a record of arrests—robbery, larceny, carrying a concealed weapon, assault, murder—dating back to 1925 but with no convictions. (When properly stoned, Alderman likes to brag about the eleven men he allegedly murdered in the old days when he ran a second-story speak in Minneapolis. Briefly, his technique consisted in pressing an icepick into the victim's ear all the way into the brain, working so quickly that no one even noticed. The dead man would slump drunkenly over the bar and Icepick Willie would laughingly chide him as he dragged the body out to a back room that was equipped with a coal chute that emptied into a waiting truck in the alley below.) Also in the group of buyers were Dave Berman, an ex-con who served time in Sing Sing for kidnaping and a former Siegel thug who was soon to become the muscle behind Greenbaum; Albert C. Abrams, a convicted brothel operator; and Jack Burke and Sam Diamond, two convicted California bookmakers. All upstanding Nevada businessmen.

With some reservations, Sedway told the Kefauver Committee in 1950 how the deal was negotiated at the Flamingo. The following text is taken from Part 10 of the minutes of the hearings.

MR. SEDWAY. Here is what happened. After Siegel died, [Morris] Rosen came to town and I was trying to get some buyers for the Flamingo. I think he talked to several groups. Finally, I told him that I had talked to somebody and I thought I could get a couple of groups together, and I think we can buy it, if we could buy it reasonably, with a small down payment. So he says, "Well, you work it out, and when you get all set, go speak to the people."

So I did. I talked to Sanford Adler and Charlie Resnick. They owned the El Rancho Hotel at the time. I talked to him and he was very much interested and he said they would be interested but they couldn't take it all. So I called Mr. Greenbaum—he went back to Phoenix since—called him and he brought some people in. Mr. [Jack] McElroy was brought in, and I got a man, a local man in town here, Mr. Mack. He put some money in, and we formed this group and bought the Flamingo for $3,900,000, with a down payment of, I think, around $500,000 or $600,000; I don't remember. The records are there.

Then when Rosen—we got closer, and Rosen says, "Well, as long as I am going—" and Rosen, incidentally, liked the new set-up and he bought in. He put in 10 and then he bought in 5 more.

MR. HALLEY. Ten what?

MR. SEDWAY. Ten per cent. And then 5 per cent more—15 per cent.

MR. HALLEY. What did he pay?

MR. SEDWAY. He paid what we all paid, except that for the first 10 he didn't have to put up any loan money.

MR. HALLEY. Why not?

MR. SEDWAY. Well, for the consideration that he was instrumental in making the—got all the proxies from all the other stockholders, and everything. So they agreed to sell it to him without a loan, the 10. But the five he loaned just like anybody else. Some people loaned more, some people loaned less.

MR. HALLEY. How much did he have to put up for the five?

MR. SEDWAY. For the five? Well, it was 10 per cent capital and 90 per cent loan.

MR. HALLEY. How much would the loan be, then?

MR. SEDWAY. I don't know what it would amount to; say, on $500,000 or $600,000, if he had 5 per cent, it would be $30,000, 10 per cent would be—

MR. HALLEY. Three thousand dollars?

MR. SEDWAY. Three thousand dollars for capital and $27,000 loan.

MR. HALLEY. So he did not have to put up $54,000 loan money on his 10 per cent?

MR. SEDWAY. No.

SENATOR TOBEY. After Mr. Siegel died, Mr. Rosen came down here, didn't he?

MR. SEDWAY. Yes.

SENATOR TOBEY. And what had been Rosen's relations with Siegel before that?

MR. SEDWAY. Rosen had an interest in the old Flamingo, in the Nevada Projects Company, and when Siegel died he came down to sort of look after the business and see what could be done to salvage it. The place was in a very bad spot. It was ready to close if they didn't get a buyer. They weren't doing much business on account of all the adverse publicity that Siegel was getting during that time.

SENATOR TOBEY. Rosen and Siegel had been pretty close in other deals in the past?

MR. SEDWAY. I don't know, but they were very close. As a matter of fact, Rosen's son just recently married Siegel's daughter [Millicent], so the families were close.

SENATOR WILEY. Who owned the 90 per cent? Who had the interest in the other 90 per cent?

MR. SEDWAY. Various stockholders. I bought a piece there, I think at the time. I bought 5½ per cent.

MR. HALLEY. Who were the other owners?

MR. SEDWAY. Mr. Greenbaum, Mr. Mack.

MR. HALLEY. This is Greenbaum of Phoenix?

MR. SEDWAY. Yes; and Sanford Adler. He bought forty-some odd shares, 48 or 49 per cent.

MR. HALLEY. Adler eventually sold out; is that right?

MR. SEDWAY. Adler eventually sold out.

SENATOR WILEY. How much do you own of it now?

MR. SEDWAY. I own 7$\frac{8}{10}$ per cent. . . .

Sedway's testimony covered thirty pages. He gave a little information here, confused matters there, and skillfully dodged all vital areas. Nevertheless, it afforded the senators an oblique glimpse into the devious machinations of the underworld.

One of the items Sedway neglected to tell the senators was that the 90-per-cent loan was held by the Mob. The $3.9 million price tag took care of their investment and the Siegel heirs suffered the loss. The money owed to Webb was to be taken from the profits. The Mob did not want cash. What they wanted was a front and Sanford Adler was the best front available at the moment. With the gambling license issued to Adler, the "hidden" interests could stay well hidden. Adler, unfortunately, did suffer from the delusion that he owned the Flamingo for a while, but when he failed to produce a substantial profit, they summarily kicked him out. In April, 1948, Adler angrily stalked off to Carson City to spill his tale of woe to the Tax Commission and was able to arouse a modicum of sympathy. Jubilant over what he considered a total victory, Adler returned to Las Vegas and promptly punched Morris Rosen in the nose. In less than an hour, Adler got the word. Rosen was going to get him. Suddenly realizing his mistake, Adler jumped into his car and drove nonstop to Beverly Hills, California, where he sobbed his fears to Police Chief Clinton H. Anderson. The next day he sold out his stock in the Flamingo and moved to Reno.

This time the Mob decided on Gus Greenbaum, a favorite of the new Capone gang, then under the triumvirate leadership of Charlie "Trigger Happy" Fischetti, Jake "Greasy Thumb" Guzik, and Tony "Joe Batters" Accardo. Determined to make the hotel a success, Greenbaum borrowed $1 million from his Chicago pals for improvements, most of it to be spent in enlarging the hotel from ninety-seven to over two hundred rooms. It was a personal loan and it gave Greenbaum a controlling interest in the Nevada Projects Corporation.

The shift in command at the Flamingo came at the time when Greenbaum was having difficulties in Arizona. A change in administration had resulted in police raids and court injunctions against his bookmaking empire. Gus and his two brothers had been in Phoenix since 1928, when they had migrated from Chicago. During the Roaring Twenties, he was a bootlegger as well as a bookmaker. Soon he was the kingpin of organized crime in Arizona, handling the Trans-America wire service, and paying tribute to Al Capone, then to Frank "The Enforcer" Nitti, and finally to the triumvirate. When Siegel came West, Greenbaum took his orders directly from him.

Gus Greenbaum was a tall, loose-jointed character with a huge lantern jaw and deep-set, brooding eyes. Like most top hoodlums, he was a fancy dresser and a fast talker who glibly mixed four-letter words with proper four-syllable words and made it all sound quite congruous. To many people in Las Vegas, even today, Gus is regarded as one of the sharpest and toughest punks ever to operate there. There is a story about Gus, Mickey Cohen, and Moe Sedway that points up how tough Gus really was. All three men were seated at a table in one of the bars in the Flamingo not long after Gus took over the operation. It was early in the morning and the place was empty. Cohen and Greenbaum got involved in a violent argument, with Little Moey looking on sort of wide-eyed and fearful. Suddenly, Greenbaum reached across the table and grabbed Cohen by the tie and began to kick him under the table, all the while shouting and cursing him. He kicked until Cohen's shins bled. When Gus finished his spiel of invectives, he gave a shove and Cohen's chair flew back, spilling the little mobster on the floor. Gus returned his attention to Sedway and calmly resumed his conversation while Cohen limped out of the room, his pudgy face pale and furious.

In his first year as manager of the "fabulous Flamingo," Greenbaum not only brought the hotel into the black, but showed a $4 million profit as well. This is the figure that was reported. What the actual figure was is something the state of Nevada and the Internal Revenue Bureau will never know. Gambling even when legalized is a hard-cash business. There is no tax collector in the counting room. It is not unusual for a casino to knock off a large amount of cash from the top of the day's receipts. One casino was reputed to knock off $10,000 daily, rain or shine. Some casinos take a certain percentage, from $5,000 to $20,000 a day, depending on the action. In a year's time it totals into millions; millions of tax-free dollars filtering back to the "hidden" interests in the underworld.

But as sharp and tough as he was, Greenbaum was a sucker for a cold pair of dice or deck of cards. In a twenty-four-hour-a-day gambling town, Gus flirted with total destruction every time he approached a table. Instead of paying off his personal loan to his Chicago friends, Greenbaum steadily flung his vast income across the green-felt tables. And he steadily lost.

Gus would have benefited from a lecture delivered by Mike Howard (*né* Meyer Horowitz) in Mickey Cohen's new Brentwood mansion one night. At the time of the lecture, the Los Angeles police had a microphone planted in Mickey's spacious living room, thereby preserving these hallowed words for posterity. Howard said:

It ain't gambling if you play gin and pick up pat hands or if you roll the right dice—it's business. You must wind up a winner every night. Every day you got to get that dough. I don't gamble. Don't be a gambler—be a businessman. Get the dough if you got to take it away from them. Knock 'em down and put a gag in their mouth. . . . I go to the races and sit there for five races, drink ice tea and bet on the last race because it's fixed and I know it. That's not gambling—that's business. To hell with this luck; every night you got to take.

Between crap games and running a busy hotel and casino, Greenbaum found time to make friends and to ingratiate himself with the natives. He served on the committees of various charitable organizations. Gus smiled a lot and had a firm handshake. He was generous with politicians and law-enforcement officers. And he was quick with the donations as Vegans hurriedly built churches, trying to stay even with the number of casinos. After a few years, everyone in town had a good word for Gus Greenbaum.

In December, 1950, Gus Greenbaum was officially proclaimed the first mayor of Paradise. Paradise valley comprises an area of fifty-four square miles, which includes the four and a half miles of U.S. Highway 91, known as the Strip, and the populated area bordering the Strip. Speaking at his inauguration, Greenbaum declared that "What is good for the valley is good for the Strip. . . . We hope this move [the creation of the valley as an unincorporated town] will bring you better roads, better schools, and better everything."

The "fabulous Flamingo" became a favorite with the locals. It was clean and attractive, and the service was the finest on the Strip. There was no violence—at least, none that was discernible to the free-spending patrons. Everybody was momentarily stunned by the deluge of gold. Greenbaum had made Siegel's dream pay off in a way even Siegel had not imagined. Suddenly, hotel–casinos sprouted along the Strip as rapidly as creosote bushes. And like the creosote bush, which has a deep and intricate root structure, only the front men were visible in the glitter of glass and stone and rare woods. But before it was over, every branch of the Combination was represented along the Strip and on Fremont Street in downtown Las Vegas. The Last Frontier was enlarged and renamed the New Frontier. The Thunderbird came next, in 1948. The Desert Inn (popularly known as Wilbur Clark's Desert Inn) opened in 1950, and in 1952 there were two grand openings, the Sands and the Sahara. Nineteen fifty-five was the biggest year, with three openings: the Riviera, the Dunes, and the Royal Nevada.

The new hotels created intense competition, not only between the casinos on the Strip but between Reno and Las Vegas as well. Up to then, Reno had been known as "the biggest little city in the world." Soon it was not even the biggest little city in Nevada.

Gus Greenbaum made many friends and some enemies during his seven-year stewardship at the Flamingo. Gus was a hard taskmaster and all employees had to toe a straight and narrow line. Once he signed a complaint against two clerks who had embezzled $47,000 from the hotel. They were prosecuted, convicted, and served four years in state prison. This was not exactly the means and methods of a professional hoodlum. But using the ways of an honest businessman gave Gus a feeling of respectability. And besides, there was a lot of insurance money involved.

But there were other times when Gus forgot about respectability and reverted to the law of the jungle. One drastic example started with an armed robbery of the commission book at the Flamingo in June, 1951. Tony Broncato and Tony Trombino, products of Kansas City's Tenderloin district, and three accomplices executed the only successful armed robbery of a Strip casino in Las Vegas history. They entered the layoff cash room on the ground floor of the hotel at ten o'clock in the morning through a rear door. There were four bookies in the room, including the operator, Hy Goldbaum, whose police record (seven aliases and fourteen convictions) was equal to that of any of the bandits. (Goldbaum is presently credit manager at the Stardust.) A moment later the robbers fled with $3,500 in cash. Broncato lost a $2.98 straw hat while dashing madly to an old gray sedan waiting at the rear entrance. Though the two Tonys had covered their faces with strips of red-flannel cloth, they were recognized immediately. An APB was sent out and roadblocks were installed. A week later they were apprehended in San Francisco. Out on bail, they fled to a hideout in Los Angeles. Between them, Broncato and Trombino had yellow sheets totaling forty-six arrests and seventeen convictions, all major crimes, from aggravated assault to rape, narcotics, armed robbery, burglary, and countless murder suspicions. They were known in the underworld as shakedown artists and free-lance torpedoes.

The two Tonys were soon ferreted out of their hole. The man assigned by the Mob to do the job was Jimmy Fratianno, the top enforcer for the Mafia on the West Coast. Captain James Hamilton, chief of the Los Angeles Police Intelligence Division, credits Fratianno with at least sixteen gangland executions. According to police conjecture, Fratianno cleverly duped the two Tonys into thinking he was going to help them raise money for their trial. He had a big card game all lined up, he told them, and he arranged to meet them on Franklin Street in Hollywood. On the night of August 6, 1951, Jimmy Fratianno walked up Franklin to a parked car and carefully slid into the back seat. The two Tonys were together on the front seat. After only a few words, Fratianno pulled out two .38-caliber automatics and calmly fired eight shots, four into each head.

Later Fratianno was arrested, questioned, and reluctantly released, for lack of witnesses and evidence. He later went up on a five-year rap for extortion. He is out again and a frequent visitor in Las Vegas.

The seven years at the Flamingo took their toll on Greenbaum. He grew tired and his health began to suffer from the long days of business and the even longer nights at the gaming tables. Since childhood Gus had suffered from asthma, and with the liquor and worry he developed ulcers. In the early part of 1955, a section of his stomach was removed, and Gus decided to call it quits. His local partners in the Flamingo operation (Icepick Willie Alderman, Dave Berman, Jack McElroy, Joe Rosenberg, Elias Atol) were incensed by his decision. Gus was adamant; besides, his wife, Bess, had finally put her foot down. She was anxious to get Gus away from the booze, the gambling, and the cheap women.

The "hidden" interests were more amenable to the proposition. It was another opportunity for them to get "loan" money out and still keep control of the hotel–casino. A group of thirty local investors, headed by Thomas E. Hull, a veteran hotel man who in 1941 had built El Rancho as a small motel, paid $7 million with less than a million down.

Gus moved back into his Tower offices in Phoenix and turned his gambling fever toward the stock market. In the thirties Gus and his two brothers had been indicted on a federal charge of stock-fraud manipulations in connection with the promotion of a Phoenix supermarket. They were tried and convicted. They appealed, and the decision was reversed. They were retried (on a technicality) and again convicted; appealed once more and again won a reversal. The government threw up its hands and surrendered. Greenbaum was as good at stock manipulation as he was bad at gambling. He had an innate talent and business acumen that could have made him a rich man if he had devoted his full time to this "legitimate" pursuit. But Gus craved a more direct and personal type of action. To win a thousand dollars from Ray Ryan or Nick the Greek in a head-to-head game was more gratifying than doping out a million-dollar swindle on the stock market.

In Phoenix, the reform movement had collapsed and Gus Greenbaum was back doing business at the same old stand. One of Greenbaum's close friends of many years was Barry Goldwater (*né* Goldwasser). Goldwater was a Phoenix councilman from 1949 to 1952. Then in '52 he ran for the U.S. Senate and was elected by a one-per-cent majority.

The junior senator from Arizona, who is the most popular rich man's candidate since John Adams, is actually a poor man who lives the life of a rich man in every sense and dimension. (As comedian Mort Sahl remarked: "Goldwater is Jewish and an Episcopalian—I admire a man who tries to better himself.") Coming from a small western state, Goldwater has traveled a long way in eleven short years. As the rich man's foremost representative, it is not strange, then, to find the Senator opposed to every social and humanitarian program in this country. He is violently against Social Security, the graduated income tax, federal aid to education, public power, TVA, the closed shop, agricultural price supports, public housing, urban renewal, medical care to the aged, and economic aid to foreign countries. And finally, but still very much in character, he is opposed to enforced desegregation. In fact, Barry Goldwater is opposed to everything except personal wealth and power.

Born the son of a shopkeeper, Goldwater allegedly married a wealthy woman, but is prompt to protest that he does not touch her money for Senate business. His Senate salary is $22,500 a year, and dividends from the family emporium in Phoenix net him another $15,000 a year. This $37,500 is not enough, Goldwater claims, and must be implemented by another $10,000 which he receives by gradually liquidating his life insurance. Since he has been a senator for eleven years, it can only be assumed that his life policies must be large indeed.

Along the Strip in Las Vegas, Barry Goldwater is known by the wags and older show girls as a real "swinger." His brother, Robert ("Bobby") is a Gold Card holder and one of the "high rollers." Bobby still gambles regularly in Las Vegas but the Senator, since Greenbaum's death and his own personal "high hopes," has steered clear of the town except for brief quiet visits.

In the old days, when Gus was Mayor of Paradise, Barry Goldwater was a frequent visitor, occupying plush suites, first at the Flamingo and then later (when Gus changed his operation) at the Riviera. Some of the Senator's speeches were written in Las Vegas. The authors know of at least one occasion, in 1955, when Greenbaum's ghost writer helped the Senator with one of his speeches.

As Gus tried to relax in Phoenix, events were shaping up in Las Vegas that would soon involve him. A group of Miami investors had just completed a new eleven-story, $10 million hotel, called the Riviera. It opened in March, 1955, and immediately the builders were in financial trouble. Then one of them suggested, "Why not get Gus Greenbaum. Look what he did for the Flamingo when it was ready to fold." Gus was approached but declined.

A few days later, Tony Accardo and Jake Guzik visited Greenbaum in Phoenix. In a series of three meetings at the Flame night club, Accardo laid down the law, while cherubic-featured Greasy Thumb Guzik smiled benevolently at both of them, enjoying his role as peace mediator. There was still the matter of the million-dollar loan Greenbaum had never repaid. Gus promised to have it within two weeks. Accardo shook his head. He didn't want the million. Not yet. There was something a lot more important on his mind. Greenbaum was to take over the management of the Riviera. It was a golden opportunity for the Chicago mob. The hotel itself was not for sale. The land and the building would remain with the original corporation, but the casino was up for grabs. And the casino was the heart of the action. Everything else was just dressing. With Gus in there running things, the boys would have a front seat in the counting room.

Greenbaum listened to the various arguments before flatly turning them all down. He was a sick man, he protested. The frenetic tempo of Las Vegas would kill him. Accardo angrily pointed out that a man could die in a number of ways. Gus was not impressed. He went home, took a couple of sleeping pills, and tried to forget it.

Then one night a few days later, Gus's brother, Charlie, and his wife, Leone, visited him. Leone was nearly hysterical with fear. Some man had threatened her on the telephone, intimating that "they" were going to teach Gus a lesson. Gus assured her she had nothing to fear, but the next day she contacted the police and pleaded for protection. A few nights later, Charlie found his wife sprawled on their bed, dead. The county medical examiner concluded she had been smothered by a "human hand." The murder was never solved.

Gus Greenbaum returned to Las Vegas.

Within a short time, Gus had re-formed his old Flamingo group and had added a few other members. Gus bought twenty-seven per cent; Elias Atol seventeen and a half per cent; Joe Rosenberg, Little Icepick Willie and Berman seven per cent each; Charlie "Kewpie" Rich two per cent; Sidney Wyman ten per cent; Jack McElroy four per cent; then Gus gave Ben Goffstein two per cent and made him vice-president. Atol became treasurer.

By the time Greenbaum took over, the Riviera was ready to slide into receivership. In the middle of the night, trucks were being loaded with linen, silverware, dishes, and even furniture. The owners gambled nightly in the casino, losing thousands of dollars and then tearing up the markers. It was the most ridiculous situation since Siegel had gone berserk in the Flamingo.

Greenbaum had his work cut out for him; he was an old-timer at the business and soon put a halt to such nonsense. Rosenberg was made casino manager and Dave Berman, who could kill a man with one hand, was suddenly everywhere, barking orders, scowling ferociously, and getting things done in a hurry. Ben Goffstein trotted dutifully behind Greenbaum, trying desperately to look as important as a vice-president.

At the "fabulous Flamingo," there was much bitterness. When selling out to Thomas E. Hull, Gus had promised not to operate within five miles of the Flamingo for five years. And then, to add insult to injury, Greenbaum and Goffstein had stolen the set of ledgers containing the names of Flamingo Gold Card holders. At that time, they had literally buried the records in the desert. Now they were dug up and dusted, and a battery of secretaries were busily mailing out gold-engraved invitations to all the old suckers on the list. Soon business was booming at the Riviera. Gus Greenbaum had done it again.

At first Greenbaum tried to stay away from the gaming tables, but gradually his resistance wore down, and he found himself in the thick of it, drinking, gambling, and gamboling with the show girls and prostitutes operating in the Riviera.

One of his buddies at this time was Willie Bioff, the convicted panderer, extortionist, and celebrated stoolie. In 1941, after a six-year reign over the motion-picture industry, Bioff had been indicted in New York City for violation of the federal anti-racketeering statute. He was convicted and sentenced to serve ten years. Three years later he and his partner, George Browne, turned informers and assisted the government in the prosecution of nine Chicago mobsters, including Mafia chieftain Frank "The Enforcer" Nitti, who committed suicide before his trial. The others were Louis Campagna, Philip D'Andrea, Charles Gioe, Paul De Lucia (alias Paul "the Waiter" Ricca), Francis Maritote, John Rosselli, Louis Kaufman, and Ralph Pierce. They were all charged with conspiring to extort $1 million from Loew's, 20th Century-Fox, and Warner Brothers. Pierce was acquitted but the others were sentenced to ten-year stretches, except Kaufman, who received seven years. Three years later they were all paroled in a scandal that echoed all the way to Washington and affable Harry Truman in the White House.

Meanwhile, Bioff had settled in Phoenix. It was only natural that he would meet Greenbaum, but not so natural that they would become bosom pals. Bioff's name was anathema to the Mob.

In 1955 Bioff found an even more unlikely friend: the junior Senator from Arizona, Barry Goldwater. The two men were often seen together, and Goldwater (who was a brigadier general in the Air Force Reserve) personally chauffeured Bioff in his private plane all over the Southwest to attend various parties. When questioned by reporters, Goldwater became indignant, protesting that he had no idea that his friend, one William Nelson, was the notorious Willie Bioff. Later, the Senator changed his story. Bioff, he said, was helping him in his study of American labor, giving him a special insight into union racketeering. (To this day, Goldwater is still pleading that he did not know Nelson was Bioff. In a recent speech in defense of Texas Senator Ralph W. Yarborough, who accepted a $1,700 contribution from Billie Sol Estes, Goldwater told his Senate colleagues that he saw nothing wrong with a man in politics accepting a campaign contribution when "nothing has been disclosed" about the contributor. On one occasion, Goldwater said, he had accepted a political contribution through a relative of a man who later turned out to be a "very notorious individual." Continuing the rationalization, he added: "All of us in politics have this problem.")

Meanwhile, Bioff was placed in charge of entertainment at the Riviera. Greenbaum's rationale was that Willie would knock down the high prices of the performers. It was a pathetic excuse and did not satisfy Accardo and Guzik, who held personal grudges against Bioff for testifying against them in a federal tax case in 1948—not to mention the earlier squeal on their *paisani* in 1943.

Marshall Caifano, Accardo's top mad-dog henchman, made a special trip to the Riviera to look into the situation. Caifano, who usually goes under the alias of Johnny Marshall, is, like Bioff, a pint-size hood, but what he lacks in height and heft, he makes up in ferocity. He is one of the most feared gunmen in the underworld. It wasn't long before Caifano collared Greenbaum and told him to "get rid of the fink or else."

Greenbaum disregarded the warning. Everywhere Gus went, little Willie tagged along. It was like walking around with a leper, for Willie had twice as many enemies in Las Vegas as Gus had friends. Soon the hate boiled over and exploded.

On November 4, 1955, Willie Bioff came out of his Phoenix home and slid behind the wheel of his car. A moment later an explosion rocked the neighborhood. Parts of Willie and parts of the car were strewn all over the driveway. The police investigated and found that a dynamite bomb had been wired to the starter. That was the beginning and the end of the investigation. The case is still open, but the folder is not any thicker. (The police did learn, however, that on his last visit to Las Vegas, two weeks before his death, Bioff had returned to Phoenix in Goldwater's private plane with the Senator and Mrs. Goldwater, and Mrs. Bioff—no doubt discussing the intricacies of unionism.)

Most large casino–hotels maintain a goon squad of psychopaths whose greatest pleasure in life is the torture of their fellow human beings. As goon squads go, Gus Greenbaum had one of the best (or worst) on the Strip. The authors know of three specific incidents where cheating dealers were dragged into the counting room to be taught a lesson. The counting room, which is behind the cashier's cage, is a soundproof room, ideal for such torture. One dealer was held by two goons, while his closed fists were placed on a table. Another goon wielded a lead-encased baseball bat and brought it down on the dealer's hands, smashing them beyond repair. The dealer was then dragged through the casino, with the blood dripping from his crushed fingers. His hands were bandaged by one of the Mob's doctors who was instructed not to set the bones. Then he was driven to the edge of town and his shoes were taken from him. "Now, you son of a bitch," he was told, "walk to Barstow. No goddamn hitchhiking, either. We're gonna check on you all the way." Barstow is over 150 miles away, all of it desert.

Two other dealers had their collarbones smashed with the same bat. The life of a dealer is a hazardous one, to say the least, in Las Vegas. This kind of treatment, though, applies also to whores, cocktail waitresses, and bartenders. Employees who handle money are in a precarious position if they think they can steal from the house.

There is no one as suspicious as a hoodlum. The bigger the hoodlum, the more suspicious he is. The suspicion is almost intuitive. In the crime business, it is a substitute for brains. They spend their days checking up on their friends and associates. If someone comes in by plane, they know the exact landing time, the distance from the airport to the hotel, and how long it takes to drive it at various times of the day. The first words spoken in any greeting are: "Where you been? You're five minutes late." Alibis have to be iron-clad. If the arrivee is a half hour late, then he's in real trouble. Phone calls are made to check his every word. They are equally suspicious about their peers and their business dealings.

Recently, at a dedication ceremony in Los Angeles, where Mayor Sam Yorty and Walter O'Malley were scheduled to preside, it was rumored that a tough Las Vegas hoodlum was going to attend as O'Malley's guest. The dedication concerned land and everyone, including Yorty, knew that if the hoodlum showed up, he was going to leave with a percentage of the deal. An employee of a friend of the hoodlum was approached by two of the Mayor's assistants. "You've got to do something," they pleaded. "If that guy shows up it will be murder for Yorty. He's got enough trouble right now without getting his picture taken with this bum." The employee promised to do what he could. That evening when he was having a drink with his boss, he casually remarked about the boss's friend attending the ceremony. The boss stared into space for a long time before answering. "I don't know nothing about that," he said thoughtfully, his brow furrowing. "Naw, I'm sure he's not going." Then he thought some more, the little wheels clicking away, no doubt wondering what his friend was pulling behind his back. "Naw, that's got to be wrong. His mama's sick in Chicago. I think he's going home to see her." The hood never showed up at the ceremony.

Bioff's death deeply shocked Greenbaum. He increased his drinking and his ulcers started acting up again. Then his asthma got worse and he visited the town's most respected and wealthiest doctor, who prescribed heroin for the asthma attacks, assuring Greenbaum that it was the only thing that could stop his wheezing and coughing and ease his breathing. And besides, he added, the heroin would dull his desire for liquor, indirectly helping his ulcers. Gus was apprehensive, but being a cold-deck gambler he decided to give it a short whirl just to see what happened. The heroin worked miracles for his asthma. Within six months he was a confirmed addict.

Being one of the most suspicious in the land of suspicion, Gus was able to cover up his new habit from the Mob for a long time. His gambling increased and his forays among the whores became so extravagant that even the jaded bellhops were astounded. Heroin never subdued Gus's libido. He surrounded himself with whores and was constantly inviting friends to share in his sexual aberrations. (The second question in Las Vegas after "Where you been?" is "Didja get laid?")

Gus's gambling luck turned from bad to worse. He gambled nightly, more often than not the entire night, retiring with one or two "broads" for what turned out to be a couple of fitful hours of sleep. By noon he would drag himself to the lobby, his pale face emaciated, his eyes puffed and ringed with dark circles. Dave Berman carried much of the load Gus was now neglecting. Then Berman was stricken with cancer and died, leaving Gus without the muscle he had depended on for so many years.

The heroin took its effect most notably in Gus's thinking. With his personal fortune completely dissipated, Gus began to cheat his partners on the count. Slowly the profits decreased and the Mob began to worry. They knew that it was virtually impossible for a casino with the Riviera's volume to lose money. The odds are always with the house, averaging perhaps 6 per cent of every dollar bet on a table. Somebody was stealing and that somebody had to be Greenbaum. By this time they knew Gus was on junk and they knew of his gambling losses.

Marshall Caifano made another trip to the Riviera. Gus did not want to talk to him. Every time Caifano approached him, Gus moved away. Finally, Caifano cornered him in the gambling pit. Shaking his fist at Gus, Caifano laid down the Mob's ultimatum. "Sell out or you're gonna be carried out in a box."

After Caifano left, Gus called a meeting of his group. "I don't want to leave," he said. "This goddamn town is in my blood. I can't leave." His group, which held the controlling interest in the casino, backed him up. Greenbaum hired himself two bodyguards and remained at the Riviera. The decision cost him his life.

During the 1958 Thanksgiving holiday, Greenbaum went back to Phoenix to be with his family, leaving the bodyguards behind in Vegas. Nothing more had been heard from Chicago. He had talked to Accardo the week before and everything seemed back to normal. But 124 miles south of Phoenix, a group of well-dressed men had assembled at the ranch of a friend in Tucson. The friend was Pete "Horse Face" Licavoli and the spread was known throughout the underworld as the Grace Ranch. At the time, Licavoli was out on bail, awaiting an appeal on a recent conviction of federal income tax evasion. His yellow sheet had thirty-four entries, starting with juvenile delinquency at the age of ten in St. Louis. At the height of prohibition, Licavoli moved his action to Detroit and married into the most powerful Mafia family in Michigan, all residents of the exclusive Grosse Pointe section. Pete married Grace Bommarito, sister of Scarface Joe Bommarito and also a sister of Mrs. Sam Zerilli. Sam Zerilli's sister, Rosalie, was the wife of Black Bill Tocco. One of Tocco's sons, Tony Joe, married Joe Profaci's daughter, Carmella. The study of the intermarriages between the Toccos, Zerillis, Licavolis, Priziolas, Polizzis, Melis, Perrones, and Bommaritos in the Detroit–Cleveland area is a study of the Mafia itself. Family ties crisscross in a complex web over the entire United States. Another of Joe Profaci's daughters married Nick Licata's son, Carlo, in Los Angeles. Profaci's niece is married to the son of Joseph Bonanno and his brother-in-law is Joseph Magliocco—Profaci and Magliocco are second cousins and their mothers are first cousins. All three Joes—Profaci, Magliocco, and Bonanno—attended the Cleveland Mafia meeting on December 6, 1929, and the Apalachin meeting on November 14, 1957, twenty-eight years later.

And now again the three Joes enjoyed thick steaks and bonded whiskey together at the Grace Ranch. Other Mafia *dons* from across the country had joined them. The conversation was mostly in a peculiar Sicilian dialect and there was much hand-shaking and emotional embracing as the variously related members greeted each other. Tony Accardo walked among them, smiling and winking, the perfect host. The decision reached at this meeting cost Accardo one million dollars.

Shortly before noon on December 3, 1958, Pearl Ray, the Greenbaum housekeeper, found Gus Greenbaum, clad in beige-silk pajamas, sprawled across two twin beds pushed together, with pillows pressed on either side of his head. He was almost decapitated. A heat pad, the television, and a table lamp were still on. Bess Greenbaum lay face down on a couch in the den, at least fifty feet away down an L-shaped hall from her husband. She was fully clothed, including a knit sweater-type jacket. Her hands were bound behind her back with one of Gus's silk ties. At her feet was a blood-smeared butcher knife (taken from the Greenbaum kitchen). It lay on a plastic bag that the killer had used to shield his hand. Bess's throat had also been severely slashed, but only after she had been knocked unconscious by a heavy glass ornamental bottle. Under her face was a section of newspaper and a bathroom towel and near her head were a bedroom pillow and a sofa throw pillow. Not a drop of blood had touched the deep carpeting. Nothing except Bess's house key was stolen. Outside, in an areaway beside the garage, police found shoe prints and cigarette ashes that indicated the presence of two men. There was much official speculation concerning the crime, but as in the Siegel murder in Beverly Hills, nothing of any importance was ever added to the basic facts. No clue, no suspicion, no arrest.

The authors wish to take this opportunity to advise the Phoenix police of the arrival of a chartered plane bearing two men on the afternoon of the murder. It departed that same day at 10:30 P.M. The plane was from Miami, Florida.

The Greenbaum funeral was attended by three hundred mourners, including Senator Barry Goldwater. Listening to Rabbi Albert L. Plotkin, an uninformed bystander would have been much impressed by the virtues of the late Gus Greenbaum.

"The lives of good people," the rabbi said, "need no eulogy. They speak for themselves. Gustave Greenbaum was loved and respected as a friend. He had an inner warmth and kindness to his soul. He gave of himself humbly and simply, without notoriety."

Warming up to his subject, Rabbi Plotkin added: "Their marriage was one of the most beautiful things in life. It was a marriage of untold years of giving, sweetly sharing, and seeking together a life of beauty." Then in conclusion he declared: "The spirit itself cannot die. Their good life is an inspiration."

CHAPTER FOUR

The Temples of Mammon

In Greek mythology, Palamedes invented dice and taught the game to his countrymen during the seige of Troy. Palamedes also invented money. The two have been inseparable ever since. In terms of Western history, Palamedes was the first professional gambler, and like all gamblers who followed in his footsteps, he was a cunning and resourceful man, though not very lovable —he was stoned to death.

Dice made of ivory, the knucklebones of sheep, stone, or metal have been excavated from cities dating back to 1,000 B.C., and were once used by Pagan priests when they wished to consult with the gods. Since the gods could control the fall of the dice, the answer to any propounded question lay in the way the numbers came up. But even then there were characters who tried to outwit divinity by loading the cubes.

Much of the mystique of old still exists in today's gamblers, though the need to cheat in Las Vegas is more psychological than pragmatic. With the prevailing odds enjoyed by the house, the cheating is mostly internal.

In fact, there have been few casino failures in Las Vegas. Except for the Moulin Rouge (which failed for other reasons), the Royal Nevada is the only Strip hotel that lost its bankroll and flopped. Its showroom was turned into a convention hall for the Stardust, which also utilizes its three hundred rooms.

Since it opened in 1955, the New Frontier has gone through the resources of nearly a hundred investors, including a large bundle from Vera Krupp, the munitions heiress, who owns a ranch in nearby Red Rock Canyon. The hotel has been plagued by bad management, and the fact that it never was "with it" as far as the Las Vegas underworld clan is concerned has no doubt helped it along the road to ruin. The New Frontier is an outgrowth of the Last Frontier, which opened in 1942, four years before the Mob moved in. Today it is operated by Warren "Doc" Bayley, a self-styled farmer from Platteville, Wisconsin, who built the Hacienda, known along the Strip as "Hayseed Heaven." Bayley operates his own fleet of planes (eight planes valued at $2 million) and last year ferried in 150,000 "package deal" guests from San Francisco, Los Angeles, St. Louis, Chicago, Detroit, and New York. The Los Angeles flight features a piano bar, champagne, and a strip-tease act. Once in Las Vegas, the tourists become "captive guests" in the last outpost along the Strip, literally miles from the center of the action. Included in the nominal package deal is ten dollars "to spend." This is in the form of ten white paper chits that can be used only for gambling. The idea is that the user will feel conspicuous at the gaming table and will secretly be glad when the last one is gone. Soon he will be digging into his wallet for real money and then it will be the house's turn to be glad.

To date Bayley is one of the few owners along the Strip who has not been connected (we think) with the underworld. Now and then a hoodlum has been seen on the premises, but the fact that it is a "hayseed" operation may very well have discouraged the boys.

The big guessing game in Las Vegas is "Who owns whom." Though there are many big hoodlums in Las Vegas operating openly as licensed owners in plush Strip casinos, there are many more who operate behind legitimate or semilegitimate fronts. One front can be divided among a half-dozen hoodlums from as many states. Or one hidden hoodlum may own a half-dozen fronts. It is a baffling and curious game that confuses the police, the Gaming Control Board, and not a few owners along the Strip. The fronts are moved about from casino to casino like pawns on a chessboard as the big boys buy and sell. Two well-known pawns, Sidney Wyman and Kewpie Rich, were moved from the Flamingo to the Riviera (Wyman was also at the Sands) and lately to the Dunes, which is having its share of trouble with Chicago. These two characters once operated a bookmaking operation in St. Louis where they used Western Union offices as bookie drops.

One national magazine greeted the opening of the Sahara Hotel in 1954 with these words: "Today, the big mystery is the identity of the owners of the Sahara Hotel, newest of the multimillion-dollar casino palaces along the Strip. Listed owners of the Sahara are A. F. Winter, Milton Prell, and Barney Morris. All are small-time gamblers out of Oregon, where they ran upstairs dice tables, poker games and race books. Such minor operators don't move in on a territory dominated by the Flamingo, Desert Inn and Sands outfits just because they feel like it. The only thing that figures is they're backed by somebody big."

Actually, Milton Prell is an ex-Los Angeles jeweler who was

once fined for operating skillball machines in Butte, Montana. Today there are thirty-four owners in the Sahara and only three of them list their address as Portland, Oregon. The "mysterious" hidden interests may be behind any of these names. Del Webb, builder of the Flamingo and the Sahara, recently erected a twenty-three-story skyscraper addition to the Sahara that was financed largely by his construction company. A group of Sahara owners also control the Mint, in Glitter Gulch.

By far the most publicized front man in Las Vegas history is Wilbur Clark, the Desert Inn's genial host, who has smiled and winked his way into the hearts of a million happy losers. A few years ago, Wilbur flashed his big smile into millions of American homes. His host was Edward R. Murrow. At that time Wilbur was a happy man with a gargantuan ego. But a few years can be a lifetime in Las Vegas, where fortunes are made and lost overnight. Wilbur still has his ego, but not much else. Caught unawares behind his expensive horseshoe desk, the snowy-haired "Ambassador of Vegas" is rather glum these days. His eyes stare morosely at the many autographed pictures of celebrities on the tastefully paneled walls, and the corners of his mouth slant downward as he nervously chews on his lower lip.

On the surface, at least, Clark appears to be clean by comparison to the odious characters that surround him at the Desert Inn. Except for an income-tax-evasion rap which he miraculously beat in 1953, the fifty-three-year-old gambler is one of the few big operators on the Strip without a police record. His background is vague and that's the way he intends to keep it. Seated before the *Person to Person* television camera, Wilbur deftly sketched in a nebulous background. He had left his Keyesport, Illinois, home at the age of nineteen, he smilingly recalled, hitch-hiking to the West Coast, washing dishes in various cafés along the way. Included was a sentimental vignette about a café owner who gave him a silver dollar with the admonishment that if he kept the dollar he'd never go broke. (Years later Wilbur had 3,500 silver dollars minted with his likeness on one side and the Desert Inn on the other.)

Finally, he settled in San Diego, California, where for a time he worked at a variety of menial jobs: dishwasher, busboy, elevator operator, bellboy. Then he switched to dice dealing and his fortune changed. He worked on a couple of gambling boats off the California coast, moved on to Saratoga, to Reno and Palm Springs. Back in San Diego, he bought four or five barrooms (with gambling in the back), and later acquired a small hotel with his brother. Next thing he knew, he was in Las Vegas and a part owner of the El Rancho Vegas on the Strip. Then, of course, he built the Desert Inn and lived happily ever after in a quarter-million-dollar house with television sets popping out of the ceiling. Murrow's visit was most amusing. The Horatio Alger image must have given the all-wise robber barons along the Strip many hearty belly laughs.

Wilbur is, has been, and always will be a well-dressed puppet to the gambling fraternity. They are not impressed by the fact that he has been presented to the Pope (his wife is Catholic) in two private audiences, or that he has been a guest at the White House on several occasions. Or that he's listed in *Who's Who* and was twice voted as one of the ten best-dressed men in America. Or that he was mayor of Paradise on two occasions, and is a member in good standing of the local PTA, the Opera Association, the Elks, and the (32nd degree) Masons.

The depth of Wilbur's ignorance is surpassed only by the height of his ego. His grinning visage is inescapable in Las Vegas. The tourist is confronted with it on napkins, match folders, gambling chips, menus, stationery, place mats, paper cups, and multicolored neons. This infantile urge for fame is welcomed by the mobsters who pull the strings on Clark. It keeps the heat of publicity off them and gives the suckers the kind of flamboyant square-john they can identify with and trust.

To judge from his clothes, his diamond accessories, his palatial home, his arrogance, Wilbur Clark has to be wealthy. But wealth in Las Vegas is most relative. Compared to his colleagues, Wilbur is far from rich—and even farther from owning the Desert Inn. In fact, he has never even come close to owning it.

The actual construction of the D.I. was started in May of 1947 by Wilbur and his brother, and two other investors. The total cash raised was a quarter of a million dollars. A few months later, the money ran out and the construction came to a halt. For nearly two years the wooden framework sat bleaching under the desert sun like the carcass of an ancient buffalo. Then, in the summer of 1949, Clark met Moe Dalitz, and two months later they made a deal. Dalitz and five of his Cleveland partners in the notorious Mayfield Road gang (Morris Kleinman, Sam Tucker, Thomas Jefferson McGinty, Ruby Kolod, Bernie Rothkopf) cut themselves in for 74 per cent of the D.I. Brought in by Dalitz to supervise the business end of the deal was Allard Roen (*né* Rosen), a young Duke University graduate. Today Roen owns 2.5 per cent of the D.I. and 2 per cent of the Stardust. (Roen was also one of sixteen defendants in the United Dye and Chemical Corporation $5 million stock-fraud-swindle trial. Involved with him were three other Las Vegas gamblers: Charles M. Berman, Sam Garfield, and Irving Pasternak. Testimony in the trial clearly showed how gambling interests could penetrate a publicly held corporation with a New York Stock Exchange listing and convert it into a "boiler room" pressure operation. The charges also included bribery in high places. Federal prosecutor Gerald Walpin charged that the late Senator Bender of Ohio had been paid $100,000 when he was an assistant secretary of the interior to "quash an SEC investigation." Roen and his associates had entered into a conspiracy with two United Dye officers, swapped almost worthless companies to United Dye in exchange for 575,000 shares of United Dye stock, four times the amount previously outstanding. They then sold the stock in a "boiler room" promotion for $10 million at vastly inflated prices. Roen and eight other defendants pleaded guilty during the trial. As of this writing, Roen is still awaiting sentencing.)

One year later, during the Kefauver Investigation, Senator Charles Tobey of New Hampshire blew his top.

"Before you got in bed with crooks to finish this proposition, didn't you look into these birds at all?" Tobey asked Clark.

"Not too much. No, sir," said Wilbur.

And then when Clark admitted he didn't know the names of the other directors or the heads of the various departments in the Desert Inn, Senator Tobey again interrupted the testimony.

"You have the most nebulous idea of your business I ever saw. You have a smile on your face but I don't know how the devil you do it."

"I have done it all my life," Wilbur answered.

Clark's testimony covered twelve pages and though he evaded questions with pleas of faulty memory, he never once hid behind the Fifth Amendment. The picture presented of the big-shot impresario was somewhat less than imposing. He came out as a confused little fish who had been bodily swallowed by the sharks from the underwater catacombs of Cleveland.

Clark's once boyish face now clearly mirrors the ravages of thirteen years of struggling in a jungle of concealed violence and chicanery, where the rules change every day with the prevailing odds. The results have been two coronaries and an apprehensive bird's-eye viewpoint on the future. Clark now visits the Desert Inn only rarely. Instead he sticks close to his home on the edge of the Inn's golf course and speculates on what his dream might have been if it had not turned into a nightmare.

Where once he literally ran to newsmen, gushing with good will and humorous anecdotes, he now shuns them in fear they will ask intimidating questions about his associates. All he will say is that they have treated him fairly, but it is obvious that Wilbur is a very frightened man, a shell of the old convivial "Ambassador of Vegas." He is even afraid to take a vacation. Recently, while on the first leg of a European tour, he received an urgent telegram from his private secretary of eleven years, Frosty Jennsen, informing him of plans afoot to remove his name and image from sundry items in the D.I. The next day Moe Dalitz stormed into Frosty's office and summarily fired her. The shocked secretary, who had a son to support, toppled over and died at her desk of a heart attack. Her funeral was dutifully attended by Dalitz and his Cleveland cronies. Wilbur is still grieving.

From the very beginning, the Desert Inn has represented the temporal power of the U.S. crime syndicate; it has been a favorite haven for the country's most sinister hoodlums. In thirteen years it has played host to more Apalachin-type meetings than Miami and Atlantic City combined. It is a favorite with the *capi mafiosi,* and to prove their love, they have been slowly usurping control, all well disguised behind respectable (for Las Vegas, that is) fronts.

Seated behind his own expansive horseshoe desk, Moe Dalitz is not inclined to smile too readily these days either. His reign as absolute potentate of the Desert Inn expired long ago. And no one knows it any better than the sanctimonious little mobster from Cleveland.

In a recent interview, Ed Reid was stunned when Dalitz burst into tears. "Why, why," he implored, his arms rising in supplication, the tears streaming from his hard little eyes, "why are they persecuting me?"

"Who?" Reid inquired.

"Them. All of them! I've fought hoodlums all my life. What are they trying to do to me?"

What eventually will happen to Dalitz may be very similar to what happened to a number of Dalitz's competitors in the old days, as Moe well knows. Meanwhile, to a corps of uninitiated magazine writers, Moe still palms himself off as a big shot and dispenses his two-bit philosophy on morality. In a recent interview with Peter Wyden of *The Saturday Evening Post,* Moe said: "Let's say gambling isn't moral. Neither is drinking to excess. I think Las Vegas has given people lots of fun. Sure, some will get hurt. But listen, they can go to Atlantic City and get into more danger in a crap game than here, where there's supervision."

Dalitz's criminal activities go back to the prohibition era. In his heyday he had a lot going for him, including many legitimate enterprises. Among his gambling interests were the Mound Club, the Pettibone Club, and the Jungle Inn, near Youngstown, Ohio; the Beverly Hills Club and the Lookout House, near Cincinnati; the Frolics Club in Miami, Florida; the Ohio Villa in Richmond Heights, Ohio; and the two swankiest clubs in Kentucky, the Lookout Club in Covington and the Beverly Country Club in Newport. Associated with Dalitz in some of these illegal gambling ventures were many of his closest friends of that period: Morris Kleinman, Lou Rothkopf, Thomas Jefferson McGinty, Sam Tucker, Cornelius Jones, Sam "Game Boy" Miller, Charles "Chuck" and Alfred "Big Owl" Polizzi, Tony and Frank Milano, Joe Massei, and Abner "Longie" Zwillman. In later years, Frank Milano and Al Polizzi, two important

Mafia *dons,* edged Dalitz out of the leadership of the Mayfield Road gang.

Milano and Polizzi were also important members of the Detroit Purple Gang, an exclusive Sicilian mob, bossed by Black Bill Tocco and his fantastic Grosse Pointe clan of relatives: the Bommaritos, the Licavolis, the Zerillis, the Melis, the Corrados, the Matrangas, the Perrones, the Priziolas, and scores of others who form the hard core of the central division of the Mafia.

Many of the same friends also joined Dalitz in his legitimate enterprises, which we will list briefly here to show the diversity of investments. Some of these, of course, Dalitz owned outright, while in others he was joined by the various friends listed above. The list does not include all his businesses but a fair proportion of the larger ones, each one capitalized in the tens or hundreds of thousands of dollars, and some in the millions: Reliance Steel Corp., Detroit Steel Corp., Michigan Industrial Laundry Co., Pioneer Laundry Co., D. J. Krause Realty Co., Michigan Modern Land Co., Colonial Laundry, Liberty Co., Union Enterprise, Buckeye Catering Co., Pioneer Linen Supply Co., Milco Sales Co., Dalitz Realty Co., Berdeen Realty Co., Liberty Ice Cream Co., Chicago & Rock Island Railroad Co., River Downs Race Track, and Coney Island Dog Track.

Those were the good old days of wealth and power. The days when Moe Dalitz had the "big fix" in a half-dozen city halls. Moe had organizational ability and he used it for corruption. His legitimate enterprises simplified the fix—stock deals and percentages are the modern ways to pay off graft. In the case of the Pioneer Laundry Co., his partner was the son of a powerful Cleveland politician, Maurice Maschke, Jr.

Dalitz's partners were not all as agile as their boss in keeping out of trouble. Kleinman was convicted of income tax evasion in 1933 and served three years of a four-year sentence in Lewisburg penitentiary. It was based on his 1929 income, estimated by the government at $931,000. All the others, including Dalitz, had yellow sheets until Dalitz managed to have them removed from the police files and destroyed.

After the 1945 murder of Nathan Weisenberg, the slot-machine king of Cleveland, the Dalitz mob was on its way out. Besides the harassment of the Cleveland Press and the presence of Eliot Ness, the Sicilians were moving in like an army of locusts. Dalitz was still on friendly terms with the Mafia, but he knew that the best way to stay friendly was to move out without losing face, and before it was too late.

Dalitz told the Kefauver committee that the investment of his group in the Desert Inn had been in the neighborhood of $1.3 million. *Time* magazine estimated it at $4 million, which is a lot closer to the actual figure of $5 million. Today, with its golf course and country club, it is valued at $10 million.

On the Desert Inn's opening night, April 24, 1950, Wilbur Clark, boyish and jaunty, warmly greeted his myriad guests beside a pink-painted Joshua tree laden with gardenias. His diamond-studden cufflinks glittered as he graciously plucked a gardenia from the tree for each lady. Inside the green-and-coral casino, the crowd surged around the gambling tables: movie stars, politicians, millionaires, and hoodlums, rubbing elbows, drinking, laughing, and tossing money away as though it had gone out of fashion. The elite corps consisted of 150 Gold Card holders, each entitled to $10,000 credit. Some of the more prominent guests were Governor Vail Pittman, Lieutenant Governor Clifford A. Jones, Mayor Ernie Cragin, former U.S. Senator E. P. Carville, Van Heflin, Ella Logan, Gail Storm, Evelyn Keyes, Abbott and Costello, and Chet "Lum" Lauck. Sprinkled among them were such *capi mafiosi* as Black Bill Tocco, Joe Massei, Sam Maceo, Pete Licavoli, and Frank Milano, all harboring a secret grin on their otherwise impassive faces. The gross play for that first night totaled $750,000.

The Sicilians had a good reason for being there. In fact, without them there wouldn't have been an opening night. Months earlier, Virgil Peterson, operating director of the Chicago Crime Commission, had sent a damning report to the Nevada Tax Commission on Dalitz and associates. The Tax Commission delayed the issuance of the licenses until "juice," in the person of the late *mafioso* Sam Maceo, Galveston's underworld chieftain, appeared at the Riverside Hotel in Reno, and presented the boys' case to the late Senator Pat McCarran. Suddenly, the opposition seemed to melt away and the licenses were issued posthaste. Again the Sicilians had succeeded where others had failed. And the reason could be found in one word: organization.

Once the operation got under way, Dalitz did not lose time cementing relationships. It soon became a well-known fact about town that Moe had juice at police headquarters. The complete demoralization of the police force shocked even the jaded citizens of the gambling camp, and a special grand jury began to look into the matter after patrolman Al Mazucca, fired for insubordination, blew the whistle on his colleagues. The following investigation shook the town. When the dust settled, Mazucca found himself alone behind bars. Police Chief Ray Sheffer resigned and Moe promptly appointed him chief security officer at the Stardust, a hotel controlled by the Desert Inn.

Dalitz is proud of his cultivated taste in the finer things in life, and surrounds himself with art objects, custom-made furniture, tailored clothes, diamond accessories, and beautiful women. The good life has softened Moe considerably: the veneer of respectability, the social and philanthropic whirl, the gay playboy, the respected rancher (cattle ranch in central Utah with private airstrip), the student of politics, the wise old man, and all the years removed from the actual battlefield of the underworld. He is still the hoodlum in conscience and mind, but the heart has weakened.

The pressure is on. The Sicilians are moving in and Moe sits and wrings his hands in desperation. Licavoli and his Detroit *paisani* have been in from the beginning, collecting their substantial tithe. But now the Capone mob is moving in and Big Tony Accardo's number-one enforcer, Marshall Caifano, has been pushing his weight around. Early in 1961, Caifano paid one of his visits to the D.I. The target this time was Morris Kleinman. The argument started in the cocktail lounge adjacent to the casino. Now, nobody in Las Vegas ever argues with an owner, not if he values his health. Unless, of course, he is a Chicago thug whose boss might control the owner. Caifano, it seems, was trying to make a point about the division of interest in the Stardust Hotel, a thousand-room monolith, owned (on record) by the D.I. group, but bossed by Johnny Drew, an old Capone mobster.

"Listen, you dumb dago," Kleinman shouted menacingly. "You can't talk to me that way."

Caifano's face darkened. He cursed and swung, slamming the heel of his hand into Kleinman's face and knocking him out of his chair. First startled, then terrified, Kleinman jumped to his feet and raced out of the lounge, across the casino and lobby, then up the stairs to his room, where he bolted the door. Caifano was right behind him all the way. The security guards stared in disbelief. The entire action in the casino stopped while dealers frowned knowingly and players looked puzzled.

The frightened Kleinman moved chairs and a dresser over to barricade the entrance. Caifano banged on the door with the butt of his gun and shouted threats. No one came to Kleinman's rescue.

Marshall Caifano, who operates under a score of aliases, such as Joe Russo, Frank Rinaldi, George Mariani, and Johnny Marshall, is one of the most feared henchmen in Las Vegas. Once a pugilist, Caifano traded in the boxing gloves for a gun at an early age. He is the brother of Leonard "Fats" Caifano, killed in 1951 while attempting to kidnap Theodore Roe, a wealthy numbers king in Chicago. Marshall was picked up for questioning in that case but Roe could (or would) not identify him. A few weeks later, Roe was killed. Caifano's name has been linked to some of the most sensational murders in the underworld. He was a key suspect in the bludgeoning and torch murder of Estelle Carey, Chicago dice girl and sweetheart of Nick "Dean" Circella, who was serving a ten-year rap on the Bioff movie-extortion case.

Another case involved the murder of former Chicago Police Lieutenant William Drury in 1950. The Drury case vividly illustrates the power of the Mob. It began during the investigation following the murder of James M. Ragen, owner of the Continental Press Service. Captain Thomas E. Connelly and Lieutenant William Drury courageously brought in Jake "Greasy Thumb" Guzik for questioning. Guzik was freed within two hours, but Connelly and Drury were indicted; the charge: depriving Guzik (ex-convict, panderer, and "bagman" for the Capone Mob) of his civil rights! In a fit of temper, Guzik had threatened to have the officers busted.

Meanwhile, three of Guzik's torpedoes had been identified as Ragen's murderers and were under indictment for murder. But soon two of the witnesses recanted, the third was murdered, and naturally the indictment was dropped.

But not so with Connelly and Drury. They were brought before a grand jury and when that body returned a "no-bill," they were brought before the Civil Service Commission and dismissed from the force. The two officers sued and were promptly reinstated by the court, but the city appealed. The Illinois Supreme Court approved the court decision, but again the city refused to accept the verdict. The case was brought up before the Appellate Court on a technicality, and there

Guzik's threat was finally and irrevocably made good. Two jurists "heartily approved the wholesome decision of the Civil Service Commission," serving notice to Chicago's seven thousand policemen to keep their hands off the Mob, proving once again that organized hoodlums are in fact untouchable.

Drury continued to fight city hall and the Mob to the day he was murdered in his garage on September 25, 1950. Caifano was questioned politely by the Chicago police, and for the eighteenth time in his sordid career, promptly released.

A lot of people along the Strip have reason to fear Mr. John Marshall (as he's respectfully referred to in newspapers across the country). Beldon Katleman, owner of El Rancho Vegas, lost his head one night and had Caifano ejected forcefully from the premises. Two weeks later, a mysterious fire completely gutted El Rancho Vegas. Nothing was ever proved, but then no investigation was undertaken. To this very day, El Rancho is still a pile of ashes.

On May 1, 1963, Caifano, Charles Delmonico (son of Charlie "The Blade" Tourine), Allen Smiley, and Nicholas "Nick the Greek" Dandolas were seized by the F.B.I. on charges of conspiring to extort money from Ray Ryan, wealthy oilman and hotel operator who is a high-rolling gambler i. Las Vegas. At this writing, they are still awaiting trial.

Caifano's hassle with Kleinman at the Desert Inn was followed by an Apalachin-type meeting attended by fourteen *capi mafiosi* at the Jackpot Motel late in 1960. One of the more obvious results of the conclave was the promotion of Nick Peter "Peanuts" Danolfo from "host" at the D.I. to commander in chief. Danolfo, a former dealer in some of Dalitz's Midwest gambling clubs, has been at the D.I. since its opening in 1950. He is a close personal friend of Tony Accardo and Pete Licavoli. In fact, when Licavoli was rousted by Sheriff Ralph Lamb in November, 1961, it was Danolfo who comforted the Sicilian mobster during the process of fingerprinting, photographing, and registering as an ex-con, which Licavoli had neglected to do. (This should not be construed to mean that all ex-cons are forced to register in Las Vegas.)

There is no doubt as to the real ownership of the Desert Inn in underworld circles. Among a dozen Sicilians, Licavoli and Accardo are at the top of the list.

Along with the Sands, the D.I. has been the most successful hotel–casino on the Strip. It attracts some of the wealthiest and most famous people in the country. Hoodlums have always enjoyed rubbing elbows with the elite. It imbues them with a sense of respectability. And conversely, many of the so-called elite are imbued with a sense of evil. It is a game of illusions and delusions.

Advertised as the world's largest resort hotel, the 1,032-room Stardust occupies thirty-six acres of desert wasteland. Its tinseled façade resembles a Dali nightmare, and the multicolored (11,-972 light bulbs) sign which blazons forth its name is over a block long. It emphasizes the astronomical theme with a gleaming earth turning in a welter of flashing planets, comets, and flaring meteors.

The originator of this monolithic monstrosity was a Runyonesque character (as colorful and conniving as any ever penned by the Broadway columnist) by the name of Antonio Cornero Stralla—better known as Tony Cornero. In a Runyon story, Cornero would have been tagged "Hard Way" Tony, and his troubles would have evoked gales of laughter and a couple of tears. But in real life Cornero's troubles were a lot more pathetic than humorous.

Born in Italy at the turn of the century, Cornero started out in America by tooling a cab over the picturesque hills of San Francisco. That was during the early years of prohibition, when there was plenty of easy money around for an ambitious young man without scruples. Soon Tony traded in his cab for a double-barrel shotgun. As a hijacker of contraband liquor Tony was an immediate success. Within a few years he became "King of the Rumrunners" along the California coast, accumulating a personal fortune estimated at well over $1 million before his thirtieth birthday. But the bad luck which was relentlessly to dog Tony's footsteps all of his life soon caught up with him. It started in 1926 after the S.S. "Lilly" had unloaded four thousand cases of liquor into motor launches off the coast of southern California. Tony was operating one of the motor launches when the Coast Guard closed in on the smugglers. After a wild chase in which he tried to turn back out to sea, Cornero was arrested and indicted on three counts: smuggling in 895 cases and four sacks of rum, conspiracy to import liquor, and dumping a rowboatload of liquor to avoid arrest.

Cornero jumped bail and headed for Canada. A farcical cops-and-robbers chase followed. Cornered by federal agents in the smoking car of a train en route to Seattle, Tony leaped from the moving train. With his clothes torn and soiled, he limped to a small northern California town and hired a plane to fly him to a point near Portland, Oregon. Unknowingly, he boarded the same train. When the chase was resumed, he jumped from the train a second time. It was an exhausted and bloodied Cornero who eventually arrived in Canada.

These antics continued for twenty years. In 1929, Tony inexplicably surrendered to federal authorities and served two years on the bootlegging charges. Then, in 1938 he ran a gambling ship, the S.S. "Rex" in Santa Monica Bay, which, after it was raided, he lost in a twenty-hour crap game. During the Second World War, he traveled in Central and South America as a United States Naval Intelligence agent "without portfolio" and claimed to have been instrumental in stamping out

74

a major smuggling ring which shipped commercial diamonds from Brazil to Germany via Cuba. In 1946 he returned to the bounding main in a new gambling ship, the S.S. "Lux," a decommissioned Navy mine-layer converted at a cost of $150,000. The Coast Guard immediately seized the "Lux" as a menace to navigation.

Defeated but undaunted, Cornero retreated to Las Vegas, where he bought a piece of the gambling casino in the Apache Hotel, at the corner of Second and Fremont. Sentimentally, he named it the S.S. "Rex." Tony had big plans for the casino but he soon got into a hassle with his partners. They bought him out and Tony moved to Beverly Hills, where he bought a house for his wife, Jeanne. His next brainstorm took him to Mexico with a plan to reopen gambling in that country. Las Vegas gamblers did not take too kindly to the idea, and one night while he was entertaining two Mexican officials in his Beverly Hills home, an assassin dressed as a messenger rang the front doorbell.

"We've got something for you, Tony," the messenger said, offering Cornero a large cardboard carton. There was a pistol shot and Tony staggered back into the living room, clutching his stomach.

Cornero was rushed to Cedars of Lebanon Hospital in critical condition, and remained on the critical list nearly two weeks. When questioned by the police, he refused to identify the gunman. A few months later, Tony's wife sustained a superficial gunshot wound which she claimed was accidental. The position of the wound, however, left some doubt as to who had pulled the trigger.

For the next few years, Cornero occupied himself with a small shipping business, transporting bananas, lumber, and beef between Pacific Coast ports. Again disaster struck. One of his ships, the S.S. "Salina Cruz," a 1,300-ton lumber schooner loaded to the gunwhale with lumber and beef, burned and sank off the coast of Washington.

Shortly after this financial reverse, Cornero returned to Las Vegas. He drank and brooded from bar to bar along the Strip. He played barbouth with Gus Greenbaum and Ray Ryan and sometimes Nick the Greek. He shot craps (his first and *last* love) in all the casinos, and never hesitated to drop to his knees when there was easy money to be won and no table in sight. "Hard Way" Tony was a born gambler. Nothing excited him more than the roll of dice or the fall of a card; unless, of course, it was some grandiose plan for a new promotion. As a free-lance bootlegger and gambler, Cornero outdreamed all the hoodlums of his time. He lived by his wits and despite his incredibly bad luck, he lived the life of a wealthy man and was always able to come up with a new stake.

Late one night, while he was having a drink with friends at Louigi's on the Strip, he was struck by a new scheme. The grandeur of the revelation was such that it brought him to his feet, his granite face creased in a rare grin. "I've got it," he cried. "The whole damn schmear." Then he proceeded to outline his plan to build the biggest resort hotel in the world. It would be called the Starlight (later changed to Stardust) and it would have the largest casino, the longest swimming pool, the greatest number of rooms, and the most fantastic supper club ever conceived by man. It would also have the brightest and largest neon sign on the Strip.

"You're crazy," his friends shouted. "There are too many places here already. And besides, where are you gonna get that kinda loot?"

"You'll see," Tony insisted. "I'll show you guys how to put on a real promotion."

Tony neglected to tell his friends that his entire bankroll at that moment was less than $10,000. But within a week, a statement had been filed with the United States Securities and Exchange Commission seeking to register 650,000 shares of preferred stock at ten dollars each and 1,300,000 shares of common stock at one cent each. The stock was to be sold at par value in units of $10.01 for one share of preferred stock and one share of common stock, with no underwriting involved. The shares would be offered and sold through the company's own representatives. The filing showed that the company was organized under Nevada law on April 19, 1954, and acquired a "contract of sale and purchase of real property" by and between Frank Fishman and A. C. Stralla, company president. The real property consisted of a thirty-six-acre tract of land valued at $600,000. The local real estate man, Frank Fishman, was also a promoter, and the year before, the Tax Commission had revoked his gambling license when it learned that he had been peddling his license to the highest bidder in his effort to raise money for a new hotel to be called the Royal Nevada. As a result of this gambit, the Tax Commission changed its policy. Since then no gambling license has been granted until a hotel is from two-thirds to three-quarters completed.

The first thing Cornero did was to purchase 650,000 shares of common stock at one cent each—a total investment of $6,500, which gave him control of the company. It was a smart deal, the kind Tony liked, but as in all his deals, the problems were not far behind him. Without waiting for approval by the SEC, Tony began selling stock all over the country. He advertised in newspapers and on billboards. His entire office consisted of a leather valise, which he kept at his side at all times. He doggedly arranged for contractors and labor and building materials, and the hotel began to take shape and form. Meanwhile, he had asked the Nevada Tax Commission for a preliminary check on himself and one partner in the deal, Miss Katherine Kastris, a former secretary in the office of the then Governor Charles Russell.

He got his answer direct from Governor Russell. "As long as I'm Governor, Cornero will never get a license."

The Governor's declaration took Tony by surprise. "I have absolutely no comment to make on the Tax Commission's statement," he told the press. "I have always dealt equitably and fairly with every human being I've met. I don't want to make any comment and I don't want to make any enemies. Stardust, Inc., is building a 1,032-room hotel and those plans are unchanged."

A week later it was the SEC's turn to take a swing at Tony. It ruled that the stock issue had not been properly registered. Cornero was instructed to paint out a portion of a billboard on Highway 91 advertising the sale, and was further instructed to file the proper registration papers with the SEC before going on with the sale. The SEC explained that no public offering of stock in interstate commerce was allowed until the issue was registered with the Commission. However, it could be sold within the state as long as all the promoters involved were residents of Nevada.

Tony painted out the offending portion of the sign, but neglected to refile with the SEC. His battle with Governor Russell continued. "I'll get a license or be carried out feet first," he threatened as the pressure mounted.

Not long afterward he made good his threat. At 11:17 A.M., July 31, 1955, while shooting craps at the Desert Inn, Antonio Cornero Stralla suddenly collapsed against the green-felt table and died. "His heart swelled up and burst," sheriff's deputy Dale Grimes told the press. Cornero's doctor urged the security guards not to call the coroner, assuring them he would personally sign the death certificate. Cornero's family sent word that the body was not to be embalmed but was to be taken immediately to their Beverly Hills home for handling by a local mortuary. Over a thousand mourners attended the funeral services, and a soloist capped the brief ceremony by singing Tony's *lucky* song, the "Wabash Cannon Ball."

Cornero's troubles did not cease with his death. They continued to plague the Stardust. The SEC announced it would probe the details of the stock promotion. Baffled auditors hired by creditors attempted to decipher the bits and pieces of papers found in Tony's valise. Stardust, Inc., went into receivership. Though Cornero had raised over $6 million from nearly three thousand investors, there was less than ten thousand dollars in the Stardust's bank account. Contractors and suppliers slapped liens against the property totaling $4.3 million. The hotel was only 70 per cent completed, and it was estimated that it would take another $3 million to finish it. Construction came to an abrupt halt.

The multimillionaire on the white charger who galloped into Las Vegas with $12 million in his saddlebag to rescue the Stardust was also a Runyonesque character. In the old days John "Jake the Barber" Factor was a crony of Capone mobsters and a stock swindler par excellence. Today he is a prominent Beverly Hills real estate dealer and a self-proclaimed philanthropist.

Jake the Barber's Capone Mob connections are better today than ever before. When he took over the Stardust early in 1958, Factor did not forget his Chicago pals. The first thing he and his wife, Rella, did was to buy off the three thousand stockholders at a promised (but never paid) thirty-four cents on the dollar, which amounted to $1.9 million. Then they paid the court-appointed trustee, Paul McDermott, $4.3 million to satisfy the lien holders. Construction was resumed and Jake applied to the Gaming Control Board for a license. His luck was no better than Cornero's. But unlike Cornero, Jake did not push the matter. Instead he announced to the press that a contract had been signed to lease the Stardust casino to United Hotels Corporation (the holding company of the Desert Inn) at a $100,000-a-month rental. (Before his death, Cornero had tentatively agreed to a similar deal with Dalitz *et al.* for a monthly stipend of $500,000. This enormous loss in revenue plainly shows that some friendships are thicker than money.)

Tony Accardo and his top lieutenant, Sam "Mooney" Giancana, accompanied by heavily armed torpedoes, visited Las Vegas early that spring to consult with their new landlord. The grandeur of Cornero's vision so dazzled the Chicago boys that they added an extra $3 million in construction costs. Factor had to grin and bear it like a good pal. And then, before returning to Chicago, Accardo whispered a name in Factor's ear.

The whispered name was John Drew, a gambler with a record for running rigged dice games. Drew's closest friend through the years has been Leslie "Killer Kane" Kruse, a top-ranking member of the Capone Mob and one of the managers of Ralph's Place, in Cook County, a Mob-owned gambling joint.

Five years earlier, when Drew had appeared before the Tax Commission to request a gambling license to cover a 25 per cent interest in the Bank Club casino in Reno, he had angrily refused to answer questions concerning his friendship with Leslie Kruse. Ordered to answer or withdraw his request for the license, Drew admitted he not only knew Kruse but had actually employed him as a "floorman" in a gambling casino. Asked to elaborate on this statement, Drew indignantly withdrew his license application. A few months later the license was mysteriously granted.

But this time the Nevada Gaming Control Board promptly licensed Drew for a 5 per cent interest in Karat, Inc., the Stardust operating company. When questioned by the Board about his frequent absences (visits to Chicago) from the Bank Club, Drew promised to be more attentive to his new duties as casino manager at the Stardust. Speaking in Drew's behalf, Allard Roen explained that Drew had been brought into the Stardust casino because "he is a colorful character" and as an outsider (not part of the D.I. group) would tend to keep the Stardust from being in competition with the Desert Inn for the same clientele.

Not all has been roses with landlord Factor. The Desert Inn crowd pulled a switch on him in December, 1959, when they sold all the assets in United Hotels Corporation to Desert Inn Associates for $10 million. The sale included the Desert Inn hotel, the golf course, several annex buildings and other properties. The D.I. Operating Company (which controls the casino) was granted a long-term lease to operate all the facilities. It was a legal maneuver calculated to provide millions of tax-free dollars without disturbing the *status quo* of the owners. When the legal smoke settled, Factor found himself in business with a dummy corporation devoid of any physical assets.

Meanwhile, cocky little Johnny Drew is ruling the roost at the Stardust. Sam Giancana makes regular visits to the hotel, casting a proprietary eye about at the gaudy decorations, dispensing advice, shaking hands with old hoodlum cronies, and whenever the occasion demands it, laying down the law, Chicago style. Morris Kleinman, a 22-per-cent owner of Karat, Inc., got the word from Giancana in the Stardust casino not long after he had received the word from Marshall Caifano in the Desert Inn. Kleinman, it seems, has a unique way of irritating the Sicilians from Chicago. "Get the hell outta here and don't never come back," Giancana shouted, pointing a lethal finger toward the exit. Kleinman left sans argument and has never returned.

Drew's wife, Jeanne, who has the temper to match her green eyes and red hair, belted Patsy Goldwater (wife of the Mob's local attorney) one night and knocked her off a bar stool at the

Desert Inn Country Club. The incident was brought up before the board of directors of the club and the vote was to eject the socially uncouth Drews from the "distinguished" roster of the membership. One phone call from Chicago was enough to convince Moe Dalitz that pasting Patsy was not such an odious *faux pas* after all. The Drews stayed on.

In 1961 the Stardust (which caters mostly to grinds, or small bettors) was the second-largest money winner in southern Nevada. Drew is taking the bows and the Capone boys are raking in the profits. It's the kind of teamwork that means to succeed.

One of the most celebrated examples of hidden ownership in Las Vegas came to light one night in a flash of gunpowder in New York.

On the evening of May 2, 1957, a fat gunman waited for his victim in the foyer of a fashionable apartment house on Central Park West. When the victim appeared, the gunman, coming up behind him, shouted: "This is for you, Frank!" The man spun around and crouched before the assassin's .38 revolver. There was a roar, and Frank Costello, known as the prime minister of organized crime in America, staggered sideways, blood streaming down his cheek. Satisfied with the visual results of his marksmanship, the pudgy triggerman waddled quickly out of the foyer, past the terrified doorman, and jumped into a waiting Cadillac double-parked just north of the building entrance.

Costello (born Francesco Castiglia in Sicily in 1891) sank onto a leather-covered bench and held a handkerchief to his bleeding head. "Somebody tried to get me," he mumbled, his hard eyes stunned by the knowledge. A few minutes later he was rushed to Roosevelt Hospital, not far away. While doctors repaired the superficial furrow plowed by the .38 slug behind

Costello's right ear, New York detectives hastily searched the pockets of his suit jacket. They found $800 in cash and a slip of paper with some astounding handwritten notations:

Gross casino wins as of 4/27/57	$651,284
Casino wins less markers	434,695
Slot wins	62,844
Markers	153,745

Mike $150 a week, totaling $600; Jake $100 a week, totaling $400; L.—$30,000; H.—$9,000.

Taken to the West 54th Street Station that same night for questioning, Costello feigned amazement when confronted with the slip of paper and asked to explain its content. An examination of the note indicated that it bore the handwriting of two persons. Costello protested he had no idea who had written the note or how it had found its way into his pocket. Brought before a grand jury, he politely but firmly claimed the privilege of the Fifth Amendment. That performance earned him a thirty-day sentence in the workhouse for contempt. (Since his contempt indictment for angrily stalking out on the Kefauver Committee in 1951, Costello has been involved—as defendant, appellant, or petitioner—in some forty-four court actions. He recently finished serving a three-and-a-half-year prison term for income tax evasion, and as of this writing he is fighting proceedings for deportation to his native Italy.)

Even without Costello's cooperation, the New York police soon traced the gambling figures to Las Vegas. The $651,284 figure matched perfectly the gross casino receipts of the Tropicana Hotel for the first twenty-four days of its operation. Then the Nevada Gaming Control Board established that the main part of the note was written by Michael J. Tanico, a Tropicana cashier who had been previously employed in the Beverly Club in New Orleans, a plush gambling joint operated by Dandy Phil Kastel, Frank Costello, Meyer Lansky, and Carlos Marcello.

No one was really surprised in Las Vegas, including the members of the Gaming Control Board. After all, Dandy Phil and his wife, Margaret, had originally given birth to the hotel, and Kastel had been a Costello stooge for nearly thirty years— in fact, since Arnold Rothstein's murder before election day in 1928. Dandy Phil had been one of Rothstein's lieutenants and his record even then included bootlegging, extortion, and mail fraud. He was just the kind of hood Costello needed in his expanding operation. In the early thirties, Costello made a deal with Huey P. Long for the gambling rights of Louisiana. Dandy Phil was selected for the top post, a job he maintained until his death in April, 1963.

Carlos Marcello, the head of the Mafia in Louisiana and presently a "legitimate" businessman and multimillionaire, was born Calorso Minicari, in Tunis, North Africa, in 1910, the son of Sicilian parents. Marcello arrived in America when only eight months old. His first arrest was at the age of twenty on a charge of bank robbery. The case was dismissed—a typical big hoodlum beginning. His police record includes aggravated assault, robbery, dope peddling, income tax evasion, and gambling.

When Dandy Phil Kastel decided to invade Las Vegas in 1954, he needed a good front, plus a few million dollars. The front turned out to be Ben Jaffe, chairman of the board of the Fontainebleau Hotel in Florida. At the time Jaffe had a background of radio-station promotions in the States and on the border of Mexico. Besides, he was in the punchboard business, operating out of Juárez and Mexicali, where his foreign radio stations broadcasted gimmick products for sale, circumventing the U.S. rules and regulations in the advertisement of undesirable products. In his spare time, he started a small insurance company, Guarantee Reserve Life Insurance Company, in Hammond, Indiana, which under his leadership grew into a fair-size business.

The contact with Jaffe was made through Leon Stoller, president of Bond Estates in Las Vegas, another Jaffe enterprise. After getting the word from Kastel, Stoller rushed down to Miami to arrange a meeting between Jaffe and "someone who is very much interested in getting into the gambling business in Las Vegas."

Ben Jaffe had been an operator all his life, but when he joined with Dandy Phil he found himself pinned against the wall. The Kastel group, which included Costello, Marcello, and singer Morton Downey, raised a million dollars to get the hotel under way. A company known as Conquistador, Inc., was formed and Kastel became nominal head. Kastel assured Jaffe that the hotel would not run over $4 million in cost. Encouraged by the low figure, Jaffe recommended the Taylor Construction Company of Miami, which had just completed the Riviera Hotel. Kastel readily approved it. Then Jaffe appointed a close friend by the name of Phil Galt to protect his interest and supervise the construction. Again Kastel was amenable. Overwhelmed by his easy success, Jaffe planed back to Miami, congratulating himself all the way on his good fortune in meeting such a fine gentleman as Mr. Phil Kastel—which went to show you couldn't trust anything the newspapers said about so-called hoodlums.

The moment Jaffe left, Kastel made it clear to everyone concerned that "when this is over I'm gonna be the captain of the ship." His wife, Margaret, a tall, striking brunette, spent a good portion of her day climbing up and down ladders, uttering little disapproving sighs and grunts as she waved her long cigarette holder, repeating to gaping workmen, "This is going to be our palace." Usually during these daytime excursions she was attired in full evening gown and mink stole, her brown hair glazed atop her head like an igloo. Her boundless enthusiasm was soon deflated in the divorce court.

After Margaret's daily visits, Phil Galt had his hands full soothing the injured feelings of the aristocratic union workers, especially those of sheet-metal boss Tom Hanley, a hard-nosed gent who demanded jurisdiction over everything at the hotel. To add to his problems, there were eight other major projects under construction in Las Vegas at that time, including the mammoth Stardust, where Tony Cornero was paying straight double-time to masons, thereby corraling all the masons in town. A local school project had to be postponed since all the available workers preferred the higher wages paid by the hotels.

The jovial Jaffe stopped smiling after a few months. The pressure mounted with every inch the building grew in those first months. The demands for more money never stopped, and finally in desperation Jaffe sold out his interest in the giant Fontainebleau for $3 million. The money was pumped into the Tropicana and for a while everything was calm again. Then in 1956 Kastel tapped Jaffe again and this time he had to milk his Hammond, Indiana, insurance company for a $2.8 million loan. The amount of the loan represented a third of the firm's total assets—an unusual practice for a licensed insurance company. As the construction of the Tropicana progressed, Jaffe retrogressed. He lost weight and became so nervous that his friends strongly advised him to seek the services of a psychiatrist. By the time the hotel was completed, Jaffe was a shell of his former ebullient self.

Meanwhile, Kastel was still ruddy-faced, still chunky, and still brash and cocky. He had a $10 million hotel and all he had personally invested was $320,000. He was turned down for a license but was not overly dismayed by the Gaming Control Board's action. Among the investors were two Chicago characters, Louis J. Lederer and Charles "Babe" Baron, who bought stocks valued at $180,000 and $120,000 respectively. Lederer and J. Kell Houssels, Sr., were placed in charge of the casino and Mike Tanico was transferred from the cashier's cage at the Beverly Club in New Orleans to the cashier's cage of the Tropicana.

As is customary on all opening nights, the Mob was in glorious attendance that spring in 1957 when the Tropicana flung open its doors. The hoodlums looked sleek and prosperous in their silk suits; their faces were tanned, their hair slickly pomaded, their fingernails brightly lacquered. Outside, in front of the hotel's porte-cochere, a sixty-foot tulip-shaped fountain set in a large shallow pool tinkled melodiously, and inside the mahogany-paneled casino the sophisticated tinkle of champagne glasses was drowned by the cacophony of the gaming tables and slot machines.

In the Celebrity Gourmet Room, Dandy Phil amused his guests with some fascinating tidbits prepared by his publicity department. The air-conditioning, he proudly told them, would cool over one thousand homes in Death Valley in midsummer; the concrete poured into the hotel was enough to build 140 miles of two-lane freeway; and the paging and canned-music system was even audible underwater in the pool.

The .38 slug fired at Costello's head shattered Kastel's dream. The Nevada Gaming Control Board, caught with its hoodlums showing, lost no time in trying to save face. Louis J. Lederer, whose handwriting appeared on the telltale memo, was ordered removed from the industry. Lederer, who also had an interest in Ed Levinson's Fremont Hotel (another mobster-controlled property), was forced to sell out for $80,000. The $80,000 needed for the purchase was advanced to Levinson by a lifelong friend, Sam Garfield, an Indiana gambler, who was a codefendant with Allard Roen in the $5 million stock-swindle indictments. Conquistador, Inc., the operating company of the Tropicana, was then instructed to retire Kastel's note in full within a reasonable time in order to remove any question of a Costello–Kastel interest of any nature. Conquistador, Inc., agreed to pay off Kastel at the rate of $40,000 a year.

One would have to be naïve, indeed, to believe that this action by the Nevada Gaming Control Board actually erased the influence of Kastel, Costello, Marcello, *et al.* in the Tropicana. In 1961 it was the biggest money winner in southern Nevada, topped only in northern Nevada by Harrah's Club at Lake Tahoe and Harold's Club in Reno. No hoodlum in history has ever been known to walk away from this kind of easy loot. It is foolish to suppose that such a precedent would be established in Nevada.

The latest casino owner in Las Vegas to embark on the hearts-and-flowers route is Francis Albert Sinatra, better known as The Leader, The General, The Dago, The Pope, and Frankie Boy. In a public announcement before departing on a recent six-week tour of seven nations, Sinatra said, "As an overprivileged adult, I'd like to help underprivileged children." Hollywood and Las Vegas swingers were at first stunned by the declaration, but soon recovered their cynical wit. Sinatra, they said, was trying to impress President Kennedy with a new image, since the President had snubbed him on a recent trip to Palm Springs, accepting Bing Crosby's invitation instead of Sinatra's —even after Sinatra had spent thousands of dollars tacking on a new Presidential Wing to his Palm Springs retreat. The Clan was also coming apart at the narrow seams, and the Rat Pack image needed some public cleansing.

Whatever the reasons for the welfare tour, Sinatra's presence was sorely missed on the Strip by the robber barons who *really* clean up when The Leader is in town. He is a swinger par excellence, and the biggest entertainment draw of all.

As of this writing, Sinatra owns 9 per cent (valued at about $850,000) of the Sands. His part ownership of the Sands should not be surprising, since Sinatra is a native of Hoboken, New Jersey, and very cozily connected with a number of notorious gangsters. Sinatra himself is of Sicilian descent and has never hidden his affection for hoodlums. In 1952, he wrote that he might well have become a gangster if he had not had a consuming interest in music. Writing about his youth in an article for *Cosmopolitan,* Adela Rogers St. Johns wrote:

> There was not much music in his life in those days, but there was enough trouble—and what he couldn't find, he created so successfully that his ability to master-mind neighborhood capers earned him the nickname of "Angles." His movie heroes were Edward G. Robinson and Paul Muni, and their pictures must have been heady, hypnotic stuff for a belligerent, antagonistic teen-ager whose blood was never far below the boiling point. Their influence was enduring. To this day, the way he wears his elegant and expensive clothes, the way he moves about at the head of an entourage composed of those who serve him plus hangers-on and friends, his long stride with its hint of swagger and menace, the angle of his hats—all testify to the accuracy of a remark his friend Bing Crosby once made about him. "I think that he's always nurtured a secret desire to be a hood," Crosby said, but added, "But, of course, he's got too much class, too much sense, to go that route—so he gets his kicks out of barking at newsmen and so forth."

Sinatra's pathological hatred of all authority, particularly "cops," qualifies him for the company he keeps. Like George Raft, he likes to brag about his days as a tough kid in the alleys of Hoboken. "We kids had no one to turn to but each other," he

89

has said. "All I knew was tough kids on street corners, gang fights, and parents who were too busy trying to make enough money for food, rent, and clothing." And again like George Raft, he had no patience for school learning, being expelled his second month in high school for general rowdiness.

A number of entertainers have been sponsored by underworld figures. It is alleged that Willie Moretti (alias Willie Moore), the Mafia chieftain of New Jersey, held that distinctive honor with Sinatra. In the files of the Narcotics Bureau in New York is a telegram Moretti sent to Sinatra when the singer decided to divorce his wife Nancy.

Willie wired: "I AM VERY MUCH SURPRISED WHAT I HAVE BEEN READING IN THE NEWSPAPERS BETWEEN YOU AND YOUR DARLING WIFE. REMEMBER YOU HAVE A DECENT WIFE AND CHILDREN. YOU SHOULD BE VERY HAPPY. REGARDS TO ALL. WILLIE MOORE."

Though there have been many stories about the warm relationship between Tommy Dorsey and Frank Sinatra, the two men were deadly enemies. The underworld rumor is that Sinatra's contract was obtained by Moretti from Dorsey by the simple hoodlum tactic of holding a gun in Dorsey's mouth. The sale price was one dollar.

Through the years Sinatra has been seen in the company of one hoodlum after another, many of them members of the board of directors of the Combination and the Grand Council of the Mafia. When Lucky Luciano sneaked into Cuba for a summit meeting with the "boys" and issued the contract on Bugsy Siegel, Sinatra flew down to Cuba to join Lucky. Luciano threw a wild party to celebrate the reunion. The next morning a group of Girl Scouts, shepherded by a nun, came to the hotel to see Frankie, whose arrival naturally had been announced in the local press. Up to the penthouse they went, tingling with excitement, their hands pressed against their mouths to suppress their girlish giggles. When they arrived they found the door was ajar, and beyond it was a scene that froze the giggles and blanched the face of the nun. Bottles and lingerie were strewn everywhere, and unconscious bodies in various stages of undress were sprawled across the sofas and floor in positions not meant for the eyes of Girl Scouts, much less a nun.

The fact that Sinatra was able to acquire 9 per cent in the hoodlum-controlled Sands is proof enough of his underworld connections. In many ways, today Sinatra *is* the Sands. His slightest wish becomes an irrevocable order. He is feared and hated by the staff. His recorded voice is omnipresent around the clock. On his order, the Sands constructed the first steam room in Vegas at a cost of $40,000—it is known as the Clubhouse of the Clan. No licensed front, no matter who he is, dares talk back to The Leader.

Actually, the Sands has been controlled by more different mobs than any other casino in Nevada. Licensed and "respectable" fronts represented the interests of gang leaders in Houston, Galveston, St. Louis, Los Angeles, San Francisco, Minneapolis, Chicago, Detroit, Cleveland, New York City, Newark, Jersey City, Brooklyn, Boston, Miami, and New Orleans.

The brains behind the operation and the biggest juice man in the Sands (even bigger than Sinatra) was (and is) Joseph "Doc" Stacher, a New Jersey gangster (see Chapter 9). Other owners of record on opening night were Jake Freedman, a Russian emigrant who bossed gambling in Houston and was in partnership in Galveston with *mafioso* Sam Maceo; Eddie Levinson, a Florida and Kentucky bookmaker, brother of the notorious Louis "Sleep Out" Levinson; Malcolm Clarke, a Chicago racketeer associated with Charles "Cherry Nose" Gioe and on a first-name basis with the country's top hoodlums; Sid Wyman, St. Louis bookmaker, previously mentioned in this book; Michael Shapiro, Los Angeles bookmaker and friend of Mickey

Cohen; Edward Levy, who told the Tax Commission he had obtained part of his investment money by winning an election bet from Wilbur Clark; Louis J. Lederer, a Chicagoan and business partner of Charles "Babe" Baron, a suspected murderer who is presently the official greeter at the Sands; and three dark horses: Lionel Brooks, who said he was a Beverly Hills broker; Hyman Abrams, who said he operated a restaurant in Boston; and Edward Torres, who said nothing that would ever give one cause to worry.

The official greeter on opening night was big Jack Entratter, a former bouncer at the Stork Club and Copacabana in New York, who is known as Mr. Six-by-Six-Plus. Entratter owned 5 per cent and was allegedly the "front" for Frank Costello and Joey Adonis, the same two men he had (again allegedly) fronted for in the Copacabana. (A brother of Entratter was once a henchman for Legs Diamond and was killed in a gang war.) Entratter started out as general manager and show producer for the Copa Room at the Sands; but when Jake Freedman died in 1958, he became president. Today he owns 12 per cent and is reputedly a millionaire.

Another investor in the Sands and Fremont was Isadore Blumenfeld, more popularly known to the law as Kid Cann, the leader of the Minneapolis underworld. His holdings (11 per cent in the Sands, 9 per cent in the Fremont) were in the name of Harry Isaacs, a member of the Kid Cann organization. The investment had been concealed through the Mid-Continent Development and Construction Company. (When the authors queried the Nevada Gaming Control Board on this recently, the reply was that Isaacs had sold his holdings in the Sands some months previously and that his interest in the Fremont was under investigation and they couldn't talk about it. "Besides, he's selling his interest," was the astounding answer.)

This information first came to light in May, 1961, when

Blumenfeld was sentenced to eight years' imprisonment and fined $30,000 on perjury and bribery charges by Federal Judge Edward J. Devitt in St. Paul, Minnesota. Blumenfeld's brothers, Harry Bloom and Yiddy Bloom, and Abe Brownstein and Eddie Berman (Dave Berman's brother) were each sentenced to three years' imprisonment and fined $20,000 in the perjury case.

While the Sands was being built, many of the hoodlums behind the project were residing in the exclusive resort town of Palm Springs, California. The list included: Joe Fusco, who in 1931 was tried with Al Capone on a liquor-conspiracy charge, Mack Kufferman, Mal Clarke, Ed Levinson, Meyer Lansky, Gerry Catena, Frank Carbo, Abraham Zwillman, Joe Stacher, Champ Segal, and Abraham Teitelbaum, a former attorney for the Capone Mob who has often stated that "Alphonse Capone was one of the most honorable men I ever met."

Four months before the Sands opened, the Nevada Tax Commission denied licenses to both Mack Kufferman and Jake Freedman. Interviewed by newsmen in his suite at the Desert Inn, Kufferman said: "I am dumfounded, amazed, and startled. I don't know what to say, and am not in a position to figure what to do. How can I pull out of the Sands with three and a half million invested? I have not yet had a chance to talk to Jake Freedman. Call me in about three days, and I will know more about it."

Jake Freedman, who was also staying at the Desert Inn, was just as nonplused. "I actually believe it hurt the members of the commission to turn me down," he said. "I think they were for me, and liked my conduct and personality. They went over me with a magnifying glass, but they just won't do any business with that other fellow [Kufferman]. I can't tell you what will be done now until I have a chance to talk it over with him."

The Tax Commission's refusal of Kufferman was based on

his relationship with Stacher, intimating that he was fronting for the New Jersey gangster. Freedman was turned down because of his association with Kufferman, which he denied under oath. "I've been the star all my life," Freedman told the commissioners. "I'm not going to stooge for anyone this late."

A month later, Jake Freedman had his state license. The commissioners reversed themselves when the Texas gambler informed them that he had purchased Kufferman's interest for $789,000 (whatever happened to Kufferman's alleged $3.5 million investment was never explained).

But Freedman's troubles were not yet over. He had forgotten about the County Commissioners. Rodney Colton, Harley Harmon, and Sheriff Glen Jones found Freedman objectionable. Harmon explained that the board was constantly running into new information that showed financial interests in resort hotels that the board knew nothing about when granting the license. He cited the case of the newly opened Sahara. "We find eight additional names connected with the Sahara," he said, "none of which were on the application when we granted the license. That is the sort of thing we are trying to stop."

However noble the effort to stop gangster infiltration on the Strip, the County Commissioners reversed themselves and granted Freedman a license three weeks later. Sheriff Jones proudly announced to the community that Freedman's character "is good and he has no criminal record."

From that moment on, the state and the county saw eye to eye on the licensing. All applicants were automatically approved. In fact, the state board altered its standing rule of requiring exhaustive financial net worth statements on the grounds that the Internal Revenue Bureau would undoubtedly subpoena such statements for possible use in income tax prosecution. Attorney Harry Claiborne said he personally would not fill one out and would advise his clients to take a similar stand. Evidently knowing their applicants, the Tax Commission agreed with Claiborne and substituted a modified statement, requiring only that a sworn affidavit showing all liabilities and the source of the funds slated for the casino be submitted.

Perhaps the Internal Revenue Bureau could discover the hidden interests in Las Vegas by checking the tax returns of all licensed casino owners. But it is doubtful that there would be a repeat of the Jake Lansky and George Sadlo experience which nearly folded the Thunderbird in 1955 (see Chapter 7).

It is a safe bet that the fronts pay the required tax before divvying up the spoils. And besides, the big income is not the reported gross to the state. It is the slicing off the top that no one but the "in group" knows anything about. As noted earlier, this is how Las Vegas contributes millions of tax-free dollars to the coffers of organized crime and why it is such a lucrative spot for the underworld.

The reported gross take of $200 million by all the casinos in Nevada for 1962 is a figure that should insult the intelligence of a third-class bookkeeper. At that rate, the seventeen million tourists lost an average of twelve dollars each. This becomes particularly ridiculous when you realize that the carpet joints cater mostly to high rollers who are classified as super-droppers.

Gambling is a hard-cash business whether legal or illegal. There are no Revenue men in the counting room at the end of each shift when the "drop boxes" beneath the tables are brought in for the count. And even if the Revenue men could manage to get into the counting room three times a day in all the casinos in Nevada, the gamblers would have a dozen other cheating tricks left that would make a straight count impossible. They could overstate the "fill slips"—slips of paper which show amount of money brought to the table—or overstate the amounts lost by shills (and keep all earnings), or hand out a large sum to a

confederate and take his IOU, which would never be repaid and
thereby become a tax deduction.

There have been reports of other ways in which legalized
gambling assists organized crime. In an article for *The Saturday
Evening Post,* Peter Wyden wrote: "The government has heard
reports that millions of untaxed dollars made by narcotics peddlers and other criminals around the country come to Las Vegas
to be 'won' at the gambling tables. That way the money can be
reported to the Internal Revenue Service as 'gambling winnings'
. . . Washington has also heard that much of this illegal cash
vanishes into numbered Swiss bank accounts and phony foreign
corporations, only to resurface for the financing of hoodlum-
controlled businesses in major American cities." Sheriff Lamb
told Wyden: "What the hell. All they gotta do is lay it aside. It's
easy."

Commenting on Nevada after visiting Las Vegas with his
U.S. Senate Crime Committee, Senator Estes Kefauver said:

As a case history of legalized gambling, Nevada speaks
eloquently in the negative . . . both morally and finan-
cially, legalized gambling in Nevada is a failure. It is true
that revenue derived from state and local levies on the
gambling dives is welcome. . . . However, the amount the
state receives is only a pitiful fraction of the millions of
dollars that the gamblers themselves drain from the pockets
of the public—not all of whom are out-of-state tourists,
either. . . . Pages could be filled with examples heard by
the committee of the old, familiar story of how fine citizens
and family men became paupers, embezzlers, and worse
because of the enticements of the gambling tables. . . . It
is my opinion that big-time gambling is amoral—I refer to
the casino type of operation, which is more often crooked
than not—and that legalizing it will not make it less so.

Gambling produces nothing and adds nothing to the economy or society of our nation. America will be in a bad way if we ever have to resort to taxing crime and immorality for the purpose of raising revenue to operate our institutions. . . . Nevada gambling centers have become headquarters for some of the nation's worst mobsters. . . . I can shed no tears over the fact that experiments being conducted at the new atomic bomb testing range near Las Vegas are rattling the windows of the gambling dives and making the sharpers nervous.

Atomic blasts may have shaken some of the owners, but as for the gamblers, the guys who risk their money on the gaming tables, it would take the wrath of Judgment Day itself to catch their attention. When one blast at Yucca Flat, some 150 miles north of Las Vegas, shattered windows and rocked gambling tables across the state, a gambler had just tossed a pair of hot dice. The dice teetered on the edge of a natural, then rolled over.

"Damn," whined the gambler, staring at snake eyes. "What made them do that?"

Whether Nevada admits it or not, it is paying an insidious price for basing its economic structure on the weaknesses of its fellow man. Vice and corruption work from within, and like the genetic effects of radiation, the moral mutation may not be evident until it is too late to reverse.

CHAPTER FIVE

Hoffa's Fountain of Pension Juice

The real gimmick in high-powered hoodlum economics is not the disposition of money but the acquisition of it. The financial labyrinths of Mob-owned corporations have confounded more than one government official through the years. A typical hotel can have as many as sixty owners of the basic corporation that owns the land and the main building, the mobsters who control it having only a minimal investment. The basic corporation leases out the gambling (always to the mobsters who underwrite the entertainment cost), the bar, the restaurants, the newsstand, and all the swank shops. The gambling equipment can be on lease from as many as a dozen different companies. If the hotel becomes a financial success, new wings of rooms are added by different finance groups and leased back to the basic corporation, which guarantees a substantial yearly return on the investment.

Two prominent legal brains assisting the mobsters in Las Vegas are David Goldwater, attorney for the Dalitz group, and Bryant R. Burton, attorney for the Stacher group. Both Dalitz and Stacher have done extremely well in multimillion-dollar sleight-of-hand business deals.

"You better believe it," one informant said. "The boys never use their own loot when they go into business. They borrow the whole bundle and pay six, seven per cent interest. It's a real cute deal. If the business makes out, it's gravy. If it flops, what have they lost? And that way they don't have nothing to explain to Uncle. You know, embarrassing questions like 'Where did you get the loot to build this big beautiful, expensive joint?' And don't forget all that interest is tax deductible. You wonder where they get the loot? That's easy. There're plenty of square johns who want to invest with the boys, usually through fronts. It gives them juice. Look at Jimmy Hoffa. Him and Dalitz are real cozy, you know. Jimmy's got dough all over Vegas. But don't ask me how much or where. I don't know. All I can tell you is that Jimmy's got plenty of juice with the boys in this town."

The Hoffa juice in Las Vegas came from the Teamsters Central States, Southeast and Southwest Areas Pension Fund (29 East Madison, Chicago) and amounted to $11,780,000. According to the union's bylaws, Teamster officials do not have to account for expenditures of pension funds they loan to corporations; in fact, they can even make loans to themselves, which they have done on more than one occasion. The $167 million Central States pension fund and its investments are self-administered by sixteen trustees equally representing employers and teamsters, but Hoffa's influence on his fellow trustees is overwhelming (about 60 per cent of this fund is invested in real estate loans and mortgages—a sharp contrast to the 2.3 per cent average of corporate pension funds reported to the Securities and Exchange Commission).

Before detailing some of these intricate financial manipulations, a little background information is necessary to show the relationship between James Riddle Hoffa and Morris B. "Moe" Dalitz. Their association can be dated back to 1949. In those days, Dalitz owned a string of laundries in the Midwest and enjoyed very satisfactory contractual terms with the Teamsters. But in 1949, Isaac Litwak, head of Detroit's Teamster Local 285, demanded a five-day week for his laundry drivers. The following excerpt is taken from Attorney General Robert F. Kennedy's book *The Enemy Within:*

When Isaac Litwak started talking strike, they got in touch with a Detroit laundry owner, Moe Dalitz, who also is a Las Vegas and Havana gambling figure. Moe Dalitz was supposed to have "connections," and indeed he did have. He arranged a few days later for Mr. Meissner and Mr. Balkwill (representatives of the Detroit Institute of Laundering—an association of laundry owners) to sit down to lunch with Jimmy Hoffa's labor consultant friends, Joseph Holtzman and Jack Bushkin. At Carl's Chop House, just a stone's throw from Hoffa's Detroit Teamster headquarters, they discussed how they might get around Isaac Litwak. After a bit, Holtzman left the restaurant to see if it was possible to go over Litwak's head. When he returned, he told them he could get them the contract they wanted—for a price.

What price?

Twenty-five thousand dollars, all in cash, said Mr. Holtzman.

Balkwill told the [McClellan] Committee: "We nearly fainted. It is a lot of money, we couldn't pay it."

And while they couldn't pay it, neither could they afford to go back to the bargaining table with Isaac Litwak—described as a man "who wouldn't take a cigar."

So Meissner and Balkwill began "negotiating" with Holtzman and found him far more "reasonable" than Isaac Litwak. They "negotiated" the fix price down to $17,500, agreeing to pay the money for Mr. Holtzman's "expenses" in three installments: $7,500 in 1949; $5,000 in 1950; and $5,000 in 1951. To raise the money, they assessed each laundry owner so much per truck: $45 in 1949 and $22.50 in 1950–51.

What did they get for their money?

Back went the officials of the Institute to the bargaining sessions with Issac Litwak. Litwak, apparently confident that the laundry owners would soon capitulate, stood by his guns on the five-day week. Balkwill, Meissner and company stalled and watched the door and waited.

Late in that last session the door opened and in came Jimmy Hoffa.

Mr. Hoffa told the group there would be no strike. He wanted the contract signed on the owners' terms and signed immediately or he would step in himself. Mr. Litwak was stunned and angry—Meissner described him as "furious"—but he had no choice. He surrendered. The contract was signed without a five-day-week provision.

This was the background that paved the way for Moe Dalitz to receive multimillion-dollar loans from the Teamsters Pension Fund ten years later.

The first loan involved Sunrise Hospital, a Dalitz-controlled copartnership which included Nathan Adelson, his son Merv Adelson, Irwin Molasky, Allard Roen, and Eli Boyer. Merv Adelson and Molasky are known in Las Vegas as "guys who fell into it" when they became socially acquainted with Dalitz at the Desert Inn Country Club. They were young and aggressive and "clean"—no police record. Before Dalitz adopted them, they owned the Colonial House on the Strip, a bistro noted as a haven for prostitutes in those days. But the moment Dalitz smiled upon them, they sold the Colonial House and fell into step behind Dalitz. They learned much and prospered enormously. Today they are both millionaires.

The hundred-bed Sunrise Hospital, an imposing edifice of glass and country rock overlooking the desert to the east of Las Vegas, is a profit-making business venture with a philanthropic sound. Public records disclose that the first tie-up between the Dalitz combine and the Teamsters Pension Fund occurred on April 14, 1959. On that date, Sunrise Hospital, Inc., executed an assignment of its account to Congress Factors, a California corporation located in Los Angeles. Merv Adelson signed the document as president of the hospital and Milton Dranow signed as vice-president of Congress Factors.

(Milton Dranow is the brother of Benjamin Dranow, who obtained $1.2 million in loans from the Teamsters Pension Fund on a Minneapolis department store which went bankrupt. Benjamin was tried and convicted of fraud and later of income tax evasion.)

Less than six months after Adelson assigned the hospital accounts to Milton Dranow, a partnership known as A & M Enterprises borrowed $1 million on the hospital property from the Teamsters Central States, Southeast and Southwest Areas Pension Fund. Signing as beneficiaries were James R. Hoffa and fourteen trustees of the Pension Fund. The officers of A & M

Enterprises were the old Dalitz group. They executed a $1 million trust deed and chattel mortgage on September 1, 1959. Hospital equipment and furnishings requiring sixteen pages to list were pledged to the Teamsters Pension Fund by the chattel mortgage. Also attached was a $1 million promissory note giving terms of the loan repayment at 6 per cent interest.

Then on December 3, 1959, Milton Dranow canceled the notice of assignment of the hospital accounts to Congress Factors. The documents were then rerecorded in Clark County and delivered to E. Parry Thomas, an officer of the Bank of Las Vegas. The legal maneuvers were handled by David Goldwater.

Sunrise Hospital has had an illustrious career in Las Vegas. First, it was permitted to open with thirty-nine building-code violations, which led to the dismissal of the county director of building and safety, Bill Rardon, who claimed he had opposed the opening but had been overruled by Harley Harmon, then chairman of the County Commission. Harmon is one of the wealthiest insurance men in Nevada, his firm having issued multi-million-dollar policies on many Strip and Glitter Gulch properties.

In the case of Sunrise Hospital, Rardon told the Las Vegas *Sun*: "Harley told me they [Sunrise] have a million invested and have already announced their opening date. Then he dictated a letter on his own office typewriter allowing the hospital to open regardless of the violations." The list included four electrical connections, nine incomplete installations, twelve building violations and fourteen plumbing violations. It also included a citation that solid-core fire doors had not been installed in the rooms.

(Political influence in licensing is a two-edged sword. An influential gambler can not only procure a license but can also prevent an opponent from receiving one. Many times the pressure can come from perfectly legitimate sources—contractors, building-supply people, labor unions, realtors, and insurance men, who stand to profit by the licensing of a new casino. Rumors today place the going price of a license in Carson City at $25,000 for an undesirable or unpopular candidate—the money going to three VIPs. But after a license has been granted by the state, the licensee must still win approval of the County Commissioners in the county in which he will operate; where the casino is within city limits, a third license is necessary.)

To insure the success of Sunrise Hospital, Hoffa provided Dalitz with thousands of "captive" patients from the rosters of the Teamsters and the Culinary Workers unions. The deal provided sick care at a cost of $6.50 a month for each union member, paid by the employers. Sunrise agreed to provide five beds and certain basic medical care. Bills were to be paid by the accumulated fund, but the catch was that union members had to use Sunrise for treatment. (This has been amended recently to include the county hospital.)

Hoffa had more on his mind than the medical problems of his union members. The International Brotherhood of Teamsters, Chauffeurs, Warehousemen and Helpers is the biggest union in America, representing nearly two million men and women. As its president, Hoffa is constantly on the alert for new members. His latest target has been the Culinary Workers union.

In February, 1962, five Molotov cocktails blew up the headquarters of the Union de los Trabajadores de la Industria Gastronomica (Culinary Workers) in San Juan, Puerto Rico—which is Local 610, Hotel and Restaurant Workers Union (AFL–CIO). Shortly after the bombing, the union members were summarily turned over to the ranks of the Teamsters and Hoffa installed Teamster official Leopoldo Ramos Duclos as boss and trustee of the Gastronomica. Hoffa had made his deal in Cincinnati with the leaders of the International Hotel and

Restaurant Workers. The character who led the Hoffistas in Puerto Rico was Frank Chavey, whose long police record includes an earlier charge of attempted murder by hurling a fire bomb.

In Las Vegas, Hoffa employed a benevolent gambit: cheap hospitalization—Teamsters and Culinary workers lying in opposite beds, on the mend together. The big medical question, though, was how could a privately owned hospital provide medical care on the same plane as the nonprofit county hospital? Part of the question was answered when the local Variety Club presented Sunrise Hospital with a $25,000 Fluoricon Image Intensifier, which takes motion pictures of the body's interior parts and intensifies the image three thousand times more than the ordinary fluoroscope. The $25,000 had been raised by Variety's many public fund drives. Why then had public money been donated to a private hospital operated with private capital for a private profit? The answer was simple enough. For many years, philanthropist Dalitz has been Chief Barker of the Las Vegas Variety Club.

Dalitz' zealous concern for the Damon Runyon Cancer Fund (the Desert Inn's "Tournament of Champions," a yearly golfing event) has resulted in many grants to local hospitals, including Sunrise, for "cancer research." Just what cancer research Las Vegas institutions have accomplished has still to be determined.

Another Dalitz associate, Israel "Icepick Willie" Alderman, was recently favored by the Teamsters Pension Fund to the tune of $850,000. Alderman, whose sinister record was outlined in an earlier chapter, has been a stockholder in the El Cortez Hotel (1945–48), the Flamingo (1948–54), and the Riviera (1954–59). In this instance, he was president of the Three-O-One Corporation (the vice-president was Allard Roen, and other directors were Moe Dalitz and Morris Kleinman).

The Three-O-One Corporation received the full $850,000

105

loan on April 17, 1961—just three days after Roen was indicted in a New York court on stock-fraud charges. The legal moves in this case are particularly interesting. As part of the property involved, four lots at the corner of Third and Fremont Streets, in the heart of Glitter Gulch, were leased July 21, 1954, by H. John Gluskin from the Las Vegas Lodge No. 32, Free and Accepted Masons. Six days later, Gluskin assigned the lease to David Goldwater. Goldwater then assigned the lease to the Three-O-One Corporation on February 2, 1955, and on October 23, 1955, Three-O-One entered into a lease with the Nevada Building Company. Then on April 17, 1961, Three-O-One executed a trust deed on its leasehold interest in the property in favor of the trustees of the Teamsters Central States, Southeast and Southwest Areas Pension Fund, as security for the $850,000 loan. Another document, executed on the same day, deeded three small adjoining lots and a portion of a fourth as additional security for the loan. As in the Sunrise Hospital loan, the documents were returned after recording to E. Parry Thomas at the Bank of Las Vegas.

Six weeks later, June 1, 1961, Fremont Hotel, Inc., gave a trust deed on its real property, plus a chattel mortgage on all the hotel's existing furnishings and those to be installed in the future addition (a fourteen-story annex), as security for a $4 million loan. The furnishings were already subject to a prior chattel mortgage and there were two previous trust deeds on the real property for loans with total unpaid balances of $3 million. These documents were signed by Edward Levinson and Bryant R. Burton, president and secretary respectively of Fremont Hotel, Inc., and E. Parry Thomas, executive vice-president of the Bank of Las Vegas.

Then, less than five months later (October 20, 1961), the Bank of Las Vegas assigned the trust deed and chattel mortgage to the trustees of the before-mentioned Teamsters Pension Fund.

106

E. Parry Thomas (now identified as president of the Bank of Las Vegas) signed the assignments, which were said to be made "for value received" and "for valuable consideration received."

What Hoffa actually ended up with for the $4 million loan was a third mortgage on an already overextended hotel and a set of drawing plans for a new fourteen-story addition, also heavily mortgaged. On February 28, 1961 (eight months before the Hoffa loan), Fremont Hotel, Inc., received a $2,513,140.13 loan from Montgomery Investments, a San Francisco limited partnership of fifteen members headed by financier Louis Lurie. This brought the total of the loans for the new expansion to more than $6.5 million—nearly $1.5 million more than the announced estimated cost. Another sterling example of a gambler's economics. The only people gambling in the deal were the partners of Montgomery Investments and thousands of Teamsters who have contributed to the Pension Fund. Levinson was safely sitting in the middle; he had nothing to lose but other people's money.

The Dunes was another hotel to enjoy the benevolence of the Teamsters Pension Fund. The original hidden interest behind the Dunes was *capo mafioso* Ray Patriarca, who bossed the Mafia in New England. His front man was Joe Sullivan, who later sold out to James "Jake" Gottlieb, the present landlord at the Dunes. (In the old days, newsmen used to page Patriarca on the house phone and break up hysterically when Sullivan, on the other side of the casino, would get up and walk around excitedly—no doubt wondering if his boss was really in the hotel.)

Gottlieb reportedly gave Major A. Riddle (Major is his first name and not a military title) $100,000 to buy control of the casino operation in the Dunes (today Riddle owns 37.28 per cent). Both Riddle and Gottlieb have interesting Chicago backgrounds. Gottlieb is the owner of the Western Transportation

Company, Chicago; president and owner of the Missouri–
Oklahoma Express, Inc., St. Louis; and owner of Pioneer Motor
Service, Chicago—all businesses directly connected with the
Teamsters.

At the time of his arrival in Las Vegas in 1956, Major Riddle
was the full owner of the Riddle Oil Company, 2300 Michigan
Avenue, Chicago, and of the Riddle Drilling Company at the
same address. In 1936 he had an interest in the Plantation Club
in Indianapolis, and in 1940 he also had an interest in the Plantation Club in Moline, near Chicago, a reputed Capone gambling
joint.

The operating company for the Dunes is M & R Investment
Company, Inc., formed as a holding company to own Western
Transportation Company, Missouri–Oklahoma Express, Inc.,
General Leasing Company, and the Dunes Hotel. Hoffa's method
in the Dunes loan differed slightly from the other loans in Las
Vegas. A letter of commitment from the Pension Fund reportedly was used to advance $4 million to the Dunes. The loan was
made in 1958 and was due to be picked up in 1962. Meanwhile,
a loan was obtained from the Bank of Las Vegas and a laundry–
dry cleaners' union. The guess is that it soon will be formalized
as a Pension Fund loan for $5 million.

Other loans from the Teamsters Pension Fund include $1.2
million to Star Investment Company, a partnership consisting
of Moe Dalitz, Merv Adelson, Irwin Molasky, Allard Roen, and
Bernard Rothkopf. The money was used to build the Stardust
Golf Course and the Paradise Palms housing development.

Two small loans, one for $475,000 and another for $255,000,
went to men not involved in gambling. Las Vegas *Sun* publisher
Hank Greenspun received a loan from the Bank of Las Vegas
which was later purchased by the pension fund; and former
Teamsters official Homer L. Woxberg secured a $255,000 loan
to set up a taxicab business in Las Vegas.

Nearly $12 million of the Teamsters Pension Fund was sunk into real estate, golf courses, and casinos, most of it precariously secured and undercollateralized. If Nevada revoked legalized gambling tomorrow, most of the big hoodlums could walk out unscathed, their numbered Swiss bank accounts fatter by untold millions; their chattel mortgages, their leases and leaseholds, their trust deeds and endless variety of assignments reduced to a pile of rubbish. The real losers would be the union members, the little men who weren't there—but whose money was.

CHAPTER SIX
Sex for Sale

There are two things Las Vegas has in greater ratio than any other city in the world: money and whores. But unlike other cities where the red-light districts are relegated to well-defined areas (New York's Tenderloin, Marseilles' waterfront, Baltimore's Hook, San Francisco's Barbary Coast, New Orleans' Story Town and old French Quarter, Boston's Scollay Square, Chicago's Levee), the green-felt jungle is one huge whorehouse. Of its 64,405 population, a conservative 10 per cent are in one way or another engaged in the pursuit of prostitution. Cabbies, bartenders, bellhops, newsboys, proprietors of various establishments (liquor stores, motels, etc.), gamblers, special deputies (the private police forces of the casinos, numbering over two thousand, many of whom have yellow sheets as fantastic as their employers'), and professional pimps make a sizable income by procuring for a veritable army of prostitutes.

Money mysteriously breeds prostitutes the way decaying flesh breeds maggots. Where there's easy money, there's whores; it's that basic. Taken in its logical sequence it goes like this: where there's gambling there's easy money, where there's easy money there's whores, where there's whores there's extortion and narcotics, and where there's narcotics there's everything else.

The line between a whore and a hustler is a shaky one at best. Many of the chorus girls and cocktail waitresses who put out for high rollers as special favors to pit bosses try to maintain their amateur standing by living what they believe to be a "normal" sex life. "Normal" in this sense can mean anything from shacking up with a celebrity or someone with juice, to bankrolling a gambling boyfriend. A large number of these girls are married and have homes and children. The husbands spend their time swimming in their pools, cutting the lawn, and taking phone messages for their wives.

The most lucrative job in Vegas is that of cocktail waitress in one of the hotel–casinos on the Strip. The salary is only eight dollars a day, but the tips can be ten times as much and more. The most sought-after position is in the "pit," where drinks are delivered "on the house" to players. Since the smallest change a player has at a gaming table is a cartwheel (silver dollar), the tips work up from there. Lucky winners have been known to drop handfuls of chips on a waitress' tray. And players, winners or losers, are an uncommonly thirsty group. Almost without exception, the girl in the pit is full of what Vegans call "juice."

Show girls are required by the house to sit in the lounge for at least an hour after each performance and "dress up the room." What is meant is that they want the girls to be ogled by the customers who saw them nude or seminude on the stage just a moment before. It is another lure to bring in business. The casino is the pay-off place of the operation. Everything else is subservient to it. In most places the girls are ordered to mix with the customers, and to keep themselves ready for whatever arrangements the house cares to make. Few girls object. "They just don't want you skipping out," one lovely chorine told Arthur Steuer in an article for *Esquire*. "You don't have to go out with anyone you don't want to. Of course, if they ask you as a special favor and you say, 'No, thank you,' you gotta watch the door don't slap you in the ass on your way out."

"I've always had fantasies of making love to the guy in the movies," another girl told Steuer, "and I really believed I would if I got the chance. So there's Frank Sinatra sitting over there, and I just turn to jelly and ask him for his autograph. This is the big leagues and I guess I belong back in the bushes. It's just a little too fast for me. Listen, I'm no prude. I've spent some of the best years of my life pinned under a steering wheel, but boy! This town! They don't even say, 'Hello, what's your name?' They just sort of point at you and you're supposed to fall over."

One of the most popular performers as far as the house is concerned is Zsa Zsa Gabor. Financier Lou Wolfson escorted the Hungarian beauty one night and gambled away close to $400,000 before dawn. Though greatly admired by the casino owners, Zsa Zsa is not as popular with the dealers; she makes dollar bets and is more likely than not to grab the dollar up again if she loses and run away giggling.

Divorcees, arriving for their six-week residence requirement, are easy prey for sharp-eyed pimps. The high cost of living, the gambling, the feeling of newly acquired freedom, or disillusionment—all contribute toward making them available. A pimp buys a divorcee a drink, listens to her sad tale, and loans her a hundred dollars. First thing she knows he's introducing her to "friends."

In a recent headline story, a thirty-one-year-old divorcee revealed to the police that she had been talked into a career of prostitution by another prostitute, Kim Harris, twenty-seven, and "her old man," Perry Dolphus Hammett, forty-three, who had served time as a draft dodger. The divorcee moved in with the couple and began to make calls. During a period of two months, she was not allowed to have any outside contacts or acquaintances. She was also told that if she disobeyed, her family would be informed she was working as a prostitute. Though she earned more than $10,000 in that period, she kept only $2,700. Forty per cent of her earnings went to a Strip hotel bellhop and 35 per cent went to Hammett for expenses and juice.

Usually the bell captain of a Strip hotel is the commander-in-chief of all assignations taking place under "his" roof, using his wife or a favorite whore as the enforcer to keep the girls in line. A sharp bell captain can satisfy the urges of the most depraved customers.

One of the most popular sex kicks in Las Vegas today is the massage parlor. There is no law against this Oriental custom in Nevada. Massage parlors advertise in the newspapers and on radio and television. Beautiful girls or boys (depending on the customer's weakness), many still in their teens, massage old men (or women) and make them feel young again. On request they will unrobe and for a small bonus will perform acts more French and American than Oriental. The bell captains use the portable kind: Have folding table, will travel around the world.

(In 1962 the City of Las Vegas passed an ordinance making it illegal for women to massage men or vice versa, unless approved by a doctor's prescription—whatever that's supposed to mean. However, most of the masseuses are still in business, the only noticeable change being a higher price.)

The "weekender" is another type of amateur prostitute. These girls are generally from southern California and arrive on a Thursday night, dressed in evening clothes, without luggage.

113

Their field of operation is the lounges of the Strip hotels. On Monday morning they are back at their jobs as secretaries, clerks, or waitresses.

The shock troops of prostitution are the hard-core whores who come from brothels across the country. They work as "call girls" and their action comes mainly from pimps—bellhops, cabbies, bartenders, etc. The rate starts at $100, but many of them can be bargained with during slow periods of the day, going for a "quickie" for fifty dollars. The pimp gets 40 per cent.

The more attractive whores operate strictly from calls from the pit bosses. These girls are generally better dressed and slightly more intelligent. Known as "pit girls," their job is to entertain high rollers while the house empties their pockets. The pit girl usually meets her date early in the evening, accompanies him to dinner (usually a ringside seat at a dinner show), and later stands beside him as he gambles. This is her big opportunity to steal chips. But she has to be very careful, not only of her date but of the eagle-eyed pit boss, who frowns upon anyone stealing what will eventually be the house's money. If she's experienced she'll find ways of secreting chips from the rack into the specially designed narrow pockets ("subs") inside her fur cape. Her next problem will be to get rid of the chips at one of the cashier's cages before accompanying the high roller to his suite. Most gamblers get angry if they find girls stealing chips from them. It makes them feel like they are actually paying for the girl's company.

The most fabulous pit girl in Las Vegas is dark-haired, brown-eyed, buxom Ruth Elizabeth Walker who has been operating on the Strip for six years, most of that time at El Rancho Hotel. When El Rancho burned down in 1960, pit bosses up and down the Strip fought for her services. She was thirty-two when she hit Las Vegas and had a police record which included prostitution, extortion, and gambling. She also had a

Texas accent, a bobbed nose, and a lift job that had erased ten years of hard living from her neck up. She started operation as a cigarette girl at El Rancho and her husband went out looking for a friendly crap game. Within two years she was the owner of a $75,000 home, a new Cadillac, numerous fur capes and stoles, and a full-length $20,000 mink. Her income fluctuated between six and eight thousand a month. The pit bosses at the El Rancho catered to her every whim and tantrum because of her great talent at enticing to the gaming tables Texas "live ones"—characters who thought nothing of dropping $50,000 or $100,000 on their visits to Las Vegas. One Mississippi live one paid for her home and spent an estimated quarter million dollars on her. He was an alcoholic and incapable of collecting his sexual dues. Later, when Ruth was linked with other whores by the grand jury investigating prostitution along the Strip, she became a nude model at $185 a week to establish a "visible means of income." Her fleecing operation continued without interruption. She was so successful that she hired a confederate to follow her around from casino to casino, the confederate darting into the ladies' room to receive the load of chips secreted in the subs of her mink stole.

Ed Reid once innocently devoted two pages in the Sunday supplement of the Las Vegas *Sun* to Ruth Walker's home. The story was written by the society editor and was the subject of the weekly "Home of the Week" feature.

Sheika "Yellowbird" Moisha had a fabulous career as a show girl at El Rancho before it burned down. She was Beldon Katleman's favorite and a great hit with the locals, who cheered whenever she walked out on stage in her yellow feathery costume. She was also a hit with the Hollywood crowd, and at one time or another has been seen with Cary Grant, Ricky Nelson, and Frank Sinatra.

For a while Yellowbird was the most popular show girl in

Las Vegas. Then she fell for Sinatra and, ignoring the standing rule that requires show girls to stick around the casino between shows and after the last show until 2:30 A.M., she began to sneak out to the Sands to see Frankie. Katleman, who has always disliked the Sands and Sinatra, swiftly laid down the law. No more Sinatra and no more Sands or out you go. Yellowbird shrugged and out she went. Sinatra, of course, assured her she had nothing to worry about; he would be more than happy to take care of her.

How well Sinatra took care of Yellowbird is not known. However, she did return to El Rancho and Katleman did forgive her and she did continue to excite the boys, but somewhere, somehow, something had been lost.

Lesbians are plentiful in Las Vegas, and can usually be found at such offbeat taverns as Maxine's and the Tail o' the Pup. Some of the more colorful habitués, past and present, include choreographer Rene Molnar, dancer Sheika Moisha, stripper Candy Barr, self-styled press agent Mimi Marlow, dancer Marilyn Appollo, singer Keely Smith, stripper Evalyn Scott, and singer Mary Kaye.

Lesbian prostitutes usually play the high rollers for all they can get—and then devote their playtime to other women. Vice officers believe that many of the "practicing" lesbians are not physiologically or psychologically lesbians but rather bisexual through degeneracy, resorting to this new kind of kick after they have tried literally everything else. They are the particular favorites of the wealthy lesbian guests who visit the Strip.

Homosexuals are also in demand and many have found a new home in Las Vegas where they can indulge their perversion with dignity and grow wealthy at the same time. A prominent Nevada judge surrounds himself with these young men and is well known to motel operators along the Strip.

Many actors and mobsters prefer hard-core prostitutes to

willing but inexperienced show girls. Besides, with a whore it's strictly a business proposition. There are no repercussions, unless you are stupid enough to get behind a one-way mirror or within range of a tape recorder. Some of these whores are proud of their influential bedmates. Others are more cynical about it. It is not too difficult to find a whore willing to describe the sexual habits and organic equipment of a long list of celebrated names, male and female.

A large number of whores operate the cocktail lounges of the various hotels. The lounge captains usually have them sitting around at tables, waiting for live ones to pop in. Since the lounges in the large Strip hotels are under the management of the casino, the pit bosses have authority over the lounge captains and keep them in line. This operation is not as lucrative for the girls, but it is not unusual for them to rake in a thousand to two thousand a week. The lounge cocktail waitress, who averages about $250 a week with tips, can also increase her income if she's so disposed. She comes into contact with a variety of night crawlers, from international hoodlums to international movie stars. An attractive waitress can make her own contacts and save the pimp's commission, although lounge captains will cut themselves in the moment their suspicion is aroused.

Of all the live ones, the blabbermouth is the most appreciated by the girls and pimps. This is the character who takes one too many and gets sentimentally sloppy, telling all about the little wife and kiddies back home in Peoria. Extortion is as natural to a prostitute as intercourse. Pictures and tape recordings can be great convincers in a shakedown and be worth their weight in diamond-studded chips.

Today there are few brothels as such in Las Vegas. Some girls may band together and work from a motel, with the motel owner bossing the operation, but most of the girls like the excitement of the Strip, not to mention the opportunity to meet live ones and steal chips. Besides, there's a Rooming House Ordinance in Clark County which prohibits the use of a hotel or motel room for the purpose of prostitution—it is construed as a nuisance. There is no such ordinance in the city of Las Vegas.

Of the 135 girls arrested on the Strip for prostitution in 1961, only two were convicted. The local ordinance is so interpreted that vice-squad officers must go to a room with a girl, give her marked money, and then arrest her. Recently, overzealous officers have forced whores to undress for nude photos to strengthen their case.

Old-timers (anyone with five years qualifies in Las Vegas) still like to talk about the night of April 28, 1954, when the FBI raided Roxie's, a sprawling motel in Formyle (exactly four miles from Las Vegas on Boulder Highway), and arrested Roxie and Eddie Clippinger, the owners of the most fabulous brothel in Las Vegas history. The federal charge was based on the Mann Act, transporting girls across state lines for immoral purposes. To make the case airtight, the special agents seized Roxie's general manager, Dick Kellogg, on a white-slave charge and three of its female entertainers as material witnesses.

Roxie's Resort, a thirty-five-girl sex factory (five dollars for fifteen minutes), had operated for ten years without interference from Clark County Sheriff Glen Jones. During that period, Roxie and Eddie had grossed more than $1 million annually. But an hour after the special agents departed with their charges, Sheriff Jones dispatched a posse and rounded up the rest of the fillies.

Then the lid blew sky high. Herman "Hank" Greenspun, crusading publisher–editor of the Las Vegas *Sun,* fired a 1,500-word broadside at portly Sheriff Jones. "After a brief stakeout of ten years," Greenspun wrote, "the sheriff's office amassed sufficient evidence to suspect that Roxie's was not on the list of the Automobile Association of America as one of the approved motels." Greenspun went on to charge that the Sheriff had a financial interest in Roxie's operation. The denunciation was accompanied by a photo of the Sheriff astride an old-fashioned bicycle. The caption read: "Sheriff Glen Jones pedaling a little on his own."

Jones denied the accusations to no avail. In a primary election shortly afterward, he ran last in a field of five candidates for the office he had occupied for twelve years. He immediately filed suit against Greenspun for $1 million, charging libel. Greenspun retaliated by rerunning the offending editorial and photo just to show his readers "what a million dollars' worth of prose looks like." But before the ink had dried on the rerun story, Greenspun had lost his key witness, a former employee at Roxie's. The garrulous gentleman turned deafmute before the Clark County grand jury. Greenspun was in a bind.

Meanwhile, in a federal court in Los Angeles, Roxie and Eddie Clippinger and Dick Kellogg went on trial. Joe Sanchez, a notorious white slaver, testified as a government witness that he had supplied Roxie's with girls for several years. Sanchez gave the details of a meeting in a restaurant with Clippinger where the brothel owner had informed him that "he had no use for any type of police authority" and that he knew people above the FBI, an important United States Senator. "He said I would only hurt myself," Sanchez told the courtroom, "if I made a statement, but that after everything was all over I would be taken care of."

Teddy Blake, a tall, dark-haired whore, testified that Sanchez had placed her in Roxie's in July of 1952. "Joe Sanchez called there [Roxie's] and said he had somebody with a lot of requirements," she said. Teddy went on to explain that the deal was made over the telephone and that she hurried to Burbank to get her "trick suit," which she explained was a dress worn by

119

prostitutes to facilitate their work. Sanchez gave her a plane ticket and when she arrived in Las Vegas she called Kellogg and was told to taxi out to the brothel. Half of her fee went to Roxie's and she was charged eight dollars a day for room and board in the dormitory wing of the motel. A count of her tricks was kept with the aid of tickets she received after the customer paid his fee.

Another prostitute, Betty Marlow, testified that Sanchez sent her to Las Vegas four times, for periods covering ten weeks in all, and that she made from three to six thousand dollars in that time. She told of staggered shifts of girls employed to keep hundreds of customers happy twenty-four hours a day and said that between eight and fifteen girls were used in a single shift.

Captain Ralph Lamb (present sheriff of Las Vegas) testified that the Strip swarmed with prostitutes who were run out of town by Sheriff Jones to cut down on Roxie's competition.

Heading the defense for Roxie and Eddie Clippinger was Louis Weiner, a Las Vegas attorney and law partner of Lieutenant Governor Clifford A. Jones (no relation to Sheriff Glen Jones). The Weiner–Jones law firm represented banks, big corporations, and numerous Strip hotel–casinos. Lieutenant Governor Jones owned 11 per cent in the Thunderbird Hotel. Interestingly enough, Weiner was found alone in Clippinger's office by the Sheriff's deputies on the night of the raid. Later, in an editorial, Greenspun hinted that Weiner had been sent there by the Sheriff after the FBI left to clean out the cash box and do away with incriminating evidence.

In the witness box, Clippinger looked gray and tired. He admitted that he had been in the business for more than twenty years. Asked if his attorney, Weiner, had ever given him advice in the operation of the brothel, Clippinger answered, "Lots of times." He then admitted that he had used girls from Sanchez, but was careful to point out that the arrangements were not made by phone. Baited by the federal prosecutor, Clippinger said he didn't "look down on anyone who cooperates with the law if they are sincere in their manner of doing it." Sanchez, he said, "was a stool pigeon. Sanchez is known to be a stool pigeon by anyone connected with the sporting world." He then excitedly defined as illustrative of "anyone," gamblers, dealers, and bartenders. "I'm speaking for the average citizen," said Clippinger as the courtroom burst into thundering laughter.

Clippinger added that he knew all the pimps who had "teams" of girls in southern California, but disliked to hire girls who had "old men" for masters. "Old men" was explained to mean pimps with teams of girls. Clippinger said that they bother these girls for money, give them narcotics, and hold over them the threat of "telling their mothers and families" about their prostitution activities.

The trial lasted ten days. All three defendants were found guilty on the four counts filed against each one. Roxie and Eddie received a sentence of three years in the federal penitentiary and Kellogg got a suspended sentence.

Back in Las Vegas, the grand jury released a report on its findings on the office of Sheriff Glen Jones, who still had six months remaining on his term of office. They found the county jail in a deplorable condition, the prisoners crowded in unsanitary quarters, and Jones's travel expenses excessive. The grand jury charged Jones with extreme promiscuity in the issuing of deputy-sheriff commissions and noted that commissions had been issued to known hoodlums, citing as an example that "a special deputy currently employed at a resort hotel has the following criminal record: felony, auto theft, grand larceny, assault and battery . . . procuring, receiving stolen property, and pandering." They also recommended that Jones be permanently relieved from the chairmanship of the County Liquor Board. But there was nothing about graft.

121

Hank Greenspun was busy in the interim. He assigned one of the authors, Ed Reid, to do a special series on the Sheriff and the Clippingers. In six scathing articles he blasted Sheriff Jones for incompetence, chicanery, and blatant corruption. He accused Jones of removing dead men from Roxie's on two occasions, and went on to document the case of Charles Patterson, who had died of a heart attack in Roxie's on the evening of December 22, 1952. Patterson's body was found slumped behind the steering wheel of his car on the edge of Highway 93, near Formyle. And before being removed from Roxie's by the Sheriff, "Patterson was relieved of his watch, a valuable ring and about $120 in cash by a ghoul at Clippinger's joint." Clippinger denied the theft. In a statement to Reid he said: "I can tell you right now that he had his money, his watch and his ring on him when he was taken out of my place." And yet when a friend of Patterson went out to Roxie's to claim these items, he was given the watch, but not the money and ring.

In another story, Reid disclosed that four of the rooms in the plush brothel were equipped with tape-recording devices which were used by Clippinger to gain control over some of the county's leading citizens. In one room there was a television "eye" set up, which was attached to a cable that brought a picture of what transpired in that crib to a TV set in Clippinger's bungalow nearby. He entertained friends by switching on the action in the crib, especially when someone important was dallying with a girl. Even Clippinger's Cadillac was wired to record conversations; he used the car to pay off county and state officials who were shy about visiting the brothel. All of these acts, Reid stated, were conducted with the Sheriff's consent and connivance.

To illustrate how flagrant the entire operation had been, Reid disclosed a petition signed by fifty-two Las Vegas cab drivers. At a meeting, a cabbie addressed the gathering as "Dear fellow pimps" before he began his little speech:

122

We members of Teamsters local 631 would like to call a special meeting and have a vote on subjects mentioned about Formyle.

It seems that at different times we have had some union members working there. We recommend that all men have a paid up union card. It seems that we are helping to build a business there which isn't appreciated.

We ask that the house use one price for every 15 minutes or whatever is suitable, whether he comes in a cab or not. If he does come in a cab the driver gets $1 out of every $6 spent. If a driver sells the customer in the beginning and he ever goes out in a private car the driver is ruined forever in getting a so called "kelly" which is always expressed several times. Several drivers have had people that would make regular customers but after one or two trips they wind up with no "kelly." This does not cover a full discussion but we would like to call a special meeting for all drivers and vote and discuss this subject.

As these events (Clippinger's trial, the grand jury investigation, and the Greenspun–Reid attack) were taking place, another even more explosive drama was surreptitiously being played in Las Vegas.

Greenspun had been left high and dry in the Sheriff's million-dollar libel suit. Ed Reid, recalling his old *Brooklyn Eagle* days, summoned Pierre LaFitte, an undercover agent and clever impersonator. LaFitte has worked with newspapers and police departments across the country, exposing the underworld and running off, only to appear again somewhere else under a new disguise and alias.

Reid's idea was that LaFitte would impersonate a notorious hoodlum with cash to invest, and that Reid and Gordon Hawkins, assistant to Clark County D.A. Roger Foley, would personally record the various conversations while hidden in a closet of LaFitte's El Rancho Vegas suite. On other occasions, LaFitte would use a wristwatch microphone. His alias would be Louis Tabet.

And thus begins a brief but intimate tour through the labyrinths of the underworld, where politicians meet hoodlums on their own ground.

Louis Tabet's first contact was with Roxie Clippinger at her home in San Bernardino, California. This was midway through their trial in Los Angeles, and the Clippingers were trying to unload their brothel. Tabet, a short, stocky man in his early fifties, expensively dressed, and with a certain degree of cockiness in his manner, was escorted by a maid to Roxie's bedroom, where he found her reclining in bed. She was wearing white satin pajamas and a pink bed jacket. There was a yellow ribbon in her hair. Two huge diamond rings sparkled on her right hand.

ROXIE (*weakly*). You'll have to excuse me. I just had a heart attack.

TABET (*speaking with a heavy Italian accent*). I'm sorry to hear that. I can come back some other time.

ROXIE. I'm all right now. I've had 'em before. It started years ago when some practical joker pulled a chair out from under me. It damaged my spine.

TABET. I can see how it would.

ROXIE. I just saw my probation officer and things look bad.

TABET. How's the trial coming?

ROXIE. Terrible. That fink Sanchez is a monster. I'd like to spit in his greasy face. I've got a doctor coming to see me pretty soon. I want to pull a fast one on that judge. You know, get a little sympathy and a suspended sentence.

TABET (*nods approvingly*). Slip the doc some dough. He'll

take care of you. A little juice will keep you out of the box.

(*The heart specialist arrives and Tabet is asked to step out of the bedroom while he performs his examination. When the doctor departs, he goes back into the bedroom.*)

ROXIE. That bastard.

TABET. What's wrong?

ROXIE (*gets out of bed*). Let's have a drink.

Tabet follows her into a gleaming kitchen. She pours two stiff drinks and hands him one.

ROXIE. Eddie always called me "half-shot." That's because I never can finish a drink. (*She empties the drink and pours herself another one.*) How do you like the place? Eddie built lots of this stuff with his own hands. He's very clever that way. Building things is his hobby.

TABET. He's a smart guy.

ROXIE. You'd be surprised. He's really just a plain Joe. He don't like to dress fancy or anything like that. I remember when we went to Honolulu. I had to force him to buy a tux. I was so surprised when he put it on I even took his picture to be sure.

TABET (*nods and empties his drink. Roxie empties hers and gets two refills*). Well, it's like I told you on the phone. I'm in the market for a place.

ROXIE. You've come to the right place. Just a minute, I'll get the books.

She leaves the room and comes back with a large gray ledger.

ROXIE. Let me show you the kind of a place the Roxie is. Here, let me pick a month at random. February, this year. See the figures. Seventy-seven thousand dollars.

TABET. Is that the total?

ROXIE. It includes two thousand from the bar, one hundred from the cig machine, and eighteen hundred from the dormitory.

TABET. Pretty sweet operation.

ROXIE. You've got to promise me one thing, though. Those

girls out there are devoted to me. I don't want to let 'em down. I expect the buyer to keep them on.

TABET. If they do their job O.K. it's O.K. by me as long as the profits keep coming in. A whore's a whore, what's the difference.

ROXIE. They're all good girls, and they're hard workers.

TABET. How about juice?

ROXIE (*smiles*). You've got nothing to worry about there. Back in Fifty-one the D.A. busted Eddie but he got nowhere with it. Glen Jones wouldn't enforce the court order and the D.A.'s hands were tied.

TABET. I've gotta talk with that Jones.

ROXIE. Get in touch with Louis Weiner. He'll put you wise on who to talk to and who not to talk to, and who to pay and not to pay. We had [Sheriff] Jones on the payroll a long time and you better do the same. But be careful. He's terrifically greedy.

TABET. What's the juice?

ROXIE. A thousand a month, and from time to time—you know, when he comes in with one of his sad stories—a little extra.

TABET. How about his boys?

ROXIE (*laughs*). They keep coming in for loans. Eddie makes them sign for the money. Hell, we knew they wasn't going to pay it back. But Eddie says it's good business. It takes the pressure off. Now, if I was you, I'd take Dick Kellogg in as general manager. He's a great asset. He knows his way in and out of Vegas. He'll put you wise to what goes on in that town.

Tabet makes an appointment to meet Kellogg. A few evenings later, a powder-blue Buick winds its way along Wingy Way at El Rancho Hotel and stops in front of a secluded cottage, set back a full three blocks from the Strip. Dick Kellogg, a tall, slim man, steps out of the car and walks jerkily to the front door.

TABET (*after greeting, both men are seated. They met two days earlier and are now ready to continue their conversation*). I don't want to make no enemies. The machine must be greased before it starts to squeak.

KELLOGG. You don't have to worry about that. I'll put you in touch with the right people.

TABET. I don't want to splurge neither. Look, I want to be fair and all that. I don't want to forget nobody.

KELLOGG. I'll bring you face to face with the Sheriff.

TABET. That's the best way. Then he can tell me to my face and then I know how to grease him so everything's O.K.

KELLOGG. Just don't give him too much.

TABET. How about five G's and then the regular one G a month?

KELLOGG. Twenty-five hundred is plenty. If you give Glen too much he will become more greedy and a nuisance.

TABET. O.K., if you say so. I just don't want to make no enemies.

KELLOGG. Glen is all right, but he has no guts and you have to back him up all the time.

TABET. I don't like that.

KELLOGG. He got panicky every time there was too much heat put on Roxie. He would come up to the place and suggest that at least the light be turned off on the motel sign. But don't worry about it. He can be argued out of doing anything.

TABET. What's gonna happen after Jones goes out of office in January?

KELLOGG. Don't worry about it. There's all kinds of juice in this town. Roxie's is good for five years yet.

TABET. How about the Commissioners?

KELLOGG. We've got a couple of them. That's all we need.

TABET. Maybe the D.A.—

KELLOGG (*angrily*). He didn't cost us a dime in four years.

127

But you get Louis Weiner and he'll clear the way. His partner is the Lieutenant Governor and he's full of juice.

Kellogg arranges a meeting between Tabet and Jones in Tabet's suite. Sheriff Glen Jones has just arrived and is explaining how he has been to the airport to get a whiff of the "oxygen" there for his health.

TABET. I want to operate in this town without no heat. I've got a wife and kids now and I don't want no heat. Years ago I didn't care nothing about heat, but now I want everything to run smooth.

JONES. You've got nothing to worry about.

TABET. I don't want no beef from nobody.

JONES (*laughs*). I handle all the beefs. Even to a couple of stiffs we had to cart out of there once. You get all smooth sailing.

TABET. You're gonna be out of office in January.

JONES. That's O.K. I can do you some good as a front man.

TABET. Dick fixed it up with Weiner. I'm gonna see him tomorrow. Then I'm gonna look Roxie's over.

JONES. I'm going over there when I leave here.

TABET. You going there to get your cut?

JONES. Yeah.

TABET. You know that when I take the joint over I give you a cut of five G's and one G a month.

JONES. O.K.

TABET. Everything is gonna run smooth. There's going to be no bar and no slot machines. We are gonna do everything we can to run the place smooth.

JONES. I like that.

TABET. And I want them whores on the Strip to be knocked out of town. They gonna hurt business.

JONES. Don't worry about that.

TABET. And today when you see Weiner and the woman who runs the joint to get your cut, make it clear that you're not gonna be able to give them protection and you'll maybe find a couple of more thousand-dollar-bills on the top of the five G's.

JONES. I'll take care of it.

TABET. That's good.

JONES. I've gotta go. I've been looking at TV sets but I'm going to wait for a while. So many changes coming up in the new models.

TABET. You don't have to wait. I'll send you one right away.

JONES. Thanks.

TABET. Don't mention it. I'll have somebody deliver it.

JONES. Never mind about that. I've got a pickup truck and I'll have my handyman pick it up here.

Tabet visits Roxie's brothel at Formyle. His guide is a whore named Billie, a chatty young redhead who was placed in charge following the convictions of Eddie and Roxie.

BILLIE (*gushing enthusiastically*). This was Eddie and Roxie's private apartment. It's cleaned out now, but they had beautiful furniture, all custom-made and everything. (*Pauses and stares hard at Tabet.*) I'm gonna be married soon. (*Giggles.*) The girls call me "square." Billie the Square, that's me. I guess they know that deep down in my heart I don't like this business. It's not for me. (*Points grandly as they walk through various richly appointed rooms and into the office behind the bar.*) This place is run very efficiently. Look here. That's an alarm system. Whenever a car enters the driveway a bell rings in the reception room so one of the girls goes to meet the customer at the door. Pretty neat, huh? (*They walk into the reception room, where a half dozen luxurious divans are spread about. There is a bar in one*

129

corner with a colored man standing behind it in a white jacket, and a row of slot machines line one wall.) There are twenty people working here besides us girls. Ten bodyguards and a chef who's been here nine years. This place runs twenty-four hours a day. We get half of what we earn, then we pay three dollars for room and five for food a day. Of course, we have to pay for towels and stuff like that, too. Come, I'll show you the dormitory. (*The dormitory is a two-story building with twelve rooms and a bathroom and kitchen on each floor.*) No men are allowed here, only Eddie and Dick. (*Coming back to the reception room, Billie checks the cash register.*) We made thirty-two hundred yesterday, one eighty from the bar. We sell more champagne than any big hotel on the Strip. We've got a flat price of nine dollars per bottle.

Tabet arranges another meeting with Sheriff Jones at El Rancho.

JONES. I want to thank you for that nice TV set.

TABET. It's nothing. I ordered you a bigger one from the Coast. This one is for the Roxie. The other one is for something else. By the way, Dick tells me I got to register to get a liquor license and that means I got to be here six months.

JONES. You should be, but what do they care? You've lived in Clark for six months. Who can prove otherwise?

TABET. O.K. But I don't want no trouble. I got a record when I was a foolish young man—

JONES. You've got nothing to worry about.

TABET. What about that guy Dickerson?

JONES. George Dickerson will probably be the next D.A. If he gets it he will try to close Roxie's when his term starts. But he's got to have the County Commissioners O.K. it. The only

130

charge he can bring is as a "nuisance." But if you operate quietly you've got nothing to worry about.

TABET. What about the newspapers?

JONES. Don't worry about the *Review–Journal*. [Lieutenant Governor] Cliff Jones has got a fix there.

TABET. What about the *Sun?*

JONES. I hear Greenspun is trying to buy into the Los Angeles *News*. Maybe you could buy him out. Only trouble there is that he plans to write his column for five years.

TABET. Dick is gonna introduce me to a couple of Commissioners. Guys who can do me some good.

JONES. I'll introduce them to you, then we'll sit down and gab for a few minutes and then I'll leave.

TABET. I'm gonna be in and out of town for a few days. I want you to trust Dick completely. When I'm gone he's got to give you your cut. With me you have a good man. You come to me and say you need ten thousand dollars and I give it to you. When you come the next day and ask for twenty thousand I say, "Glen, take it easy." To me you are worth so much. To me, at the same time, everybody is a human being. If you put in a fix for me, I don't care if I give you ten thousand. I do it with pleasure. Why not? We're not little babies.

JONES. Sure.

TABET. When the time comes I want help, I get it.

JONES. You can depend on it.

After the Sheriff leaves, Tabet falls into a chair and laughs. The irony of the exit line will soon come back to haunt the accommodating Sheriff.

CHAPTER SEVEN

Politicians for Hire

Pierre "Louis Tabet" LaFitte was progressing a lot faster than Greenspun had ever anticipated. Ed Reid and Gordon Hawkins had done a lot of sweating over the noisy recording equipment behind that closet door in the El Rancho suite. They both knew the Sheriff was capable of shooting holes through the door if he got rattled. But as far as LaFitte was concerned it was merely the beginning. His next three targets were much bigger game: Rodney Colton, Clark County Commissioner; Lieutenant Governor Cliff Jones, a powerful politician who had just been elected Democratic National Committeeman for Nevada; and Louis Weiner, local attorney and law partner of Cliff Jones.

As it happened, 1954 was an election year in Nevada. The gubernatorial candidates were the incumbent Republican governor, Charles H. Russell, who was seeking a second term, and Democrat Vail Pittman, a former governor and brother of the late Nevada Senator Key Pittman. Pittman had the support of the powerful Democratic machine of the then recently deceased Senator Pat McCarran, the most potent political force in Nevada history. Pittman's election was considered in the bag. However, the local barons never really gamble on anything. With typical wariness, they decided to play both sides, with Pittman getting the lion's share of the spoils: $60,000 to Pittman's campaign and $15,000 to Russell's. Their meeting, which was supposed to be ultraconfidential, became front-page news the next day in the Las Vegas *Sun.* How had the *Sun* got the secret story? Vegans shook their heads and grinned slyly. They knew, all right. The "bug" was still king in Las Vegas.

What they didn't know, of course, was the drama being acted out at that very moment in the El Rancho suite between Louis Tabet and County Commissioner Rodney Colton. This was the fourth in a series of meetings between the two men. At this point Colton, a small, bookish man with thick-lensed glasses, was exulting over an expensive Scintillator, a uranium-detection device, just presented to him by Tabet.

COLTON. Oh, Louis! Oh, gee! (*Fondles it tenderly.*) That is the gadget. (*Pauses, as he's overcome with gratitude.*) My hinting wasn't intentional. This is the McCoy.

TABET. That is a little bit on the top of your cut. The ten grand, you still have it.

COLTON. This puts me in business. This is a beautiful gadget. It's in a nice case.

TABET. Well, that's a little cut. You'll get your ten grand.

COLTON. You want a license, is that right?

TABET. Yes. I want to go right down the line.

COLTON. What can I do to help?

TABET. Now, nothing. In a couple of days you're going to find out. I've got one Commissioner and we've got Glen and we've got yourself.

COLTON. That'll be the three of us.

TABET. Yes, there will be three of you, who'll be on my side. Now, the other two—I don't know. Can we talk to the other two?

COLTON. Personally, I would rather keep it between the three of us. The D.A. is a moral reformer. Why, he even had Lili St. Cyr arrested, wanted to close up Roxie and Searchlight.

TABET. The only thing I need, I want your support.

COLTON. I just want to make sure that when it comes up to a vote, I don't want to be the only one. So long as you assure me that Glen—I've got that straight? One thing was bothering me, I have other friends who have done things for me, and I don't want to vote against them.

TABET. We've got three, O.K.

COLTON. I'm thinking of buying a house on East College.

TABET. If there's anything I can do for you, all you've got to do is ring the bell.

COLTON. I've got to come up with the money in a matter of seven or eight days.

TABET. Well, you're going to have ten grand.

COLTON. Well, we'll keep that out of circulation. (*Chuckles.*) I sat here the other day and watched you squirm trying to find out how I felt before you offered anything.

TABET. That's O.K.

COLTON. You better come before the Commission before the first of the year. Then you'd be sure of getting the license through.

Five weeks after Tabet first talked to Roxie, he and Dick Kellogg meet in a plush office in the Thunderbird hotel. They

134

*are awaiting the arrival of Lieutenant Governor Cliff Jones for
a conference arranged by Louis Weiner, Jones's law partner. It
is early evening and Kellogg is leaning against the large mahog-
any desk while Tabet walks around the office, studying the signed
photographs of celebrities and politicians lining the walls.*

KELLOGG (*excitedly*). We know he can help in Carson City.
We know he's one of the few who can give us the green light.
I want to make him happy.

TABET. Louie [Weiner] told him all about me. Everything is
set.

KELLOGG. The guy is riding on a gravy train. When he goes
back to work they all go and see him. The top dog. He is sure
a hell of a man.

TABET. It's best we see him now. Colton is a nice guy but he
can't do everything.

KELLOGG. Colton is O.K. for the county. But now you're talking to the state. That's something else again. (*Slaps his hands
together.*) I showed you Marion Hicks when we came through
the casino.

TABET. Yeah. He is all front.

KELLOGG. Nevertheless, you've got to see the front.

TABET. There's big dough in here, big boys.

*The door opens and a tall, handsome man steps into the room.
He is smiling as he offers his hand to Tabet.*

LT. GOV. JONES. Sorry to be late. Had to take my wife to a
bridge party. . . . Make yourselves comfortable. Like a drink?

TABET (*shakes his head impatiently*). Cliff, I'm going to let
my hair down now. Ordinarily, in cases like this, where a man
like me has to grease the wheels to eliminate the squeak, a witness is not desirable. But, in this situation, Dick being my right-
hand man, I do not see the necessity of leaving him out of the
office.

135

JONES. Dick's O.K. (*Turns to Kellogg.*) There's a couple things I want to straighten out first. I haven't had a chance to check on you personally, Louis—it's O.K. to call you Louis, isn't it?

TABET. Sure.

JONES (*to Kellogg*). What did you find out about Louis's connections?

KELLOGG. He's O.K. He knows important people in Florida, Chicago, and other places.

JONES (*turns to Tabet*). You have a record?

TABET. Nothing recent. A few things when I was young, a little narcotics, bootlegging, murder, manslaughter.

JONES. Anything recently?

TABET. Not in the past eleven years.

JONES. You're all right but not until after the first of the year when Pittman takes office. After this election we're going to be stronger than ever. To make an application for a gambling license during election time would be poor judgment, especially for you with your criminal record. Wait until the first of the year, then we're going to boot Robbins Cahill out of his job. After that everything is going to be smoothed out.

TABET. Cahill?

JONES. He's the secretary of the State Tax Commission. He's the big boss in Carson City. He says whether you get a gambling license or not. And what he says goes up there right now, but it's going to change damn quick after the election.

TABET. Well, I've taken care of the county. I've got Harley Harmon, Colton, and Sheriff Jones.

JONES. You're with the right people. I talk for the state. Louie Weiner, my partner, takes care of the legal end of the deals and the finances.

TABET. Louie told me.

JONES. I hear you're going to buy the *Sun*. What a relief! I heard that your mouthpiece from New York is in Los Angeles dickering with that son of a bitch Greenspun.

TABET. Look, I'm a very nervous man. Twenty years ago it takes me two minutes to get rid of that guy. But today, I'm set with a family and money—

JONES (*interrupting*). Let me tell you, Louis. Believe me, we've got to get that son of a bitch out of town. He's bad for all of us. And if he finds out who you are, he's going to give you the business too. When you buy the paper you buy insurance —believe me, Louis.

TABET. But what am I gonna do with a newspaper? And more —what about the *Review–Journal* in here?

JONES. What? Louis Weiner didn't tell you about the *Review* here? My sister is married to Johnny Cahlan, brother of the owner, and what I say over there goes. Also, Louis, don't think you're throwing your money away. We'll print the two papers on the same press and save a lot of dough, and I'm pretty sure I can take it off your hands after the election. To give you an example, the Democratic and Republican papers are printed on the same press in Reno. Again, I tell you, Louis, believe me, I'm a lawyer. Get your mouthpiece from New York to draw the contract, and if you've got to pay that son of a bitch twenty-five thousand a year for ten years it is still a bargain. But the most important point to put in the contract is that you have the right to censor his column or pull his writing if we don't like it. And, anyway, before you sign anything, I want to see what kind of deal you enter into and rewrite, if necessary, the contract to our mutual satisfaction. Believe me, Louis, you're buying insurance and all the boys are going to be everlastingly thankful to you when we get rid of that bastard.

TABET. My mouthpiece don't like it.

JONES. Louis, believe me. I've been called a lot of names. But everybody in the state knows me, and believe me, I can deliver. Only one thing nobody ever called me and that's stupid.

Later, Tabet invites Attorney Louis Weiner, law partner of Lieutenant Governor Clifford Jones, to his suite at El Rancho. Weiner is seated in a large overstuffed chair. He is a small man and the big chair makes him appear even smaller. Tabet is stretched out on a red sofa, his legs crossed, smoking a long Corona-Corona.

TABET. I'm not as bad as Meyer Lansky or anybody you want to call it or Joe Henschel, or anybody like that, but I'm a nervous man. I don't like that. I got kids and a wife and things like that. What's past is past and I think I have an opportunity now. I know what he be working there for about a week now, and I know that guy needs dough very bad. He tell newspaper in Los Angeles that he wants to sell that goddamn rag he got, and I feel that Greenspun very touchy. Now he wants to accept a sum of cash and is most important, he wants it twenty years at twenty-five thousand a year and the right to write his column, and in the case somebody is going to censor that column or throw it in the basket, he has the right to open another newspaper. What's the use—I mean, we don't clamp the man down.

WEINER. That's ridiculous. You furnish a paper for him at your expense for him to write with no worry to him.

TABET. So I got a man from New York who's a lawyer. He's a good man and he tell me, he says, "Louie, what the hell, you tell me you going to buy a apple tree someplace, a mustard tree, I understand it, but for you, a newspaper, no." I say look, don't ask me no questions. I talk to Cliff and he give me very good advice. And that man is a very wonderful guy, a good guy.

WEINER. There's a kid that's taken a lot of abuse, and nothing bothers him. I talked to him last night for about twenty-five minutes and on this National Committee deal—that's important. It's important to us to have Cliff in there, because there are a lot of things that Cliff can get. He knows what's going on. We've got to have a pipeline to know what's going on, because if you don't know what's going on, you can be in bad shape. I mean, it gets here before you know it's coming.

TABET. Look, Louie, let me tell you one thing. Cliff can tell you I'm not throwing dough by the window and at the same time I'm not a miser. Well, it's like that, I'm a gentleman. Maybe my language is not—what you call that—refined. That's not my fault.

WEINER. That's right.

TABET. You know if I gave you my word, it's done. I know a lot of people. I know a lot of good people. Somebody going to throw mud on it.

WEINER. We'll just sit here and let them throw it.

TABET. I talk to Cliff, he tell me, he say, "Listen, you see the Thunderbird here, it runs smooth. We never have anything happen. We don't want that."

WEINER. They run their business and let everybody else run theirs.

TABET. I know that on the back, Jake Lansky, Meyer Lansky, everybody's in it, on the Algiers, everything runs smooth. The Rancho over here, I got a very good friend from New Orleans over there—

WEINER. But nobody bothers them—they don't care. What everybody else does is their business.

TABET. Of course.

WEINER. And every place should be run like that. You shouldn't be trying all your business in the newspapers.

TABET. What is the name of the capital?

WEINER. Carson City.

TABET. Yeah, Carson. I have very good friend fly over there and try to talk to the man—he's boss of that goddamn Commission there.

WEINER. Cahill.

TABET. Cahill, he is a—

WEINER. Oh, the worst!

TABET. You can't do business with that bum if you bring him diamonds on a platter, so I walk far away. I don't talk with him, nothing. But you know I will holler for somebody—not me, no man, no place, nothing. I ducked. Christ, boy, did I jump on the air. He's going out for blood.

WEINER. I tell you something, Louis. If Pittman is elected, this guy is out. In fact, one of the conditions on which the biggest majority—not the big—I mean fellows like myself . . . Now, I have no bones to pick with anybody, but one of the conditions on which he is getting a tremendous amount of support is that he changes the Tax Commission. That will be the first thing that will be changed. Now the Tax Commission listens to Cahill. Whatever he says, they do, and he will be out. When Pittman is in and Cliff is top dog in the state . . . But that fellow Russell is nobody. Russell doesn't know which way to turn now. He is afraid to say yes to this one for fear of Pittman. But when Pittman is in and changes that Commission and sits on that himself, you got no problem.

TABET. Like I say to Cliff, I say, "Look, I'm a gentleman. You see the point? You don't have to worry about it. Everything you have to put on the top, I take care of it. I'm a big boy. I know what is coming. That's nothing, anything on the cuff or anything like that right away." If Cliff tells me he got to take care of it in Washington, I take care of it. He said O.K., like before. Listen, I got to keep myself from now on in the hands of you guys. You got to guide me, because I'm walking on edge now, but still I understand one thing that—if you think I could be blackballed someplace.

WEINER. Listen, here's what I say. I wouldn't make a move until after the election.

TABET. Because don't forget—

WEINER. If you get hit bad to start with, you can't overcome it. If the way is smooth, there's nothing to it.

TABET. But Cliff tells me, "Don't be worried about Carson City." He says, "I can take care of it."

WEINER. Cliff can take care of it but not for the next—while Russell is in you commit suicide doing it while he's in office, because he's not going to help anything.

TABET. But tell me—well, I'm not more—

WEINER. This guy Cahill is the guy.

TABET. I'm not more dirty than—for Christ's sake—than a lot of guys in here. Listen, I'm not more dirty or perfect than a lot of guys around town.

WEINER. No question about it.

TABET. I'm—I've got no convictions—

WEINER. But they know Doc's in there. They know Doc Stacher is in the Sands. What do you think—they don't know Doc's in there? You think they don't know Meyer and Jake [Lansky] are in the Thunderbird, huh?

TABET. I want to be your friend. I'm taking Dick with me. I want to fix him up. I got power over there. I know it costs big dough, but it got to be done, because them guys are going to put a beef about him. Forget entirely Roxie's, and all that. That's out. Can't mix the two businesses together. That's very foolish.

WEINER. No, certainly, you have to take one or the other.

TABET. Not only that, but it's too much, and what's the use of playing around with that? I thought I might just play around with that and then dump it.

WEINER. You can't do that if you're going to be in gambling. Not if you're going to do something legitimate.

TABET. No, no. I'm going legit. I want to go right down the line. I don't want nobody to front for me, because on the end that's no good.

WEINER. Then you get twisted.

TABET. At the same time, I've invested so much dough I don't want to have anybody run with my dough. I don't want to run with anybody's dough.

WEINER. You want to depend on your own.

TABET. So you see, it's a little bit ticklish and difficult and right now I need you, and I need you very bad, and I need your advice, and sometime I got a headache. You know I got a (*leans forward and raps three times on the lamp table beside Weiner's chair*) *testa dura,* but still I listen to what you tell me, and I'm O.K. I believe in you. When I know other Dagos, I don't have to tell you the first day. You do a lot of good things. If you do one-tenth of what you do for people I know, is good enough for me. You don't tell me you hurt my feelings by coming here. And don't be cheap, because if you're cheap, I—

WEINER. Well, cheap is not good, because if you're going to be cheap, then you can't give the man the time. When you're cheap, it's no good, then you call up; if it's cheap, you can't give the man the time.

TABET. Well, this thing is going to be quite a big outfit, and like I said, you are maybe— I take a piece of that Bond Road over there. You handle the deal now and I got Big Tony in here asking me what I think about it, the promotion deal he want to make with me. But that I got to make a lot of talk about.

WEINER (*surprised*). Tony Cornero?

TABET. Yes, I want to ask your advice about it and if you think—

WEINER. Now, there's a funny thing. There's a man they should never turn down for a license. He's never done anything, he's never done a thing wrong. Tony Cornero is cleaner than ninety-five per cent, ninety-nine per cent of the people. Tony's never done anything in his life.

TABET. He says he was bootlegger.

WEINER. So what the hell's a bootlegger when everybody else in town did business with a bootlegger.

TABET. I know a judge who make gin in his bathtub.

WEINER. But Tony was a bootlegger when everybody else was doing it. There was nothing to it. Hell, one of our former city commissioners, two of them, were. There was nothing to it, particularly in this town; this way—they used to close the front doors and open the back door. The next month they would close the back door and they would open the front door. They ran just like they ran the bawdy houses. I mean, this was every month the big houses would send a bartender over to get a hundred-dollar fine. There wasn't anything to it. That was all Tony ever did.

TABET. Well, I think—well, I heard—but don't tell him it come from me. He came clean—I don't think that's right. He wanted to make a promotion, you see. That is the ticklish point, you see.

WEINER. If you make it a promotion, it's no good, because if you make it a promotion, you are dealing with too many little people. When you are in with little people you can't handle the business. Is that right?

TABET. That's right.

WEINER. You can't handle with little people.

TABET. That's it, but what arrangements can be made between the guys? But we don't need to worry about that now. I

143

thought maybe I take this step right away and I'm going to be left alone. Because I can't help being left alone for the moment because the way he do, the way Cliff explain to me, he said, "You going to apply," and I thought it was the county first but he said no, Carson City first, and he said the license, and thirty days after that they inquire and make investigations about you and all that crap in there, and the next month they pass it. You know that thirty days, if the press blasts around in here, what you gonna do? You can't close it.

WEINER. No, that's right.

TABET. You have to keep one guy, one of the partners, to sit around in there.

WEINER. Theoretically, you have to more or less escrow it. Technically, you are not supposed to take out any of the profits or share any of the losses during the period of investigation. You have got to have somebody in there that's on the license to manage the place. A couple of years ago when we handled the Horseshoe Club, we had it that way a couple of years ago, and a complete new group coming in. Well, we just escrowed it, and we kept some of the old fellows running—we had a new man in there working on the payroll, so he could be there and see what's going on, and we put it up in an escrow and kept the old men in.

TABET. Well, you make a very wonderful job with Georgetti.

WEINER. Yes, I know, we did a good job for Georgetti.

TABET. Now, you tell me something; you think about it and tell me how much I owe you for the year, and I pay you right away and everything that Cliff do, every fix he do for me, name it, cash, and we no get no discussions for money. I mean, let's not be—that's nothing, that. We don't talk about dough. But I want to be comfortable; I want you to be at ease; I want to be at ease.

144

WEINER. That's right. It's no good if you can't.

TABET. I don't want to take your time and things like that. I don't want to ask you for five minutes, and you say—

WEINER. I know, when you want to get ahold of me without an appointment, I can come out here.

TABET. I don' wanna disturb your wife and things like that.

WEINER. You want to know that when you call me, I'm getting something when I come out and I'm gonna—

TABET. That's right, I don't want to be complicated. I want to be clean. I want to keep my reputation of my own, my own things, you see. I don't want to walk on the feet of somebody and after that, I mean, nobody walk on my feet.

WEINER. You really want a deal.

TABET. I want to be clean; if somebody wanna be rough, I be rough. Somebody wanna start to be tricky, I am gonna be tricky. And I don't want that.

WEINER. That's right, you want to live and let live.

TABET. That's right—I mean, we got to have something here with Dick. A lot of people tell me, I know that I can put Dick someplace, and I can go to China, in one sense; so for him too I want to draw a contract with him and keep him happy, and if the guy is glad, I'm so happy.

WEINER. I'd put all the money I have on the floor and walk out and leave Dick there and know it will be there when I come back.

TABET. Everything is in the bag. Now we shall see—and I don't know—what's going to pop up now. We got to wait until after the election. What chance we got? Suppose the other fellow gets elected?

WEINER. Russell? He hasn't got as much chance to be elected as I have, and I'm not even running.

TABET. Yeah.

145

WEINER. If he doesn't get beat three to two or two to one, I'm a monkey's uncle. Oh, he hasn't got a prayer. The only chance he would have would be if sometime between now and the day of the election the nominee dropped dead, so that they don't have anybody to run against him. That's about the only chance he's got.

TABET. Yeah.

WEINER. My God, he couldn't even get his own man appointed Senator. You'd think that in an election year his own committee would go along with him.

TABET. Yeah.

WEINER. His own committee refused to go with him, and they wouldn't appoint the man. Now they appointed a man who is a relative unknown out there. He's nothing.

TABET. Yeah.

WEINER. He's a wonderful guy, but he's a nobody. We are going to get our own Senator in, and he will be McCarran's protégé. With McCarran we were—we just sat right up there.

TABET. Now look, when you going in I want to get on the bandwagon too.

WEINER. Yeah, I know.

TABET. Don't be worried if you need anything—let me know. I don't say that you got to—

WEINER. Oh, no sense in talking and pulling your arm.

TABET. No, not pull my arm. Pull my hand, yes. I'll do it with pleasure, because I know that in the end I'm going to get—

WEINER. Ten back for one.

TABET. That's all right. I know the game for a long time. I do that for many years now. O.K., Louie.

WEINER. I'm going to go home.

TABET. You should have a drink.

WEINER. No, thanks. I'm going to walk over and get the papers and go on home.

146

While attorney Louis Weiner was walking home, hoodlum impersonator Louis Tabet was packing his bags and calling for a bellhop. The tab for his six-week stay at El Rancho, plus liquor, food, and Corona-Coronas, totaled $3,900. But it was worth every penny to Hank Greenspun and Ed Reid. The next day, Reid began a series of twelve articles, revealing all of Tabet's intimate conversations with Roxie, Kellogg, Colton, Sheriff Jones, Weiner, and Lieutenant Governor Jones. The exposé shook the entire state.

The Clark County grand jury indicted Sheriff Jones and County Commissioner Rodney Colton on charges of accepting gifts and offers of money with the agreement to use their official positions to further the welfare of a self-proclaimed hoodlum.

Lieutenant Governor Clifford A. Jones tendered his resignation as Democratic National Committeeman and the Democratic leaders hastily accepted it.

Sheriff Jones meekly dropped his $1 million suit against the Las Vegas *Sun*.

And Governor Russell, the man who couldn't win unless Pittman dropped dead, won the election hands down.

Then the Nevada Tax Commission started proceedings against the Thunderbird Hotel, charging that it was unfit to hold a gaming license. Lieutenant Governor Jones denied before the Commission that Meyer and Jake Lansky had a piece of the Thunderbird, but the Commission (in some inexplicable way) produced a copy of the federal income tax returns of George Sadlo, a Lansky flunky, and Jake Lansky himself. Between the two of them they had paid taxes on $200,000 worth of income from the T-Bird. The hotel's gaming license was revoked. The hotel fought the ruling and the State Supreme Court came to their assistance, reversing the Commission's decision.

Louis Weiner took it all stoically. He admitted he had made the prediction that if Pittman were elected, he would change the personnel of the Tax Commission. But when it came to Lansky, the attorney became vague and evasive. "I have no independent recollections of making such a statement," he said. "But if you have a tape recording of my voice at the El Rancho, I presume I said what it says."

In the end nothing very drastic happened to anyone. Sheriff Jones surrendered the television set but Commissioner Colton never produced the Geiger counter. The charges themselves were quashed after a couple of years of irritating suspense. The politicians in Carson City set up the Nevada Gaming Control Board to screen applicants for gaming licenses, placing a former FBI agent at its head. This was tantamount to locking the barn door after the horse is gone. Nobody said a word about "the hidden interests." It was all very noble and the citizens applauded and no one was really hurt. And soon it was business as usual in the jungle.

CHAPTER EIGHT

Kingmakers and Tax Dodgers

If set to music, Nevada's political chicanery would rival *Guys and Dolls* as a smash Broadway musical. Since gambling was legalized in 1931, elections have been reduced to political contests between the "kingmakers" of Reno and the wealthy mobsters of Las Vegas. Both groups are zealously watching out for their own special interests. And these interests are concerned solely with greater individual profit and stronger personal power. The voters, known as citizens in the other forty-nine states, are mostly indolent transients—temporary lodgers seated at the end of a rainbow, stubbornly waiting for their pot of gold. Except for a few irascible natives, no one takes the state of Nevada seriously. It is like living inside a gas-filled balloon. They know that sooner or later somebody is bound to come along and punch a hole in it. And yet the years slip away, families are raised, the old are buried, and life wears on senselessly.

The most powerful politician in Nevada history was the late U.S. Senator Pat McCarran, who rode into office in 1932 on FDR's coattails, and then promptly broke with the Administration. It is said that when Adlai Stevenson ran for president in 1952, McCarran made a deal with Jake Arvey of Chicago to put the entire Chicago Capone Mob in Nevada gambling if Stevenson won. The main purpose was, allegedly, to provide an outlet for huge sums of black money from the Chicago area. Stevenson did not win, but the Chicago Mob came to Las Vegas anyway.

Another story about Nevada politics involves the late U.S. Senator Key Pittman, McCarran's colleague. It seems that Pittman died in November, 1940, just a few days before the election. Zealous Democrats, who knew that Pittman's opponent would be elected automatically if his death were announced before the voting took place, concealed the Senator's body in a bathtub in the Mizpah hotel in Tonopah and covered it with cracked ice to preserve it.

The announcement of his death came a few days after the election and the Republicans attempted to get the story into circulation to circumvent the results of the election. Senator McCarran and his cronies denied the story. But the fact remains that Governor E. P. Carville promptly appointed himself to the vacated Senate post. Key Pittman's brother, Vail, who was Lieutenant Governor, then became Governor—a maneuver that lends credence to the story.

McCarran worked hand in glove with Norman Biltz, a self-made Reno millionaire. The two made a formidable pair. Their combined economic and political power was close to absolute in the state. And the Washington favors that McCarran per-

150

formed for Biltz and his many wealthy friends and clients were generously reciprocated in kind.

"Nevada must be kept small," Biltz preached. "Let industry go elsewhere. Large industrial payrolls bring in large families, which cost more money in taxes for public services." Though not personally interested in gambling ("It makes me nervous"), Biltz is nevertheless a friend of gamblers, and with McCarran bossed Nevada gambling for years.

Curiously enough, Biltz is a Republican. "All that matters is good government," he told the press time and again when they questioned his friendship with Democrat McCarran. "In the Nevada elections what most of us are interested in is getting the right kind of people and we don't give a damn whether they are Democrats or Republicans."

In an attempt to bankrupt his consistent critic, *Sun* publisher Greenspun, McCarran passed the word along to his hoodlum friends on the Strip, and the *Sun* was shorn of its advertising from most of the Las Vegas gambling houses. Greenspun immediately sued the gamblers and McCarran for conspiracy to drive him out of business, and won an out-of-court settlement for about $86,000. With his advertising restored and a national reputation acquired in the bargain, he increased his excoriation of McCarran and Biltz. And he never forgot that mobster Moe Dalitz at the Desert Inn had been the first to follow the Senator's prompting.

During the 1952 elections, Thomas B. Mechling, a young "upstart" from Washington, D.C., took advantage of Nevada's negligible residence requirements and decided to file in the Democratic primary contest against McCarran's protégé, Alan Bible, for the post of United States Senator. Campaigning in a trailer and assisted by his wife, Mechling, a journalist, shook hands with most of the voters in the state, promising them that

151

the day of the bosses was over. Impressed by his courage and arguments, the voters selected Mechling over Bible to represent the Democratic ticket.

Dismayed by the results, the seventy-six-year-old McCarran switched his support to the Republican candidate, George H. "Molly" Malone. Norman Biltz then stepped into the picture. He invited candidate Mechling to his office for a friendly chat. Still unwise about Nevada politics, Mechling visited Biltz without notifying his friends and backers.

The next day, a smiling Norman Biltz entertained the press with a tape recording that suggested Mechling had offered Biltz a deal in return for political favors.

Mechling protested that the tape had been cut and spliced to make it appear as if he wanted a political deal. Biltz answered Mechling's charge by playing the tape on radio across the state. Mechling went down to defeat even though he had been far ahead of Malone in the pre-election straw voting prior to the recording session.

After the elections, Biltz had something to say about outsiders like Mechling. "You couldn't elect an alderman in New York City for $30,000, and yet that's all it costs to elect a Nevada Senator. That's why outsiders think they can move in here and take over. They want to tear down everything that took so long and so much sweat to build up, and we're determined to stop them. Sure we have a lot of influence around here, but damn it, we earned it. We worked hard to bring in the right kind of people, and to make this a decent place to live. It's going to stay that way." What Biltz overlooked was the fact that he also was an outsider. Speaking of McCarran, Biltz said: "Pat is as stubborn as a mule, and he and I have lots of arguments. On the other hand, he is the greatest Senator Nevada could possibly have."

It was no secret in Nevada that McCarran was a friend of the

152

gambling fraternity, and his friendship often exceeded the state's boundaries. On January 23, 1951, a long list of influential hoodlums and racketeers were brought up for contempt citations before the Senate by Senator Estes Kefauver. McCarran tried desperately to block the action by citing a Supreme Court decision regarding an alleged Communist, Mrs. Patricia Blau, of Colorado. It soon became apparent that McCarran's overweaning interest in the constitutional rights of Joe Adonis, Jack Dragna, Arthur Longano, Pat Manno, Salvatore Moretti, *et al.,* was far greater than his concern for the rights of many witnesses before his own Communist-hunting committee.

McCarran's ploy was to hide the hoodlums behind the legal skirts of Mrs. Blau, who had refused to answer questions in Denver concerning the Communist Party and her employment by it. He asked that the contempt resolution be referred to his Judiciary Committee for "further study"—a move wholly without precedent at the time in the Senate. The Senate rejected McCarran's motion by a roll-call vote of 12–59, then passed the contempt resolution by voice vote. In the next nine months the Senate cited thirty-nine other hoodlums for contempt without a dissent from McCarran.

For years headquarters for the McCarran clan in Las Vegas was the Thunderbird hotel (in Reno it was the Riverside—then operated by Mert Wertheimer, a Detroit hoodlum). McCarran's disciple Lieutenant Governor Cliff Jones (known in gambling circles as "Big Juice") owned 11 per cent of the T-Bird. Jones's other gambling interests included 2.5 per cent of the Pioneer Club, which netted him approximately $14,000 a year on an original investment of $5,000, and one per cent in the Golden Nugget, a $23,310 investment which netted him about $12,000.

Commenting on this situation in his report to the Senate, Kefauver said:

153

The profits which have been taken from gambling operations are far greater than those which can be earned quickly in any other business. The availability of huge sums of cash and the incentive to control political action result in gamblers and racketeers too often taking part in government.

In states where gambling is illegal, this alliance of gamblers, gangsters, and government will yield to the spotlight of publicity and the pressure of public opinion, but where gambling receives a cloak of respectability through legalization, there is no weapon which can be used to keep the gamblers and their money out of politics.

In Nevada it is more likely that the crooks are the politicians rather than the politicians being crooked. Lucius Beebe, former publisher of the Virginia City *Territorial Enterprise,* once observed about the convening of the state legislature in Carson City:

"Adult Nevadans with business affairs at stake almost unanimously regard the legislature as an unavoidable public calamity and recall Thoreau's remark when told by a neighbor that the Massachusetts legislature was about to convene, 'I must go to town and buy a lock for my back door.' "

Considering the matter, Beebe suggested that the "bicameral zoo" should meet only every twenty years and then for a maximum of five minutes. "The damage to everyone they could do in even that minimum period would take sane and industrious citizens the ensuing two decades to repair."

Once when McCarran and Jones had trouble convincing the legislature that it should not raise the state gaming tax, the Thunderbird played host to fifty lawmakers for several days. The junket, which became known as the "lost weekend" in Las Vegas, cost the robber barons (it was split among them)

$22,000. One Senator, who explained to Marion Hicks that he was trying to get a Washington job, stayed on at the T-Bird for a month, running up a bill of close to $1,000. "Well," Hicks explained, shrugging in resignation, "we needed his vote."

The results were well worth the tab. The proposed tax increase passed the assembly but did not even get to the floor of the senate for a vote. Senator Rene LeMaire summed it up for his colleagues: "I feel I would have been derelict in my duty as a state senator if I had not gone to Las Vegas to see and understand the problems created by the phenomenal growth and expansion of that area."

This noble sentiment has been embraced by numerous public servants over the years, while visiting Las Vegas on one pretext or another at the taxpayers' expense. As late as April, 1962, Senators Barry Goldwater (R., Ariz.), Howard Cannon (D., Nev.), and Frank Moss (D., Utah), along with fifty Air Force Reserve members (from Goldwater's unit), arrived in Las Vegas in President John F. Kennedy's official airplane, for an "inspection tour" of Nellis Air Force Base on the outskirts of Las Vegas. The inspection consisted of a half-hour look at a static display of F-105s. There was no advance notice to the press. "All they used Nellis for was a landing strip and for transportation to town," Lieutenant James Franz, base information officer, explained to angry newsmen. "They went straight to town. They mostly wanted to see the sights and sounds of Las Vegas." (On April 30, 1962, Senator Goldwater was elevated to the rank of major general in the Air Force Reserve.)

It was as a sentimental gesture, no doubt, that Senator Goldwater checked into the Riviera, where the gracious traditions of the late Gus Greenbaum are preserved by such old gambling buddies as Elias Atol and Ben Goffstein.

Commenting on the "lost weekend" junket of the state senators and the defeated tax bill, Governor Russell said: "I am

155

helpless. I have been under all sorts of pressure. I found that after I was elected I was supposed to do certain things which I won't mention. They were in the nature of favors. I did not do these things and I lost some friends I thought were good friends. I know better now."

After McCarran's death in 1954, the political power of Norman Biltz and his Reno millionaire friends was usurped by the robber barons along the Las Vegas Strip. Biltz's miserly $30,000 campaign fund became sadly inadequate. The casino owners passed the hat and raised a million dollars every two years to elect friendly candidates. Perhaps that kind of money could not elect every friendly aspirant, but it could lick just about any unfriendly one in a state where the entire population was less than that of Omaha, Nebraska, in the 1960 Census.

In Nevada, when it comes to electing men of good will and intelligence to the U.S. Congress, the state assembly, and local offices, the slim pickings are enough to confound the most astute voter. Rogues and oddballs, selected by the powers that be, constantly defeat the few impressive candidates who have the courage to leap into the public arena. Now and then there is a flash of color along the thorny campaign path, such as coffee heiress Eugenia Clair Smith, a wealthy Renoite, who repeatedly has sought the state's only seat in the U.S. House of Representatives. Flame-haired Eugenia's last attempt, in 1956, was directed by author Ed Reid, who served as speech writer, publicist, chauffeur, and bodyguard.

Eugenia campaigned in a limousine, her lovely neck and hands set aglow by a quarter-million dollars' worth of gems, her graceful figure hidden under a six-foot-square chinchilla throw rug during cool afternoons in the hills. Cautioned by Reid to remove her jewelry while addressing the populace, she would reluctantly strip it off before stepping out of the limousine at each whistle stop. As she went into her pitch, Reid would blow on his chilled hands and stamp his feet to the accompaniment of the clicking stones in his pocket. A tot with a slingshot could have pulled off the biggest gem robbery in Southwest history.

Eugenia's platform was as lush as her attire. Among a long list of promises was her pledge to construct a red-brick building in the nation's capital to be known as the Nevada House. It would contain offices for a dozen experts whom she would personally pay $10,000 a year to advise her in such complex fields as mining, farming, ranching, industry, business, recreation, etc. Furthermore, she would maintain a private airliner to be used free of charge by any Nevadan who had a legitimate complaint he wished to voice in Washington.

It was a "swell" campaign, but Eugenia had not reckoned with the seasoned manipulators in Las Vegas. She ran last in a list of five candidates. The winner of that election, Walter Baring (present incumbent) has had a lackluster career, and was recently criticized in the Nevada press for supporting the John Birch Society.

Another colorful campaigner was celluloid cowboy Rex Bell, the husband of the "It Girl," Clara Bow, a "smoothie" who charmed the natives with his costly western wardrobe and verbal gymnastics. Bell talked himself into the lieutenant governorship of the state in 1954 (replacing Cliff Jones) and managed to retain the office until his death on July 4, 1962. A few weeks before his death, Bell had filed as G.O.P. candidate for governor in the November elections.

In a move that startled both the kingmakers and the robber barons, *Sun* publisher Greenspun promptly filed to replace Bell on the Republican ticket. "I feel it is my duty as a newspaperman to bring before Nevada's tax-paying public the shortcomings of the present spendthrift state administration," said Greenspun. In the spring he had expressed a different philosophy: "Too many newspapers have been destroyed by publishers with

157

political ambitions. This I will never permit, for this little old paper means more to me than all the rewards which high office can bring."

Greenspun's opponent in the primary was Oran Gragson, Las Vegas' mayor, who had enjoyed the *Sun's* support in his election four years earlier. The *Sun* also had backed Democrat Sawyer for governor, and as late as 1959, Greenspun had written: "He has exceeded our most extravagant hopes and predictions. Grant Sawyer is a man among men."

In January, 1962, the new Las Vegas Resort Hotel Association, headed by Moe Dalitz at the Desert Inn, had been formed to take joint action on "problems of mutual interest." Coming on the eve of the 1962 election campaigns, when every important political office (except one U.S. Senator) was on the ballot, the "mutual interest" became quite transparent to Greenspun, who labeled it an ominous portent and filed his own candidacy.

A gigantic statewide smear was Greenspun's reward for his troubles. In the primary, he lost to Gragson by a two-to-one margin. A jubilant Moe Dalitz summed up the campaign in an interview with Ed Reid. "Hank [Greenspun] says it cost a quarter of a million? Hah, it cost almost twice that, but we got results! Why, we threw the money away like water. And I'm telling you in front of witnesses. Now go on, go on and print it!"

The Mob had dug up and distorted everything they could in Greenspun's past, including his guilty plea to running arms to Israel in 1950, for which he was fined $10,000 (his civil rights were restored in 1961 by President Kennedy). Smear advertisements appeared in newspapers throughout the state, and anti-Semitic literature was distributed to homes and handed out on the streets. Greenspun was called a Red because he had worked as a law clerk in the office of Vito Marcantonio in New York.

158

The ads neglected to mention that Fiorello La Guardia had been a member of the same law firm.

Casino employees were forced to re-register Republican in order to vote against Greenspun and were ordered to put Gragson stickers on their cars and signs on their lawns. In the heat of the battle, Greenspun warned the voters that if Gragson won the primary the Hotel Association would desert him and support Sawyer in the general election. And that was exactly what happened. The day after the primary, the Gragson stickers came down and Sawyer's went up. Sawyer won the general election by a three-to-one margin.

In the aftermath, it was interesting to note that in all the dirt thrown at Greenspun, not once was there any mention that the *Sun* publisher had begun his Las Vegas career as a publicity man for Bugsy Siegel at the Flamingo hotel. That, it seems, would have been knocking a little too close to home.

The two biggest political issues in Las Vegas today concern water and civil rights. Las Vegas sits atop an artesian basin which for over one hundred years has provided the area with all the sweet, potable water necessary to preserve life and promote growth. But the development of the area and the drilling of wells by home owners, ranchers, and the Las Vegas Valley Water District has dangerously depleted the water basin. Today Las Vegas is using 200 per cent more water than is replaced through melting snows of the nearby Spring range of mountains and the scant annual rainfall. The water table is sinking lower each year, and the only solution for the arid town appears to be the Colorado River, which feeds into Lake Mead (the world's largest man-made lake) behind Boulder Dam. The only drawback is the $57 million necessary for the pipeline and the equipment to pump it over a thousand-foot elevation to Las Vegas.

159

A recent survey by the U.S. Bureau of Reclamation proposed a four-mile-long tunnel through the mountains surrounding Lake Mead at an estimated cost of $42 million. The tunnel would supply the area with 110 million gallons of water daily. The plan calls for a long-term, low-interest loan with the government, but so far it is still in the nebulous future.

Experts figure that the situation will be critical by 1967. But residents say the town is already in trouble. Each year wells have to be redrilled, going deeper into the water zone. In many areas the ground in the valley has buckled and cracked as the water pressure decreases. This sinking has been attributed to "earthquakes." Not long ago the newly built St. Viator's Roman Catholic church buckled as the ground sank. It had to be torn down.

Nevertheless, nature's warnings had no influence on the owners of the Dunes, the Tropicana, and the Desert Inn as late as 1962. They went blithely ahead with plans to construct eighteen-hole golf courses, which required up to 1.5 million gallons of water each day to stay green under a scorching sun— enough water to provide for the needs of four thousand families. The Desert Inn plans included a housing project and a golf course with streams flowing through it, and several lakes. Since the D.I. already had a golf course, the new course, besides raising the value of the housing development, was set aside for the guests of the Stardust hotel. Even without the golf course, the Tropicana was already pumping 700,000 gallons a day more than was allowed on its permits.

There was plenty of water available for the golf courses in the form of effluent (water processed from the sewage plants and the water from the steam-generating plant south of Las Vegas, which provides electric power for much of the town) but the hotel owners were determined to sink their own wells and get all the water they needed free of charge—and to hell with posterity.

Since there were already three golf courses in Las Vegas, the Ground Water Board and the State Engineer, Edmund Muth, had categorically denied well permits to the three hotels. But the robber barons are not used to being turned down. Soon the phones in the state capital started to jangle. Then Hugh Shamberger, Nevada's Director of Conservation and Natural Resources, put in a call to George Monahan, chairman of the Ground Water Board. "George," said Hugh, "you must get Riddle [the boss at the Dunes] off the Governor's back!" Monahan did the only thing he could. He granted the permits. In due course, Moe Dalitz at the Desert Inn and Ben Jaffe at the Tropicana received their permits. The only holdout on the Ground Water Board after the call from Carson City was Donal O'Callaghan. Monahan, who had originally agreed with O'Callaghan, now berated him angrily. "By God, you are a thickheaded Irishman if I ever saw one. Just because you are against golf courses doesn't have anything to do with whether we can set a policy." The board then denied permits for domestic use to the city of North Las Vegas!

"It is difficult to determine what motivated the governor's intercession. Could it be paying off political favors, past, present or future?" the *Sun* inquired. "We don't know and would not dare guess. But we do know that whatever the motivations, it was not in the public interest."

Before 1931 Negroes were welcome in Nevada society. There was no discrimination or segregation. The hardy pioneer was interested only in his fellow man's character and ability—not in his color, race, or creed. Then the poor whites from Texas, Louisiana, Florida, and other points south moved into the state with their gaming devices and bootlegged money and took over not only the gambling but the social and political life of the state as well. They were thugs and thieves and murderers, but they

161

were white, and segregation set in overnight. When the eastern and northern gangsters arrived they were quick to protect the *status quo*. They didn't want any Nigrahs upsetting their high-rolling southern gentlemen, who had more oil wells than the gangsters had slot machines. And besides, many of the mobsters had been brought up in teeming slums where they had rumbled against the colored gangs, and they had not forgotten their own prejudice and hatred.

The inhabitants of Westside live behind what they call the "Concrete Curtain"—so named because of the railroad underpass that separates their community from the commercial section of downtown Las Vegas. Though some dusty streets have been paved and some new homes built, much of Westside still qualifies as slum.

Las Vegas, or "Lost Wages," as it's known in Westside, is off limits to all Negroes—except entertainers and janitors. This holds for the plushest Strip casinos and the tiniest dives in Glitter Gulch. A Negro cannot rent a room, buy a sandwich, order a drink, or even drop a nickel in a slot machine. Even with entertainers, the house keeps a watchful eye. Not too long ago a fledgling publicist at the Sahara received a phone call from an *Ebony* magazine reporter who wanted to interview a Negro movie star then appearing in the hotel's show. "Certainly," said the naïve young man. "Come right over." But it wasn't that easy. "Hell," his boss explained after turning down the request, "the guy probably won't even be able to get a taxi driver to bring him here." As it turned out, the reporter was met at the airport and told the facts of life; later he caught the show from the wings, interviewed the star, and left on the next plane out.

Negroes like Louie Armstrong and Eartha Kitt are acceptable to the hoodlums so long as they stay out of the way and don't invite their relatives and friends to the shows.

In recent years some of the Strip hotels have relented in

favor of famous Negro artists, permitting them to stay on the premises, though it is made clear in most cases that they are not welcome in the casinos or restaurants. Negro singer Herb Jeffries, when arriving at a hotel, was once told that his room would be among the white guests (an almost unheard-of concession), but that his accompanist, Dick Hazzard, would have to stay in special Negro quarters.

"If he does, I do," said Jeffries. The owner's face collapsed when Jeffries introduced his accompanist: Hazzard is white.

In 1955, when Sammy Davis, Jr., opened in the Venus Room at the New Frontier, the occasion was sensational in more ways than one. Seated down front in the audience was his grandmother, stepmother and sister—the first of their race to sit among the princely whites on the Strip. In the intervening eight years, the color line has become more elastic in a few Strip casinos, but even in the most liberal ones it is still far from erased.

The boldest attempt at breaking down the racial barriers came with the building of the luxurious Moulin Rouge, the first interracial hotel–casino in Las Vegas history. It was not on the Strip, nor even in Glitter Gulch; but a half mile up Bonanza Road and across the railroad tracks. It featured a mixed chorus line of shapely white and colored girls, and a lively group of African dancers who throbbed to the frenetic beat of Lionel Hampton. The hotel offered all the comfort, entertainment, and gaming devices of the finest Strip casino. Former heavyweight champ Joe Louis was the chief greeter for a time, shaking hands in a sad but sincere way. The owners hoped to attract a moneyed polyglot clientele, but it did not appeal to the country's wealthier Negroes, who resented being restricted to the Moulin Rouge. Today it is dark and empty.

The 1961 state legislature, after stormy debates over civil rights, created the Nevada Commission on Equal Rights of

Citizens. Bert Goldwater, a Reno attorney, was made its chairman. The Commission ran headlong into disaster at its very first meeting in July, 1961, when it tried to investigate two separate incidents of discrimination in downtown business establishments. One of the complaints was filed by a paraplegic veteran of World War II, who claimed he was forcefully ejected from the Golden Gate casino seconds after he had limped through the entrance assisted by two canes. "We don't want any niggers in this place," a security guard allegedly shouted. The second charge was filed by a Negro salesman who was allegedly refused service at a restaurant.

But four subpoenaed witnesses refused to testify in the cases, claiming that the newspapers had placed them in the role of defendants. Attorney Goldwater asked the witnesses if they would testify if no oaths were required and the questions were limited to a general nature and not related to the casino incident. They refused to comment. Goldwater found himself powerless to take any action against the witnesses. Shortly thereafter he resigned his post, stating that a lack of support from any of the governmental branches made his job worthless and unworkable. Laws without rigid enforcement are not worth the paper they are written on.

It has long been the argument of honest law-enforcement officers that the federal government could easily crack down on organized crime any time it so desired. For example, until Mickey Cohen's trial and conviction for income tax evasion in 1952, not one racketeer, hoodlum, or gangster of first-rank importance had ever been convicted of income tax fraud in California. In fact, not one had ever been prosecuted.

Corruption is as much a part of crime as violence. But the big question for crime fighters is: Where does it start? Who gets to whom first? Or better still, which way does it travel? Up or down? After some extensive research on this subject, the California Special Crime Study Commission on Organized Crime concluded that corruption travels both ways, and quite often at the same time. The Commission's final report, in 1950, stated:

The implications of these matters are far-reaching, and of real importance in any study of the factors contributing to organized crime or in any consideration of the means available for its elimination. If the tax laws which the Federal and State Governments are now enforcing against legitimate business were applied literally to racketeers, hoodlums and gangsters, as the law contemplates, and were backed up with either actual collection of the full amount of the tax due or prosecution for evasion, organized crime could not produce the tremendous profits which are now notorious. The wealth which is being accumulated year after year by racketeers in California is proof that professional gamblers, white slavers, narcotics peddlers and other criminals, in marked contrast to honest businessmen, are evading payment of their lawful income taxes in very large amounts.

After all, we might as well face up to it: who else but a hoodlum can build a quarter-million-dollar house without explaining where he got the money? There is not one major hoodlum today who doesn't live in a palace or its equivalent and spend a half million a year for incidentals.

Do they really pay taxes on that money? We'll never find out for certain from the Federal Bureau of Internal Revenue because those reports are largely inaccessible. But there are other ways to find out, or at least to arrive at a pretty fair judgment.

165

The Commission estimated that "if federal and state taxes are paid, and if due allowance for modest living expense is made, it would require an annual income of not less than $1,270,000 for 10 years to accumulate $500,000."

Costello's worth today, including fashionable hotels, breweries, etc., is over $25 million. Jake Guzik was reputedly (on the best authorities) worth $200 million. The authors are too poor in higher mathematics to figure how many *billions* Jake had to earn, assuming he paid his income taxes faithfully, to end up with that kind of booty. It could be funny if it weren't so sad.

How is this fantastic sleight-of-hand accomplished? It can be very simple when the bottom meets the top or vice versa. Or to be more specific, when you know a Patrick Mooney; and when that Patrick Mooney is Chief Field Deputy in the Office of the Collector of Internal Revenue, District of Nevada.

Patrick Mooney did not mind meeting a hoodlum halfway, or further. Of course, there had to be a dodge, and in this case it was the Mountain City Consolidated Copper Company (not to be confused with the Mountain City Copper Company). M.C.C.C.C. was a Nevada corporation formed in 1937. Its organizer and principal promoter and general manager at all times was Mooney, who at the same time held his post with the Internal Revenue Bureau. The company, a paper organization, never produced a single ton of ore. All of M.C.C.C.C.'s officers and directors, except one, were federal officials. The company's first president was a prominent Nevada attorney, who died while in office and was never replaced.

The vice-president, Thomas W. Miller, also a director, was Staff Field Representative, covering ten western states for the U.S. Veteran's Employment Service. Miller was an ex-convict who had served a term in the federal penitentiary, having been convicted in 1927 for conspiring to defraud the United States when he held the office of Alien Property Custodian in the Harding Administration. In 1933 he received a Presidential pardon with restoration of civil rights.

Patrick Mooney was the secretary–treasurer, general manager, and a director. Another director was John B. Williams, who was a revenue agent in the bureau's Office of Accountancy and Collections. William J. Forman, a prominent Reno attorney, was the only director who was not in federal service.

According to the Securities and Exchange Commission, M.C.C.C. had 2,254,690 shares of stock outstanding in June of 1946. Of this total, 1,067,500 shares were issued as payment for the company's real property and as promotional stock. The remaining 1,187,190 shares had been sold for cash at prices varying from forty to ten cents per share.

To show for all this money, M.C.C.C. had two short prospecting tunnels, two log cabins, each with an outhouse, a corrugated-iron shed containing an air compressor and a generating set, and outside the building a boiler and a second compressor. The only evidence of actual mining were the cores from half a dozen test holes. The entire property wasn't worth $15,000.

The company's most valuable asset was a salesman named Martin M. Hartmann, who was a friend of Mooney of thirty-five years' standing. Hartmann was also an ex-convict, with a record as a swindler going back a quarter century.

When Hartmann wasn't using the stock as an extortion club, he was duping unwary buyers into thinking they were buying Mountain City Copper Company stocks, a bona fide company listed on the New York Stock Exchange. In January, 1944, Hartmann was indicted in California on three counts of grand theft, each count based on the worthless M.C.C.C. stock.

167

There was a fourth count, charging a violation of the Corporate Securities Act. Hartmann pleaded guilty and received a five-year suspended sentence.

After an investigation of M.C.C.C.C., the Securities and Exchange Commission submitted a report which stated in part:

The fact that Mooney, being Chief Field Agent of the Internal Revenue Service and of the politically powerful law firm of Thatcher and Woodburn being connected with the enterprise, appears to be most persuasive in affecting stock sales. Many stockholders are owners of gambling clubs, bars, nightclubs, and like establishments, who may be expected to court favor of employees of Internal Revenue Service and persons of political importance.

Now, you would suppose that this little item would have alerted someone in the Treasury Department in Washington. But nothing happened.

A year later, the Securities and Exchange Commission, after more complaints from swindled investors, took another and even closer look at M.C.C.C.C. What they learned more than substantiated their earlier report. They found that nine Las Vegas gamblers, owners of casinos, had purchased large blocks of stock at forty cents per share. In every case the gambler's tax return was under investigation. In two instances the purchasers actually admitted that Hartmann had told them that their income tax cases would be settled if they bought the stock. They all felt it was the best investment they had ever made. *Not one of the gambler–stockholders was ever prosecuted for income tax evasion.* But a Las Vegas businessman, Robert Kaltenborn, who refused to buy M.C.C.C. stock, was prosecuted and convicted of income tax evasion on February 21, 1949, and sentenced to a term of imprisonment. Kaltenborn had the sad distinction of being the first Nevadan in Mooney's reign to be prosecuted for income tax fraud.

Mooney's influence transcended state lines. When the United States filed a lien for more than $800,000 for unpaid income taxes and penalties against property of the notorious hoodlum Elmer "Bones" Remmer, of San Francisco, it was discovered that Mooney had personally prepared Remmer's tax returns. In going over the accounts of Remmer's Cal–Neva Lodge on the Nevada side of Lake Tahoe, agents of the Bureau's Intelligence Unit found some interesting check manipulations. One check, dated August 28, 1946, was made payable to the Collector of Internal Revenue in the amount of $7,724.11. The signature had been torn off and the check never cashed. However, a second check, in the amount of $5,324.11, also payable to the Collector of Internal Revenue, was dated August 31, 1946, and cashed by the Bureau on September 4, 1946. The number of this check was 226. The next check, No. 227, dated the same day, August 31, was made out in the amount of $2,400 (the exact difference between the first and second checks), and this check was made payable to the Mountain City Consolidated Copper Company. It was endorsed on the back with the company's stamp and signed by Pat Mooney. There was no criminal prosecution of Remmer for income tax evasion, notwithstanding the tax lien exceeding $800,000 filed against him.

What the Intelligence Unit did with this bit of juicy information is not known. Whatever it was, it didn't affect Patrick Mooney. M.C.C.C.C. and Mooney were allowed to carry on business as usual.

One of Mooney's more wholesome victims was a San Francisco abortionist. At the time of her arrest, police officers ran across records disclosing the willful evasion of more than $50,-000 in back income taxes and penalties. The Intelligence Unit began another investigation. Hartmann, it was learned, had collected $5,000 from the abortionist by promising that her back taxes and penalties would be cut down to $15,000. Tape recordings were made of two conversations between the abortionist's lawyer and Hartmann. In these recorded sessions, Hartmann recounted the story of the $5,000 extortion and named various federal officials whose intervention had been sought and obtained in avoiding criminal prosecution for the woman. Bragging a little, Hartmann mentioned a Fresno gambler whose income tax case had been compromised in the same manner by Mooney. He himself, Hartmann boasted, had not paid any income tax for years; and, in fact, had not even filed any returns. (Later investigation proved this statement to be correct.)

When Intelligence officers interviewed Mooney, he admitted receiving the $5,000 in cash from the abortionist but claimed it was for a block of M.C.C.C. stock and had no relation to income tax matters. A check of the company's records showed that no stock had ever been issued to the abortionist, and that except for the so-called sales commissions which he had paid to Hartmann, the money had been deposited in Mooney's personal bank account.

In June of 1950, the investigation by the Intelligence Unit was ordered closed. *Mooney and his associates were fully exonerated by the Bureau of Internal Revenue* and the eighty-year-old Mooney, in the harsh glare of publicity created by the release of the Crime Commission's findings, quietly resigned from the Bureau.

Thanks to Senator Kefauver, the early fifties were rougher on the personnel of the Internal Revenue Bureau. Nine high officials were involved in charges of corruption. The list read like a *Who's Who* of the Treasury Department. Massachusetts Collector of Internal Revenue Denis Delaney served nine months for bribery; St. Louis Collector James Finnegan served eighteen months for taking legal retainers from firms holding government contracts; and U.S. Commissioner of Internal Revenue Joseph D. Nunan, Jr., in office from March 1, 1944, to June 30, 1947, was sentenced to five years in prison for evading $91,000 in income taxes for the years 1946 through 1950. Assistant Commissioner Daniel Bolich, California Deputy Collector Michael Schino, and Nevada Chief Field Deputy Patrick Mooney were convicted on tax-fraud conspiracy charges. Commissioner George Schoeneman and his Chief Counsel, Charles Oliphant, resigned under fire. And, of course, there was Lamarr Caudell (Chief Tax Fraud Prosecutor), the most celebrated influence peddler since Teapot Dome.

Nevada does not have a monopoly on corruption. But it does have somewhat of a special priority. Today there is nothing sacred in Nevada, nothing immune from political corruption. Everything is for sale—from the life-giving force of water to the personal freedoms and human rights guaranteed to every American citizen under the constitution. When Nevada legalized gambling one score and twelve years ago, "It made," as one Senator later asserted, "an agreement to walk down the path to destruction with the devil." This pact has never been violated. It is the only contract still intact after these many years.

CHAPTER NINE

How to Make Friends and Stay Out of Jail

The most significant factor that separates the big-time hoodlum from the punk is the political–judicial fix. No criminal, no matter how clever, can long remain "on the bricks" without juice in the right places.

Joseph "Doc" Stacher, the Sands' number-one man, illustrates this point, although a similar case could be made for any of the rich hoodlums mentioned in this book. Stacher, a New Jersey gangster, a former bootlegger, hijacker, and narcotics smuggler, has more aliases than Lon Chaney had disguises. Some of his favorite cognomens are: Morris Rose, Joseph Rosen, Joe J. Stein, Doc Rosen, Doc Harris, Doc Weiner, George Kent, Harry Goldman, and J. P. Harris. Under just *one*

172

of these aliases, Joseph Rosen, Stacher has the following police record in Newark:

DATE OF ARREST	CRIME	DISPOSITION
11/26/24	Breaking, Entering and Larceny	Held for Grand Jury but no disposition
4/21/26	Larceny by trickery	Discharged
8/18/26	Assault and Battery	Dismissed
6/7/27	Atrocious Assault and Battery (two charges)	Dismissed
7/11/27	Atrocious Assault and Battery	Dismissed
8/15/27	Robbery	Nol-prossed
12/4/27	Interfering with officer guarding still for Federal Government	Adjourned without date
12/9/27	Atrocious Assault and Battery	Fined $50.00
5/29/28	Open charge	Dismissed
11/5/30	Atrocious Assault and Battery	Dismissed

Under the same alias, Stacher was rousted from the Franconia Hotel, 20 West 72nd Street, New York City, on November 11, 1931, by Captain Michael F. McDermott of the Alien Squad. In the room with Stacher at the time were eight other notorious racketeers: Bugsy Siegel, Louis "Lepke" Buchalter, Jacob "Gurrah" Shapiro, Philip "Little Farvel" Kovalick, Hyman "Curly" Holtz, Louis "Shadows" Kravitz, Harry Tietlebaum, and Harry "Big Greenie" Greenberg, who eight years later was murdered in Los Angeles. Siegel and Frankie Carbo (one of the promoters behind Sonny Liston) were tried and

173

acquitted on the murder charge. Carbo is presently serving time on an extortion rap. (Of the entire group, Stacher is the only one alive today. The others were either executed legally, were murdered, are missing, or died of natural causes.)

Typical of all politically connected hoodlums, somewhere between arrest and conviction, Stacher has been able to break the legal chain and escape punishment. Born in the Russian sector of Poland in 1902, Stacher came to this country in 1912, settling in Newark, where he shined shoes, sold newspapers, and later peddled fruit from a pushcart. One of his boyhood playmates, who also started out in life behind a pushcart, was Abner "Longie" Zwillman, who later became Stacher's mentor. Other boyhood pals included Willie Moretti (murdered in a Palisades, New Jersey, tavern in 1951) and Gerardo "Gerry" Catena—both Mafia leaders in New Jersey.

A confidential report by a highly placed informant to the Chicago Crime Commission, dated December 19, 1951, said in part:

> There is absolutely no doubt of the activity of Joe Stacher and who he represents. . . . In the month of October last, there was some activity with the boys at the Kenilworth Hotel in Hollywood, Florida. I was advised that Zwillman and others were there. At about the same time I learned that the higher-up were traveling around and were having "a meeting. . . ." I learned that Nevada was also an important meeting place, though the city was not mentioned and I was not in a position to ask questions. I later learned also that Gerry Catena took off for Nevada. Zwillman, it is confidentially stated, has purchased property at Lake Tahoe, Nevada, where it is alleged he intends to make his home. Zwillman found it necessary to send for Joe Stacher, who was at Las Vegas. Stacher, it is alleged,

was requested to "bring some of the boys with him" and Stacher came to these parts with four others. From other New York sources I learned that at the present time there is a great amount of distrust manifested amongst the higher-up in the crime business and includes many of those who had appeared before the Kefauver Committee. . . . If this all be a fact, and all information is absolutely reliable, it would appear that the higher-up will concentrate on Florida and Nevada.

In an effort to verify this report, the Chicago Crime Commission communicated with the Miami Crime Commission. The answer read in parts:

Up until a few months ago the [Kenilworth] hotel was owned by Tom Raffington, who has been in legitimate hotel business in the Miami Beach area for at least ten years. He sold the Kenilworth Hotel three or four months ago to the Kirkeby hotel chain. You may recall some information that there may have been some mob money in the Kirkeby hotel chain.

I have no information of any meeting of mobsters at the Kenilworth Hotel. I did receive two different reports on the weekend of October 5, 1951, concerning hoodlums. One was a report later corroborated that Max Weisberg and Big Shooey Segal, of the Nig Rosen mob of Philadelphia, were registered at the Saxony Hotel. They were seen at the time of their registration in the company of either Bennie Street or Dave Glass, numbers operators who operate at the Sands Hotel.

On the same weekend I received a report that "Big Al" Polizzi, Lou Rothkopf, Morris Kleinman, Joseph Massei, a man named Friedman, from New Jersey (first name not known), and possibly Longie Zwillman were to have a meeting at the Palm Beach Ambassador Hotel in Palm Beach, Florida.

In reply to a similar request from the Chicago Crime Commission, Al H. Kennedy, Chief of Police of Las Vegas, answered:

> Your sources of information concerning the movements of these men in this area seems to be very reliable from what I have observed and known as taking place in Las Vegas and Clark County, Nevada. There has been a very predominant rumor that Longie Zwillman has purchased some property in the Lake Tahoe area; that the property was purchased through a front man and that the present plans for it are that it will be a residence. It will probably also be used as a meeting place for his business associates and probably a hideout for some of the Eastern mob.
>
> Joe (Doc) Stacher was in Las Vegas the latter part of November and the early part of December. Also both the Lansky brothers were here at that time and there did seem to be a close association with them and the people who are now local citizens, but formerly were connected with the syndicate in the East. I personally observed Meyer Lansky and Doc Stacher in close conversation—I believe a total of three different times. I also saw Meyer Lansky in close conversation with Moe Sedway, who as you probably know is now deceased—died in Florida. Prior to his death he was supposed to have sold half interest in some property he owned out on what is known as the "strip" to the Lansky brothers. It is also stated that Lansky was instrumental in buying two other pieces of property. This was

through a man from Beverly Hills. Both of these pieces of property being in the resort hotel area and are now supposed to be in the name of one of the large owners of the Empire Race Track in New York. . . .

. . . I checked on a man who was driving Doc Stacher around in a 1950 Cadillac sedan bearing Nevada license 25-808. Stacher had a set of plans for a building which he was showing around to different people. I was convinced that this was the plans for the new hotel [Sands] to be built on the property of what was formerly the LaRue Club, the one that Mack Kufferman is interested in and is attempting to get a license for.

Even with his yellow sheet and associations, Stacher was admitted to citizenship in 1930. The federal government has been trying to rectify this mistake ever since Senator Kefauver chatted with Stacher over network television in 1951.

A 1955 denaturalization proceeding in federal court in Los Angeles suddenly aborted when depositions from Longie Zwillman, James "Niggy" Rutkin, Felix Arnold, and John Callahan, all of New Jersey, were canceled because it was decided that such depositions would be inadmissible. The charge was that Stacher had concealed his arrest record when he had applied for naturalization, and that he was not of good moral character in the five years preceding his application. The hook is that Stacher is Russian born and there is a ban against deporting such aliens to their homeland. (By law, if he were deported it would be to a country of his own choice.)

As late as the summer of 1962, Stacher was again investigated by a federal grand jury in Los Angeles. Some thirty Strip and Glitter Gulch gamblers were subpoenaed along with their records to testify at the hearings. At first the Sands management refused to give up their private gamblers' records for fear of losing customers, but when a U.S. attorney warned, "We'll throw a padlock on the Sands if you don't," they reluctantly complied.

One of the aims of the federal probe was to learn whether Stacher had a secret interest in the Sands. During the investigation, Marvin R. Cole (*né* Cohen) was charged with trying to intimidate a federal grand jury witness. Cole heads the advertising agency of Cole, Fischer and Rogow, a Beverly Hills (9833 Wilshire Boulevard) firm that represents several Las Vegas casinos. Originally a Brooklyn boy, Cole has long been a friend and business front of Stacher and presently owns 9 per cent of the Fremont and 2 per cent of the Horseshoe, two downtown Las Vegas clubs. Cole was accused of obstructing justice by trying to intimidate Joel R. Benton, also an advertising man and a witness before the same federal grand jury. In a week-long trial (May, 1963), Benton testified that Cole had warned him, "Jimmy Hoffa's boys are mighty rough" and "Doc Stacher is the number-two man in the syndicate and I am his boy." Cole was convicted and fined $1,000 by U.S. Judge Harry C. Westover.

Six other casino executives flatly refused to answer any question relating to Stacher's income before the same federal grand jury and were held in contempt. The witnesses were Carl Cohen, Aaron Weisberg, Charles Kandel and Leo Durr, all of the Sands; Eddie Levinson and Edward Torres of the Fremont. Brought to trial before U.S. Judge Thurmond Clarke they were promptly released. Judge Clarke pointed out he had been apprised that the witnesses were interviewed recently by FBI and Treasury agents. "Electronic listening devices were recently discovered in the Sands Hotel [Imagine, of all places!] and in a place where witness Durr conducts business," the Judge announced. "It is

178

the opinion of this court that under the circumstances explained to the court, these witnesses have sufficiently shown their fear was neither groundless nor clearly mistaken." Judge Clarke then denied the government's petition for an order compelling the witnesses to answer.

In August, 1963, after fourteen months of continuous investigation, the federal grand jury returned a true bill, charging Stacher with income tax evasion amounting to $43,000. Stacher merely dipped in his pocket and produced the bail in hard cash—$10,000.

This is what usually happens when Stacher is involved with the law. One or two associates are inconvenienced, but the New Jersey mobster goes serenely on forever. A typical example of this hoodlum's adroit footwork in the political–judicial arena dates back to 1952. In September of that year, Stacher and twenty-six other hoodlums, including Meyer Lansky, were indicted by a New York grand jury on charges of gambling, forgery, and conspiracy in connection with the operation of the swank Arrowhead Inn on the outskirts of Saratoga Springs, New York. Stacher was arrested in Las Vegas under a fugitive warrant and complaint. The Governor of New York transmitted to the Governor of Nevada the papers required by U.S. statutes, duly certified and authenticated, demanding the extradition of Joseph Stacher as a fugitive from justice. Stacher demanded a Governor's hearing in Nevada and received it. Governor Charles Russell held a "full and impartial" hearing in Carson City, and then issued an executive warrant for Stacher's arrest and delivery to the authorized agents to receive and convey him to New York, there to be dealt with according to law. On that same day, Stacher surrendered himself under that warrant in Las Vegas, and there petitioned the district court for a writ of habeas corpus. This was temporarily granted and Stacher was released upon deposit of $5,000 cash bail. A hearing was set for one week later.

When the hearing came up, Stacher was among the missing. The $5,000 cash bail was forfeited. In a stage play, Stacher would be on the lam with half a dozen thugs and a trunkful of weapons. Not so in real life. Stacher was living comfortably and spending much of his time on the telephone. On December 9, six days before the Sands' grand opening, Stacher made another courtroom appearance, this time before White Pine County Judge Harry Watson in Ely, Nevada, where he was granted an alternate writ of habeas corpus and placed on $10,000 bail for appearance at a hearing to be held on January 12, 1953. Stacher was now free to circulate again and he hurried back to Las Vegas and the Sands.

In a letter to the authors, Jack Streeter, District Attorney of Reno, explains what happened next:

> I appeared at the Stacher hearing in Ely as amicus curiae [friend of the court] along with White Pine District Attorney Jon Collins, Assistant District Attorney George Dickerson, and a special Assistant Attorney General and two State Troopers from New York.
>
> The last day of the hearing I noted four or five armed deputy sheriffs in the halls of the court house. I assured the Sheriff that Stacher would not escape if the judge ordered extradition. The Sheriff informed me that his purpose in having extra deputies was to guard Stacher against being kidnapped by us and taken back to New York.
>
> The Judge [Harry Watson] was the same one who released Fitzgerald and Sullivan from extradition to Michigan in the late Forties. After the decision [Watson made the writ permanent, explaining that Stacher had not been sub-

stantially charged with a crime in New York and therefore was not a fugitive subject to extradition and was illegally restrained of his liberty] I immediately took steps to appeal to the U.S. Supreme Court on behalf of Nevada and New York—and was successful in having a hearing granted.

It soon became apparent that I would have to make the argument in Washington because I had done all the research and briefing. Then began the bribe offers starting at $25,000 and when these failed, several threatening phone calls. These, of course, only strengthened my determination to make the argument.

When I applied to the Nevada Attorney General's office for expenses I was turned down. I asked Charlie Russell to use some of his promotional fund for expenses (I felt it was good public relations for the state) but was turned down.

So I paid my own way to Washington (I was later reimbursed) and obtained a reversal.

The next session of the legislature I lobbied for and obtained amendments so that Writs of Habeas Corpus can be appealed from the district court to our State Supreme Court —thus alleviating the necessity to appeal to the U.S. Supreme Court. This makes it tougher for future hoodlums to hide behind a cow county judge.

Nearly a year later, Stacher, Lansky, and the other defendants were in Saratoga Springs awaiting trial on twenty-one counts, eight of them specifically charging Stacher with violations of the New York Penal Code. The long legal maneuvers were time-consuming and expensive for both states, but finally Joseph Stacher stood before the bar of justice. If found guilty, he faced a maximum sentence of thirty-four years in prison and a $10,500 fine. The court, of course, was in possession of Stacher's police record—not only New Jersey's, but the FBI's and New York State's.

The decision of Supreme Court Justice Leo J. Hagerty is self-explanatory:

> . . . *In regard to you, Stacher, your record is practically clear* [italics added]. Something occurred in your youth, as you tell it, which may be designated as disorderly conduct charge. Outside of that, you have gone on and kept out of the clutches of the law. You have cost the State of New York some money in trying to get you back. The Court feels so far as the financial end of it is concerned, something should be done to take care of that. In your case, the Court is informed that you are apparently living in the State of Nevada. You are apparently engaged in legal gambling out there, or at least have some interest in it. There the situation is quite different than Saratoga. You can do it out there, you don't have to be looking around the corner to see if you can operate, and you don't have to pay somebody to go ahead with it.
>
> The Court is going to fine you $500 for each count of each violation. You pleaded guilty. That means you have pleaded guilty to twenty violations and therefore the total fine will be $10,000. The Court is going to help you in case you have any inclination to return to Saratoga again. In your case, on your plea of guilty to the first count, the Court will sentence you to Saratoga County Jail at Ballston Spa for the term of one year. Execution of that sentence will be suspended and you are placed on [two years'] probation.

For Joe "Doc" Stacher this was the beginning of a decade of prosperity and power. On the Strip, Stacher is a big man, constantly surrounded by young show girls and old hoodlums. His investment in the jungle is large and diversified. Besides the Sands, it includes the Fremont Hotel and the Horseshoe Club, both in Glitter Gulch and "fronted" by Ed Levinson (who dabbles frantically in charitable causes and community projects).

Without a doubt, Doc Stacher and his equally untouchable pal, Meyer Lansky, are the two richest and most powerful Jewish mobsters in America today. And the most amazing part of their success has been their ability to survive at the top in an underworld that is almost totally dominated by the Sicilians. The explanation of this phenomenon, though not simple, is clear enough. Even an organization as ruthless as the Mafia cannot ignore a juice man of the first magnitude.

CHAPTER TEN

Jungle Warfare, Las Vegas Style

There are more "socially prominent" hoodlums per square foot in Las Vegas than in any other community in the world. To fully document the sinister deeds of all these thugs, panderers, thieves, hopheads, and murderers would require a shelf of volumes the size of the *Encyclopaedia Britannica*. They hail from every section of the country, and all of them are men of enormous wealth, power, connection, ego, appetite, temper, and ignorance.

A case in point is the story of the illiterate L. B. "Benny the Cowboy" Binion, a retired and much respected denizen of the gambling town. When Binion arrived in Las Vegas in 1946, he was still the kingpin of crime in Dallas, Texas. His FBI record went back to 1924 and listed such offenses as theft, carrying concealed weapons, and two murder raps—one in which he received a two-year suspended sentence and another which was dismissed with a notation of "self-defense." His Dallas yellow sheet was a lot more extensive, and buried in the secret files of that police department were the details of crimes that would stagger the imagination of even the most prolific detective writer.

And yet in 1951 Governor Charles Russell and the Nevada Tax Commission saw fit to grant Binion a gambling license. In a statement to the press at that time, Governor Russell said: "The license is predicated on Binion's sworn affidavit and proof that he is not engaged in gambling in any other state where gambling is illegal. . . . Our investigation of his activities in Dallas, as made recently by William Gallagher and Commissioner Paul McDermott, has disclosed there is not concrete evidence that Binion in any way was involved in the [Herbert] Noble slaying."

The late State Senator E. L. Nores, one of the Cowboy's most ardent apologists, appeared before the Commission as a character witness. A few weeks earlier, the Senator had written a column for his own newspaper, *Pioche Record,* defending Binion against an attack by a United Press reporter:

Binion is a sporting man in every sense of the word, and doesn't assume it to be a military secret. His personality is decidedly dynamic, his disposition extremely affable. However, he admits that his limitations are as numerous as those of the other fellow, one of which is denied by him, extolled by his friends, and a constant thorn in the side of his enemies—that is, generosity, if you choose to call it a limitation.

Charitable organizations hail him as a philanthropist, and unfortunate individuals look upon him as a sweet Prince of

185

"Touch." The fact remains that the man is successful—to so many, a benediction, to so few, a rub!

What Senator Nores forgot to mention about Binion's generosity was the gift of a new automobile, which he accepted. The Senator's new Hudson Hornet later became known in underworld circles as the "Binion Bullet."

At that particular moment, Benny Binion was under grand-jury indictment in Texas for the operation of a multimillion-dollar policy-wheel racket, and two previous attempts by Texas to extradite him had been rejected by the Nevada courts. In other words, the state of Nevada was as anxious to keep this pudgy thug as he was eager to remain. Their interests were mutual and so were their benefits.

To document this story (which in every way is typical of mob morality, the ruthlessness and brutal tactics that form the background of all successful hoodlums), the authors journeyed to Dallas to meet with a recently retired police captain who had been active during the gang wars of the Binion era. The following is an edited transcription of that interview.

Q. How did Binion start out in the rackets?
A. He started out as a thief at a very early age. Then later, in the mid-Twenties, he got into bootlegging. He was just a kid but he was tough.
Q. Place and date of birth?
A. Pilot Grove, Texas, 1905.
Q. Who was running the rackets in those days?
A. Warren Diamond. He first organized gambling back in 1924. But by 1930 Binion was the No. 1 bootlegger. Had the town all buttoned up.
Q. What about that murder rap in '31?

A. That involved a Negro rumrunner. He was giving Binion a hard time and so he decided to knock him off, cowboy style. That's how he got that nickname. Anyway, he received a two-year suspended sentence.

Q. Was it cold-blooded?

A. Yes, it was cold-blooded, all right. But his connections were good even then, but nothing compared to five years later. In '33 Diamond committed suicide and Binion stepped into his gambling setup. At that time, Benny had two top men with him, Harry Urban and Raymond Laudermilk. I remember they opened up a bookie joint at Allen and Ross, had one or two "jump-up" crap games and two policy wheels. After Diamond's suicide they had it all. By '36 Binion was top dog and had a fix with Mr. Big.

Q. Who was Mr. Big?

A. There were a lot of Mr. Bigs through the years. I don't think we better go into that phase of it. Those were bad days. The police force was rotten from top to bottom. Oh, there were some good cops. But, Christ, it was a dangerous place to work in. You never knew what side your boss or partner was on. There was plenty of money floating around. All you had to do was raise your hand.

Q. Can you give us some insight into Binion's M.O.?

A. His M.O. was always the same. Kill 'em dead and they won't give you no more trouble. Binion eliminated four competitors in a hurry. The first to go was a gambler by the name of Ben Frieden. He operated three or four policy wheels and was making a pile of dough. On September 12, 1936, Binion and his top gun, Buddy Malone, blasted Frieden on Allen Street while he waited for his policy pickups. They emptied their .45 automatics into Frieden, who was unarmed, and then Binion shot himself in the shoulder. Just a superficial wound. Then he

187

promptly turned himself over to the sheriff. Well, both men were indicted for murder but the next month the indictments were dismissed. Here, let me read what it said: "Evidence conclusively shows that the defendant Benny Binion acted in his own necessary self-defense at the time he killed the deceased." In '38 there was a change in administration and the new Mr. Big made a deal with a gambler by the name of Sam Murray. Suddenly, Murray was in and Binion was out. Of course, Binion was still operating. In fact, his gang was known as the Southland Hotel Group. That hotel was owned by Sam Maceo of Galveston. Maceo, as you know, was a *mafioso* and those dagos stick pretty close together. Anyway, in those days, he and Binion were pretty chummy. It took Binion two years to get Murray, but in the end he got him in the old cowboy style. One day he got word that Murray was on a certain street without his two bodyguards, T. Yates and Herbert Noble. Benny and Ivy Miller hurried over there and each took one side of the street and waited for Murray. Murray finally showed on Miller's side. Miller stepped out of a doorway and drew his gun. Murray made a grab at his shoulder holster but he never reached it. Six months later the murder indictment against Miller was dismissed by the D.A. on his last day in office for "insufficient evidence." This murder really iced it for Binion. He had the whole show. He had it, that is, until one of the charter members of his gang began messing around with Murray's widow, Sue. Ray Laudermilk took her to California and when they came back, Laudermilk got grandiose ideas of taking over not only Murray's widow but his rackets as well. He teamed up with Herbert Noble and in the next two years they set up three or four lucrative policy wheels, plus a couple of crap games. Binion was furious but Laudermilk was a cagey punk who knew enough about Benny's M.O. to keep clear of any obvious trap. But Benny pulled a switch on him. There was a bum by the name of Bob Minyard who lived in the Negro section. He was a nobody but he knew Laudermilk and had borrowed money from him from time to time. So when Minyard approached him one day while he was seated in his car, Laudermilk didn't think anything of it. Minyard shot him cold turkey. This job made Minyard a big man with Binion and in no time he was rolling in the dough.

Q. What about the murder rap?

A. He was no-billed.

Q. What did Noble do about it?

A. Not much then. He realized he couldn't fight city hall and Binion at the same time. Too much money and power. Binion let him run a crap game in downtown Dallas during the war years, and cut in for 25 per cent of the take. Business was really booming in Dallas and Binion began looking toward Fort Worth. Lewis Tindell bossed that operation. Soon after Binion decided to move in, Tindell was blasted and Tiffin Hall, a Binion man, took over the operation. Now, that's pretty much the setup as it existed before the feud started. There's one other character I should mention here at this time, Hollis DeLois Green, who went by the name of Lois Green. For my money he was the most desperate, the most depraved thug that ever operated in this section. He was only thirty-four years old when he died and I personally know of twenty-two men he murdered or had murdered. He was the leader of a band of hijackers, dope peddlers, safe men, burglars, tie-up men, car thieves, professional assassins, whores, and pimps known as the "Forty Thieves." His operations were nationwide. At the time of his death his FBI record showed thirty-five arrests for major crimes and he was wanted in four states. Members of his gang had served time in twenty-six different states, plus various federal prisons. And sixteen of the members were murdered by their own gang.

189

Q. Did Noble have a gang?

A. Oh, yes. He had quite a few boys. But what Noble wanted most of all was to find the main fix in city hall. He was making lots of money and he couldn't wait to branch out. Binion got wind of it and he upped his cut from 25 to 40 per cent.

Q. What did Noble say about that?

A. He told Benny to go to hell. Well, Benny wasn't about to stand for any revolt in the ranks. At that time he had a lot of percentage deals around town, and he couldn't afford to let anyone break loose.

Q. What happened then?

A. A few nights after Noble threw down the challenge, Benny's boys made their first attempt on his life.

Q. Did Noble have any guts?

A. I think Noble had more downright cold-blooded nerve than anyone I've ever known. He was ice water in a tight place.

Q. What happened when they tried to kill him?

A. He first became aware he was being tailed that night shortly after leaving his joint in downtown Dallas. He noticed the headlights of a car behind him, became suspicious, made several unsuccessful sashays around a few blocks, and then took off for home at top speed. When he got on the main highway, the other car tried to pull up alongside. He kept out in front the best he could, swerving all over the road. Often the two cars were bumper to bumper and bullets were splattering into the back and sides of Noble's car. He said he felt like a duck in a shooting gallery. Finally, he missed a curve and landed in a ditch near a farmhouse close to his own ranch. He jumped out and ran for the house. The boys were right behind him and he caught a slug in his spine. He fell and rolled, then crawled in the dark until he was under the farmhouse. The killers were running all over the place, yelling and shooting. Noble lay there, unarmed, his gun somewhere in the wrecked car. Then the lights came on in the farmhouse and the farmer came charging out to see what the shooting was all about. The punks took off and the farmer brought Noble to the hospital.

Q. Did he know who they were?

A. He said it was Lois Green, Bob Minyard, and Little Johnny Grissaffi.

Q. Did he take it lying down?

A. Not Herbert. While he was still in the hospital, three of his boys bushwhacked Bob Minyard in his back yard and killed him. Now the fat was really in the fire. It became a race between him and Binion to see which one could get the other killed first. Noble got shot at so often he became known as The Clay Pigeon.

Q. Didn't he have other nicknames?

A. Yes, he was called The Cat after the first nine attempts on his life. Believe me, he was a double-tough cat. He had so many bullet holes and scars that he was sometimes called The Sieve.

Q. Who were the boys who killed Minyard?

A. A punk called The Groceryman, Slim Hays, and The Groceryman's brother. For my money The Groceryman was as sorry a punk as we had around here.

Q. Wasn't this about the time Binion moved on to Vegas?

A. Yes. He lost his fix in the '46 elections, so he packed his bag and moved his wife and five kids to Vegas, leaving the whole operation in the hands of Harry Urban.

Q. With Benny 1,500 miles away, it looks like the feud would have died a natural death.

A. Maybe so with any normal trouble. But with Minyard's murder Benny was on the spot. It was the first time someone had actually defied him and lived. He was losing face with everybody in the rackets and he had to patch the breach quickly. And,

191

besides, Benny never could stand to be beaten at anything. Of course, Noble was just as stubborn. Binion posted a reward on Noble's scalp.

Q. How much was put up?

A. At first it was ten grand, then it jumped to twenty-five and finally to fifty, plus a Dallas crap game as an extra inducement.

Q. That's a lot of money.

A. You're not kidding. A lot of gunsels sniffed at the proposition but three of them suddenly found themselves very dead before they could even take a crack at it. Noble might have been a clay pigeon but he was no patsy. He knew the score.

Q. Was Lois Green working for Binion?

A. Only on contracts. He was no stooge. For example, he handled hijackers for Benny. Take the case of Otto Freyer, a real tough monkey who shook down gamblers, pimps, and even raided some of Benny's games. Now, Lois had a system, a regular procedure he followed when he wanted to plant a victim. He would send a couple of his boys out ahead to dig a pit and leave some quicklime stashed nearby. Otto Freyer was taken to one of these pits, stripped naked, shot in the guts with a double-barrel shotgun, kicked into the hole, and covered with lime while he screamed for mercy. He was still alive when they finally buried him.

Q. They weren't fooling around. Looks like it would have discouraged the competition.

A. Naw. It never does. People don't realize that. They hear that a guy has been a big-shot bootlegger and think all he did was make a little brew illegally. Big-shot bootleggers like big-shot gamblers have to kill to stay in business. Otherwise they wouldn't be in business long enough to earn the title. Show me a big-shot bootlegger or a big-shot gambler, and I'll show you a cold-blooded murderer every time.

Q. What was the story on Nelson Harris and his wife?

A. Harris and another thug, Tincy Eggleston, tried to muscle in on Binion's operation. One morning Harris got into his car, stepped on the starter, and was blown to bits by a nitro bomb. The hell of it was that his pregnant wife was also killed. Tincy got the shotgun treatment a few weeks later and was buried. Then some Dallas shyster had to produce the body to make good on a bond, and the boys dug him up and placed him in a well where the law could find him. You never heard such a story as the D.A. had to put up by way of explanation.

Q. How about some of the attempts on Noble's life?

A. Lois Green made two attempts on Noble's life in 1947 and missed both times. Once with a high-powered rifle and another time with a shotgun. Then in April, 1948, Noble was shot in the hand and arm by Green, who lay in ambush along the road near Noble's ranch. Then on St. Valentine's day, 1949, a friend noticed someone tampering with Noble's car and found several sticks of explosives attached to the ignition system. Just a short time later, Noble was again ambushed near his ranch, this time wounded in the leg by a rifle slug.

Q. Wasn't Noble's wife killed at about this time?

A. Yes, and that was a shame, too. Mildred Noble was a fine woman, a really wonderful person. And though she was strongly opposed to Herbert's way of life, she loved him too much to leave him. And believe me, the love was mutual. Anyway, Noble had gone to Fort Worth that morning, taking Mildred's Cadillac and leaving his Mercury behind for her to use. At this time, the Nobles were renting a house in Oak Cliff. Mildred came out that morning and slid behind the steering wheel of the Mercury, turning on the ignition. A charge of nitro-jell blew that car and her to pieces. The whole top structure of the car was blown two blocks, landing in a yard within inches of some youngsters at play. The undertaker said Herbert came

193

right over, grabbed up what was left of Mildred in his arms and nearly went berserk. His mind never worked the same after that.

Q. Did the police ever find out anything?

A. Oh, we had the rumors, and our informants, but nothing we could go on. Knowing a thing and proving it are two different propositions.

Q. What did Noble do about it?

A. It didn't take long. In fact, on Christmas Eve, less than a month after Mildred's death, Lois Green walked out of a night club with a girl friend, leaving his henchmen inside the club. A load of buckshot nearly took his head off.

Q. Was it Noble?

A. It was Noble's No. 1 boy, The Groceryman.

Q. What kind of a character was he?

A. He was a fink and a double-crosser. Noble sent him to Vegas to look over the situation and gave him a .38 super automatic, just in case the opportunity presented itself. But Binion had the town covered so well that it was impossible for a man to even ask a question without his hearing about it. Binion and some of his boys grabbed The Groceryman and took him out on the desert. The boys wanted to plant him but Benny was more interested in a deal. In exchange for his life, The Groceryman agreed to help Benny get Noble. Not long after his return to Dallas, Slim Hays, a dice dealer and one of Noble's most trusted henchmen, was slain in an East Dallas motel. Then, on New Year's Eve, Noble came out on the front porch of his Oak Cliff house and caught two slugs. He was rushed to the Methodist Hospital in critical condition. A few nights later, a marksman pumped bullets into his fifth-floor hospital room from a building across the street.

Q. Looks like a one-sided battle.

A. Well, Benny had all the luck. Like Napoleon said, "The

Lord is on the side with the heaviest artillery." Nevertheless, Noble came up with a fantastic plan.

Q. What was that?

A. Noble was a pilot. As a matter of fact, he operated an airplane-used-parts business and also owned five airplanes. His big plan was to bomb Binion's house in Vegas. So he bought a Navy fighter surplus plane, which was supposed to be delivered to his ranch, where he had a landing strip. The plane crashed and burned as it was being delivered, killing the pilot. So chalk up another life.

Q. Did it put a stop to his plan?

A. Made him more determined. More treachery and double-cross followed. There was a con man by the name of Harold Shimley who Binion had taken into his Las Vegas home when he was broke and sick. This was at the time of the Kefauver Investigation and all the noise in Dallas was making some of the big boys in Vegas nervous. Dave Berman at the Flamingo had talked to Benny a number of times about it, warning him that unless the matter was settled soon he was going to find himself minus a head. Shimley was a hell of a smooth talker and he conned Binion into sending him to Dallas to make peace with Noble, claiming he knew Noble well and could fix everything in no time.

Q. Did Binion send him?

A. Yeah. Shimley arranged a meet with Noble in a Dallas motel. What they didn't know, of course, was that we had a bug in the room and recorded the entire conversation. Would you like to hear it?

Q. Very much.

A. Let me explain about the Phillip Stein in this tape. He was just somebody dragged in against his will. He had no business being there. Actually, Shimley was pulling a fast one. He

195

knew that Noble trusted Stein and was using him to get closer to Noble. Notice how Shimley maneuvered Stein into an impossible corner. That's so typical of these characters. They'll do it every time.

EXPURGATED EXCERPTS OF CONVERSATIONS RECORDED
ON MARCH 10, 1950, BY DALLAS POLICE DEPARTMENT

SHIMLEY. . . . I've been all over the country. Every ——— place out there, just like I told you. Now, I've made up with some people out there that own the big Flamingo hotel—this eastern outfit that owns that joint. Your name and his name [Binion] is the talk of the ——— country. The man swears by the all God, and hopes that his five kids will all die, if he knows one ——— thing about the whole proposition from start to finish. Now, I'm just going to tell you what the ——— facts are. They know where that Bowers bought the ——— dynamite. They know the whole ——— thing, and the ——— himself claims he spent $10,000 on the investigation, and has it ironclad, and he hasn't had a thing, and swears and hopes his children will die if he's ever had one thing ever done to you in any way, shape, or form.

NOBLE. Now, I—

SHIMLEY. I don't know, you understand, I'm merely telling you what I know and what I've been told.

NOBLE. Well, now—

SHIMLEY. So now Dave Berman tells me—

NOBLE. Who? Who?

SHIMLEY. Dave Berman. Owns the Flamingo hotel. You understand?

NOBLE. I—I know him. I—

SHIMLEY. Now, Dave Berman—said to me—

NOBLE. Just take it slow, now.

SHIMLEY. He says, "Shimley," he says, "do you know this fellow in Texas?" I says, "I've known the man twenty years."

NOBLE. That's right.

SHIMLEY. I says I don't know a ———— bad thing about him. I says that I don't know what in hell this thing is all about, Dave. He says, "We don't believe out here this man is our friend. The man's got the sheriff, the police, the judges—he's got everything in the state—through that outfit that owns everything there." And I says, "Well, I want to tell you something, Dave. I don't know what the proposition is about." He says, "We've got people investigating it now, finding out through our sources of investigation, and—"

NOBLE. Who's he talking about?

SHIMLEY. Talking about you.

NOBLE. Yeh.

SHIMLEY. And he says, "Well, why in the hell don't you get together and straighten this thing up?" And I said, "How in hell can I straighten it up?" "Do you know anybody that's connected with it?" And I said, "Yeh, I know a Jew boy down there that's his friend, that I've known for fifteen years, too." He says, "What's his name?" And I told him ———— who his name was ———— Phillip Stein. Well, he knows about [*indistinct*] and Jerry and them in the oil business, because he's got some oil leases with old Max Cohn, and things in Oklahoma. So he knows all about you, you understand. Now, how he knows about Phillips, I don't know. So I tell him, so he says, "Well, why in the hell don't you straighten this thing up and get to the bottom of it?" He says, "———— it, and get that ———— all stopped and kill those three ———— down there in Texas." Not talking about you, talking about some other people, understand, connected with this Bowers, now I'm telling you.

NOBLE. Who? Who are they? Tell me.

SHIMLEY. I don't know who they are.

NOBLE. Oh, you do know.

SHIMLEY. No, I don't. I don't know who they are, but I will know who they are, and I think he [Stein] can help me to find out.

STEIN. I don't want to be in on that.

NOBLE. No, no. He's—

SHIMLEY. And the name—

NOBLE. No. Well, now, here—

SHIMLEY. Here, let me show you something.

NOBLE. O.K.

SHIMLEY. Now, here's what this man says—now after Dave gets him, and I talked to him. I said, "Yeh."

NOBLE. What man? Who—who?

SHIMLEY. Dave Berman is the man that brought me in to Benny. Don't you understand? 'Cause I done talked to him. He offered—

NOBLE. But Dave's a big man out there.

SHIMLEY. He's a big man out there. He owns the Flamingo hotel.

NOBLE. I've known him through some friends of mine.

SHIMLEY. Now, now—on top of this, when we get to talking about it, he sits down at the table, me, him, and Dave, and two other people. He says, "I hope my five children will die this minute"—and holds his hand up like this—"if I know one thing on earth about it."

NOBLE. Who—who said that?

SHIMLEY. Oh, Benny [Binion] said that, himself. "Now," he said, "I'm going to get to the bottom of it—this whole ——— thing, and I've got people working on it now." Now, when I left there, I told him that I was coming to see Phillip, not you. Understand what I mean? So that was my mission here, was to try to get you two to talk together over the telephone—and let me and Phillip go out there and Phillip straighten the whole ———

198

thing out. And he's got to get in the middle of it, because he's your friend, and he can't do any more, and I don't do it by myself.

STEIN. No, Herbert.

NOBLE. No, thank you. Well, even—even after that, the ———— town is in such a mess, how in the hell you going to—

SHIMLEY. Well, you and him know how to straighten it out.

NOBLE. I don't know—

SHIMLEY. Well, by God, he said you could. I'm telling you what the man said. Would you talk to the man over the phone?

NOBLE. Yes.

SHIMLEY. All right.

NOBLE. Yeh, get him on the ———— phone right now. I'll talk to him.

SHIMLEY. I'm going to tell you something. I done stuck my neck clear up to here. You understand.

NOBLE. Yeh.

SHIMLEY. Give me long distance, please. Yes, I want 3669W, Las Vegas, Nev. Nevada, that's right. [*Indistinct whispering.*]

SHIMLEY. Now, listen, Phillip, you are the only man that can help me with this proposition.

NOBLE. Now, if you ever—tell what name I'm using—

SHIMLEY. Say, listen, don't you worry about me ———— man. Are you afraid of me, Herbert?

NOBLE. No, I'm not. If I was, I wouldn't even be talking to you.

SHIMLEY. Listen, let me tell you something. You know what I've done. Now, I'm just telling you, I don't give a ————. I've spent $6,500 on this.

NOBLE. ———— I still—if—unless he can do something with somebody here—how in the hell—but even at that, I don't see how—

SHIMLEY. By gosh, he can stop it.

199

NOBLE. That man out yonder?

SHIMLEY. You ain't kiddin'. He'll stop it, or we'll kill three of them—one or the other. And you won't have to have nothing to do with it, either. You know that man—I mean loves them kids just like you do your daughter.

NOBLE. That's right, that's right.

SHIMLEY. He [Binion] stood like this, Phillip, and he says, "I hope God will kill all five of them, now, if I know one thing about it, at all." He didn't only convince me, he convinced the biggest mob in the United States. If he wanted to get something done, he wouldn't have nobody do it like that. I'll tell you that.

NOBLE. I know he and Mickey [Cohen] are just like that.

SHIMLEY. One of the biggest outfits in the United States.

NOBLE. That's right, that's right. O.K. I know he—he's got a connection that won't quit. Hell, now, I'm not calling him.

SHIMLEY. I'm calling him.

NOBLE. You're calling him.

SHIMLEY. You're ——— right.

NOBLE. Hell, say, I get—

SHIMLEY. Hello, Mrs. Binion? Is Mr. Binion there? This is Shimley—hello, this is Harold Shimley, Harold Shimley. Yes, I'd like to talk to him, please, if you can get him on the phone. Hello, Benny, this is Shimley. Well, I'm in Dallas and I have done what I told you I thought I could do. And I think this whole thing can be straightened out 100 per cent. And, of course, I know what I've been told, and you know the whole score from start to finish. I know you wouldn't have spent $10,000 if you hadn't have known. I don't get that from you. I get it from the other people. And this is my friend, just like you are. Now wait a minute. I want you to talk to somebody a minute.

NOBLE. Ask him what he wants to tell me.

SHIMLEY. Well, come on and talk to him. ——— it. Man's 1,500 miles away. Just talk to the ———.

NOBLE. Hello, Benny, this is Herbert. All right, how are you? Oh, I've got a little cold. Yeh, yeh. We are way out in the country, partly, anyway. We are out in the country, partly, anyway. Oh, I'm all right, perfect. Yeh. Well, what about Shimley here? Yeh, yeh. Well, I just wondered—I just wondered—I didn't know what—what the score was. Yeh, wait a minute, then I'll let you talk to him. Yeh, yeh. No, never heard of him. Oh, yeh, I know the son of a ———— hey, I know him. I—I— He gave me some pretty bad write-ups. Yeh—well, I don't know but they—they done something to my wife here in the paper. I didn't like a damn bit. Yeh. Wait just a minute, then, and I'll let you talk to Shimley.

SHIMLEY. Listen, Mr. Binion, I'm here with the only man that—that we can get this whole thing straightened out with—and that's Phillip Stein. Understand? I want you to talk with him a minute. Come here, Phillip.

STEIN. Hello—hello, Benny. O.K. Yeh, well, that's him. I got—I wasn't supposed even to be here, but I am. I—I didn't want to get involved in all of this stuff. Well, I know, but—I mean I'm getting caught in something when I'm an innocent party. Yeh. Well, they just wanted me to talk with you.

SHIMLEY. Let me talk to him.

STEIN. Yeh, I know it. Wait a minute, Shimley wants to talk to you.

SHIMLEY. Now, do I have, just as you said when I left there, the power to go ahead and try to straighten the whole thing out? Well, do you know me now? Well, did you recognize the other two men? Yeh. Well, now listen—now, uh—this thing has gone far enough, just as Dave and everybody out there says, and let—let's straighten the whole thing out. Yeh. Well, then, me and Phillip might come out there to see you. Well, and in the meantime—uh—do you think that fat man—does he know anything about the thing at all? He doesn't—he doesn't? Oh, he don't even

know them. Uh-huh, yeh. Well. I'll tell you what I'll do. I don't
know just how soon I'll seen you, or when I'll call you, but I'll
get in touch with you just as soon as possible. And everything
will be careful here until we can straighten the whole thing out.
Well, every precaution will be taken. Well, no, you won't be
responsible, but still, them other people—we've got to take care
of that. So then, I'll get right on it and me and Phillip will
probably see you within the next two or three days anyhow,
maybe tomorrow. All right then, you be good, and we'll see you
soon. All right.

That ———— I'm telling you, boy, there ain't no ———— about
it, that Benny is on the square about this thing. And it's the talk
of the ———— country, it's the talk of the ———— country, and
there ain't no ———— about it. I mean the talk of the country.

NOBLE. You know—

SHIMLEY. He said right there over the phone—he said, he
said, "Now, be careful until we can get things taken care of."
You understand?

NOBLE. What did he mean by that?

SHIMLEY. Well, I guess he means that he don't want nobody
to get out in the open, you understand what I mean, and put
yourself in a spot, or something else. Just like you remember,
when I left the house, now you remember this. I'm not bawling
you out or nothing, but you told me you would not go out that
door at night, didn't you?

NOBLE. Yeh.

SHIMLEY. Then you turned right around and did it.

NOBLE. Well, ———— it. Hell. I—I—let's don't go back now.

SHIMLEY. Now, wait—

NOBLE. No; don't go back now—I am going to tell you that's
—on you. When I lost my wife—[*Crossed voices.*]

SHIMLEY. I know that—I know that.

202

NOBLE. And ———— it, I'll tell you one ———— thing ————

SHIMLEY. And I'll tell you, you are going to know the ———— that done it.

NOBLE. All right. Who? You know, now.

SHIMLEY. And the ————, by God, done it was the man that was trying to get you.

NOBLE. Yeh. Who—who is he?

SHIMLEY. You know who he is as well as I do.

NOBLE. No, I don't. No, I don't.

SHIMLEY. You know that ———— down there that got life in the pen as well as I do.

NOBLE. Who, Delbert [Bowers]?

SHIMLEY. You ain't—

NOBLE. He didn't do it by hisself.

SHIMLEY. Well, he done it with some of his ———— burglar friends.

NOBLE. I don't doubt your word. Don't doubt your word a bit, but still—

SHIMLEY. I'm telling you, and you're—you are going to find it out for your own satisfaction.

NOBLE. O.K. That's what I want to do, but I don't want to make no ———— mistakes. But—uh—well, here's the thing about it—

SHIMLEY. I know, but I'm telling you, understand? The man thinks that you think it's him. The man is as crazy as any betsy bug you've ever seen, and I saw tears rolling down the man's eyes, about your wife.

NOBLE. Well, ———— it [*Indistinct stuttering.*] I'm the one. I ain't got my right mind half of the time.

SHIMLEY. Well, I'm willing to try to handle it any way you think. I've told you the truth.

NOBLE. O.K. Well, what's the deal?

203

SHIMLEY. I say that I think that the two of you ought to get together and go ahead and get straightened, and let these other ———— be taken care of. Understand what I mean?

NOBLE. Yeh.

SHIMLEY. And they will be taken care of from the other end, not from this end. Understand what I am talking about?

NOBLE. Yeh.

SHIMLEY. 'Course, you ain't going to take care of that one [Bowers, in prison] unless you take care of him down there in that joint. [*Indistinct.*] But he tells me that the ———— can be taken care of down there.

NOBLE. Probably can, if you have the right kind of connections.

SHIMLEY. Well, I don't know about that business, you understand. All I know is what he says. He could get him killed in there if he wanted to.

NOBLE. ————, now we are talking business.

SHIMLEY. And when I'm telling you this, I'm not lying to you. The man sat there and there was five people at the table, and tears rolled down the man's cheeks when he talked about your wife, and talked about the way this thing happened. And when they found out, they know exactly where the ———— even bought the ———— dynamite, and everything, in Fort Worth. And I'll find it out for you and tell you.

NOBLE. That's what I want to know.

SHIMLEY. 'Course, they are never to know that it came from me, understand what I mean?

NOBLE. Hell, there ain't nobody ever know it, Shimley.

SHIMLEY. But I don't want to know it, because here's the thing about it—I don't want to put anybody in the electric chair. I'd rather see a ———— get murdered. I'd rather get killed myself than put a ———— in the electric chair.

NOBLE. No need to talk like that. Let's don't talk about it.

SHIMLEY. Well, here's the thing about it. I'm to straighten the thing out between you and this other man, and I know me and Phillip can get the job done.

NOBLE. I'd rather that you'd just deal around Phillip now, because ——— it ———.

STEIN. Don't pull me in. I don't really want it. You all are pulling me in something that I don't even want, and I told you I wasn't even—didn't want to come in here, and you wanted me to.

NOBLE. Well, well, now, how about this?

SHIMLEY. Well, all right, now look here, ———, you're a friend of mine, and you are his friend, so what the hell?

NOBLE. Well, how about this? . . .

NOBLE. Was it three of them?

SHIMLEY. Oh, yes; three of the ——— altogether. So I don't—

NOBLE. The hell there was. One of them to drive the car, one of them to shoot, and the other to do the job, l guess. The ———.

SHIMLEY. Every one of them ——— bank burglars, ——— knob-knockers, ———.

NOBLE. Who were they, Shimley? You know them.

SHIMLEY. I really don't know their names. No. And if I knew I'd tell you.

NOBLE. All right.

SHIMLEY. I don't know, I done told you.

NOBLE. I'd expect you to.

SHIMLEY. I don't know, I don't know, you understand. I told you the truth about it, and I wouldn't lie to you, understand, and I'll guarantee that if I can't help you I won't do you any harm. I told you that all the time, from start to finish, and I honestly believe this ——— is telling the truth. I am convinced of it, by God, because he wouldn't lie to them ——— people. They

would kill him just like they would me, if they caught the ———
in a lie and a double-crossing ————.

END OF RECORD

Q. What kind of a sale did Shimley make?

A. Let me tell you what happened. It's hard to believe that a man could be as stupid and as devious as Shimley. He had another meet with Noble a few days later and this time he told Noble that Binion was behind all his trouble. Binion, he claimed, had offered him the usual $25,000 and a Dallas crap game for the kill. Noble was naturally suspicious and wanted to know why Shimley was spilling all that stuff to him. Shimley flatly admitted he hated Binion and wanted to see him done in.

Q. Did Noble buy it?

A. Well, he wanted proof of Shimley's intentions and Shimley provided it by drawing an airman's map of Las Vegas, pinpointing Binion's house on Bonanza Road. He told Noble where Benny slept, what time he went to bed and got up, and gave him a complete rundown on Binion's daily activities.

Q. We're back with the bombing plan?

A. Yes.

Q. First, what about that Delbert Bowers? Anything to his being implicated in the death of Mildred Noble?

A. Nothing we could ever tie up. I think Shimley was conning Noble. You know, a red herring. You couldn't believe anything Shimley said.

Q. Dave Berman gets a lot more credit than he deserves. He never owned the Flamingo. Just a few points.

A. Well, the way I understand it, Berman was the muscle around the place. That meeting Shimley referred to where Binion swore his innocence on the heads of his five kids happened after he received an ultimatum. The big eastern mob wanted an end put to the feud. It was bad for business. Too much publicity. Binion was really sweating.

Q. Well, Dave Berman made a lot of guys sweat. He was a tough punk and Greenbaum's right-hand man. But it shows how big that eastern mob really was in the eyes of the underworld. What about Noble's bombing plan?

A. Noble bought himself a powerful stagger-wing Beech with extra wing tanks. Even so he wouldn't have enough fuel to fly to Vegas and back nonstop. What he needed was a landing strip along the way to refuel, and he found one a few miles out of Tucson, Arizona.

Q. You don't mean the Grace Ranch?

A. I sure do. The big "G" himself, Pete Licavoli. Pete had been trying for a foothold in Dallas for years. The idea was that Noble would take over in Dallas after Binion was knocked off and Pete would get 50 per cent of the take. Noble told him he was a hog, but he wanted Binion dead so badly that he agreed to the deal. Noble then flew down to Monterey, Mexico, and bought himself a bombing rack and two large bombs, one incendiary, the other high-explosive. Then he worked out a deal with some Mexican officials for an alibi after the bombing. He had already given them some fine guns and several substantial money gifts.

Q. What happened then?

A. Noble caught a couple loads of buckshot and was back in the hospital. Going through his clothing in the hospital, the officers found the map. It showed the airfield in Vegas, a schoolhouse, Bonanza Road, and other landmarks that pinpointed Binion's house. He even had a snapshot of the house. Soon afterward Binion turned up with a copy of the map.

Q. Binion was ready for him then?

A. Yes. Remember, he had The Groceryman spying for him. It wasn't long before he had the whole story. A pit boss in Vegas by the name of Chink Rothman was approached to kill Noble and offered the usual $25,000 and a Dallas crap game. What the boys didn't know was that Chinky was a stoolie for the FBI. Some punk called Short Count or Miscount found out about it and picked up a bundle by tipping the boys. Chinky, of course, was planted in the desert. That old desert holds a lot of unmarked graves. Another cute one by the name of Pug Miller disappeared at the same time.

Q. What happened to Shimley?

A. His string ran out in Oklahoma. I understand the boys beat in the top of his head, placed him in a car, pushed the car out on the road, and waited for an accident to happen. They were expecting a truck that time of night. However, some crazy kids plowed into Shimley's car. It was crude but it worked.

Q. What was Noble doing during this time?

A. He was having his troubles. A bomb was tossed into his place of business in downtown Dallas. Nobody was hurt. Then one day Noble attempted to start one of his planes and the engine blew up. He was saved by a steel plate. Five days later, a mechanic found nitroglycerin packed in two cylinders of an engine being overhauled for another of Noble's planes.

Q. How did he take all this?

A. I'm afraid it got to him after a while. He dropped from 200 pounds to 150, and his hair, which was gray to start with, soon turned snow white. He aged quickly. He was only forty-one and he looked like a very old man. He stayed at his ranch now most of the time and had a dozen dogs around to bark a warning if anyone approached within a half mile of the place. He slept in a small room, with a shotgun, a carbine, and a couple of hand pieces. His mind was slipping, too. He couldn't get over Mildred's death. The man was really hurting, and there was nothing he could do about it. He was so busy protecting himself he had no time to retaliate.

Q. Whatever happened to his bombing plane?

A. Lieutenant Butler finally put a stop to that. Drove up to the ranch one day. He knew Noble had been to Mexico and also to Tucson, and he wanted to find out what it was all about. Going to the Noble ranch was always a dangerous thing to do, even for a cop, especially a cop like Butler. Butler found Noble under a red stagger-wing Beech with cross-country tanks. He was sitting on the ground and was trying to adjust a bomb rack on the bottom wing. Just beyond the plane were two bombs about ten inches in diameter and three feet in length, with fins at the rear. Butler knew about the airman's map and he blew his stack. Noble had an Army carbine resting on top of the bottom wing and during the argument he made a grab for it. Butler hissed a warning and made for his own gun. Noble threw himself on the ground and cried like a baby, mumbling that Binion had all the money in the world and could buy protection and that all he, Noble, had were these two bombs. Butler explained about the five Binion children and Mrs. Binion, and Noble nodded his head in despair. He said the loss of his wife in that horrible manner had unbalanced him but he promised to get rid of the bombs. There was nothing Butler could do about the bombs since he was out of his territory.

Q. Did Noble get rid of the bombs?

A. I guess so. Anyway, he went downhill fast just about then. Started drinking heavily and sometimes took pills to knock himself out. I think the man wanted to die. The strain on him was terrific. He had a girl friend. She probably was all that saved him from going insane. In spite of all her kindness to him, he would sometimes whip her unmercifully. Everyone expected him to get killed at any time and it took a lot of nerve on her part to even be around him.

Q. But they got him finally?

A. Yeah, they got him real good. They split him into a mil-

lion little pieces with a full case of nitrojell. Blew the top part
of his body clear over a tree. There was nothing left of the bottom part. The charge was hidden under a cattle guard next to
his rural mailbox. At 11:35 A.M. on August 7, 1951, three
assassins waited in the bushes some two hundred feet from the
mailbox. When Noble stopped the Ford sedan and reached into
the mailbox, one of the assassins touched a wire against a fence,
the resulting ground setting off the stuff. Seconds later, a teen-
age boy saw a blue Chevrolet pickup truck heading north at a
high rate of speed. There were two or three men in it. He wasn't
sure.

Q. Did the police ever trace the truck?

A. Well, we picked up a gangster by the name of Finley
Donica who drove a blue Chevrolet pickup truck but we never
could pin anything on him. We knew he did jobs for Jim
Thomas, a member of the Green gang who had made plenty of
trips to Vegas to see Binion. So we picked up Thomas and
shook him down some. This plug-ugly had escaped the hot seat
a few years back for the hired murders of a doctor and his wife.
That deal got him as far as Death Row but he beat the case on
appeal. We had a pretty good lead there but it didn't pan out. A
a few days later, Thomas was eliminated with a twelve-gauge
shotgun in Durant, Oklahoma, by Hubert Deere, an old thiev-
ing pal. Lots of people think he was killed when he went after
the payoff. Deere indicated that a gambler and stockman named
George in Fort Worth had been the go-between on the Noble
job.

Q. What happened to Deere?

A. Nothing. Claimed self-defense and got away with it.

Q. What happened to The Groceryman?

A. We gave him the Sodium Pentothal treatment and he
copped out to carrying the nitrojell to the Noble ranch the night
before the trap was planted. But we couldn't use it in court. He

210

went up to the ranch the same day Noble was killed and got Noble's cash stash. Then he robbed Noble's brother of $17,000. We sent him up for burglary.

Q. Noble never had a chance in this battle?

A. No, but he got Binion just the same. All that publicity queered Binion with the Combination. They let Uncle Sam take care of him. Of course, they helped a little bit along the way. Binion didn't know what was coming off. They patted him on the back with one hand, telling him what a wonderful guy he was, and with the other hand they were cutting his throat. It's not the first time the big mob has helped the government salt away a competitor. Hell, they even conned Benny into helping them negotiate some big loans from the Dallas moneybags. Soon they had all his old connections lined up. You had better believe me, when those boys moved into Dallas they had a lot of big people over a barrel.

Q. It's been an interesting story. Thank you very much.

A. You're welcome. This stuff I just told you should put a lot of heat in a lot of sensitive places.

Benny Binion was never a big man in Las Vegas. His operation was always in Glitter Gulch. Rumors have it that he invested money in both the Flamingo and the Desert Inn, and it's probably true that he did; but true or false, he never had juice on the Strip. Even in a den of thieves and murderers, Binion lacked class. He was a barbarian as well as an illiterate. Instead of the silk suits and Italian loafers, Binion preferred cowboy boots and ten-gallon hats. He was loud, coarse, and a pompous bore.

In Glitter Gulch, Binion bought a half interest in the Las Vegas Club with J. Kell Houssels. Later they sold out to Tutor Scherer. Binion then built the Westerner Club, which he later sold to Emilio Georgetti after one of his four bodyguards, Cliff Helms, killed Johnny Beasley, a shakedown artist, in the men's room. Binion spent a lot of money trying to fix this, but Helms went to prison anyway, where he later died. Binion lost his gambling license and had to wait until 1951 for a new license. By that time he had built the Horseshoe Club.

Then in 1953, everything suddenly crumbled and Binion found himself behind bars in Leavenworth Federal Prison on a five-year income-tax-evasion rap. He's out again and once more living the good life of a Nevada gentleman. His son, Jack, following in his father's footsteps, was recently licensed for a 25 per cent interest in the Horseshoe.

CHAPTER ELEVEN

The Mafia Code of the Jungle

There was a big grin on Louis "Russian Louie" Strauss's face as the black Cadillac limousine eased out of the Desert Inn parking lot and headed south on U.S. 91. His two companions were also smiling. And why not? Russian Louie had just won $86,000 at a private poker party. The three men were headed for Palm Springs for a few days of relaxation. Seated beside Russian Louie in the back of the limousine was his good friend Jack I. Dragna. And behind the steering wheel was another good friend, Marshall Caifano. For months Russian Louie and Caifano had been as inseparable as Siamese twins. Caifano was registered at the Desert Inn in those days, but spent most of his time at the Sands with Russian Louie. Dragna was also a Las Vegan, residing in Paradise Valley, near his brother Tom and his nephew Louis Tom Dragna. As a *capo mafioso,* Jack Dragna bossed the Mafia in California and Nevada.

They had wired ahead to Palm Springs for three rooms before starting out across the desert, but when the black Cadillac rolled into Palm Springs, there were only two men in the car. Russian Louie hasn't been seen since that day—April 16, 1953.

Meyer Lansky said dryly, "That's the last time a Jew will cheat a Sicilian in this town." The underworld rumor was that Russian Louie had used too many aces. Today, the disappearance of Russian Louie has become an inside joke: when you owe someone money, you say, "I'll pay when Russian Louie hits town." The police are still waiting for Louie's four-and-a-half-carat diamond ring to show up. They have a long wait. It is more likely that some old prospector will strike it rich one of these days, and when he does, he is going to be on the other side of the Nevada line.

Las Vegas has been an "open city" (off limits to mob violence) since the wild days of Bugsy Siegel. The boys don't want any blood splattering the "fun in the sun" image of the jungle. That might frighten the tourists and their fat bankrolls away from the gaming tables. Because of this policy, there have been no gangland slayings in Las Vegas. The slayings of Siegel, Greenbaum and his wife, William "The Saint" Skally, and countless others, including another old pal of Caifano, Benedict Macri (who also disappeared), were out-of-town jobs.

This is not to say that Las Vegas is without murder and other heinous crimes. The FBI Uniform Crime Report (July, 1962), which is based on a ratio of incidence per 100,000 population on seven major crimes, bluntly testifies to the lawlessness in the jungle. Even when compared to New York City, the figures are shocking. Included in the following statistical comparison is the average for 154 cities with a population of 50,000 to 100,000.

	Las Vegas	New York City	154 Cities
Murder and non-			
negligent manslaughter	10.2	4.9	3.8
Forcible rape	10.2	7.9	4.9
Robbery	115.7	58.9	20.0
Aggravated assault	85.0	115.6	44.6
Burglary	965.2	442.3	121.7
Larceny—$50			
and over	689.7	577.3	251.3
Auto theft	486.6	237.7	60.6

No matter how black the Nevada crime picture may appear statistically, it is worse than it seems, for the city fosters crime as a stone thrown into water creates concentric ripples. A tourist who loses his life savings in Las Vegas is just as apt to return home and embezzle, or rob, or burglarize, or steal, or commit suicide, as the criminal resident. Nevertheless, studying the statistics alone, it is interesting to note that even with all the prostitution in Las Vegas, forcible rape is more than double that of any city its size, and over 20 per cent greater than New York City. In 1960, the incidence for this crime in Las Vegas was 19.7, nearly four times the average for any city its size. Only in aggravated assaults does it bow to New York City. And in crimes that spring from monetary desperation, it bows only to Los Angeles, which has the highest metropolitan crime rate in the country. (It must be remembered that Los Angeles furnishes some 80 per cent of the Las Vegas sucker trade.) Even so, Las Vegas still has the edge on murder, larceny, and auto theft. Nevada leads California, as well as the rest of the nation, in total crime figures, with an incidence of 2,184.3 as compared to 1,928.5 for California and an average of 1,053 for the rest of the country. In metropolitan figures, Las Vegas had to bow to

215

Reno, whose crime rate of 3,348 was the highest in the nation.

Ever since the days of Bugsy Siegel, the Mafia has been an integral part of Las Vegas. The first Mafia chieftain to move into town was Emilio "Gambo" Georgetti, who transferred his criminal activities from northern California to Las Vegas in 1947 when his friend, San Mateo County Sheriff James Mc-Grath, was defeated after a twenty-six-year reign. Georgetti started out by buying 10.5 per cent of the Las Vegas Club in Glitter Gulch. A year later he bought a piece of Benny Binion's Westerner Club. In six weeks, he had squeezed Binion out and controlled the whole operation.

Testifying before the Kefauver Committee, Georgetti was quick to assure the Senators that he was a reformed man.

I want you to understand I am glad to testify to the committee. I am sorry I have been in the gambling business all my life. I am glad of an opportunity to fight with you people because I want to clear myself. . . . The last couple of years the newspapers took after me and blasted me for no reason at all for what I do in San Mateo County. They informed the grand jury. They sent an investigator and he find out that I was active in San Mateo County. The newspapers been blasting me. So then to keep from that I went down to Las Vegas and bought this interest in the Las Vegas. Unfortunately, I got in with Binion, who looked down on me, but today I make this statement: If I get clear now, I am in the soup. I had to borrow $275,000 out of a building that I bought for $20,000 years ago before I got in any gambling, and today it is worth a million. I was certainly fortunate that it went up in price. But I make this statement: If anybody wants to buy, I am willing to lose $100,000. Out in Nevada gambling is called legitimate. . . . I am in honest business. I have a packing plant. We enjoy $6 million a year of business. I got a restaurant. We do nice business.

Georgetti was of the old Mafia school, known as the Mustache Petes. He was illiterate and tough, and though a multimillionaire, he had no taste for fancy clothes and palatial homes. Speaking of one of his hirelings, Sam Termini, Georgetti expressed his contempt for such ostentatious trappings. "My house is worth $12,500. I bought it in 1938, and I think his [Termini's] gate is worth more than all of my house together. He spent more on the gate than I spent on my whole house. I was the boss, and he was working for me."

Not long after his appearance before the Committee, Georgetti died of cancer. At a meeting of the Grand Council of the Mafia, Jack I. Dragna was appointed to replace Georgetti in Las Vegas. Dragna, who was known as "The Al Capone of Los Angeles," was also a quiet man of the old school. Born in Corleone, province of Palermo, Sicily, in 1891, Dragna first came to this country with his parents in 1898. They returned to Sicily ten years later, and in 1914 Dragna came back to this country to stay, settling in southern California. A year later he was convicted of extortion and served three years in San Quentin. Though frequently arrested in later years, he was never again convicted—a legal immunity typical of a *mafioso*'s cunning and power.

And also typical of a *mafioso*, Dragna had many legitimate business interests, including a ranch, a 538-acre vineyard near Puente, California, and a winery. He owned the "Santa Maria," a vessel under Panamanian registry, which plied between Long Beach and Central and South America in the banana trade.

On February 14, 1950, the Los Angeles police seized papers from Dragna and one of his henchmen, Mo Mo Adamo. Several small address books read like a *Who's Who* of the Mafia. There were also a sprinkling of names of police officers, district attorneys' investigators, bail-bond brokers, lawyers, and lobbyists—most of these business contacts rather than social, as indicated in many instances by canceled checks. The papers also showed that gangster funds were being invested in certain legitimate businesses, such as clothing, fruit, wine, olive oil, and importing.

Two weeks after the police seized the records, Abraham Davidian, a dope pusher, was murdered in Fresno while hiding out in his mother's home. Davidian had testified before a federal grand jury in Los Angeles concerning his purchase of heroin from Joe Sica, Dragna's lieutenant in charge of narcotics. The case against Sica was subsequently dismissed.

One of the most succinct descriptions of the Mafia (which coincides in every significant detail to the recent disclosures of Joseph Valachi, the first *mafioso* to ever break the bond of silence imposed by *Omertà*) was presented by John T. Cusack, a district supervisor for the United States Bureau of Narcotics, when he appeared before the New York State Investigating Commission following the infamous Apalachin meeting of fifty-eight *mafiosi* on November 14, 1957:

We consider the Mafia a well-organized secret-fraternal order originating and probably still controlled from the Palermo area of Sicily. Its members, with a few exceptions, are all of Sicilian origin and are located in every prosperous city in the world, principally cities of Europe and North and South America where the profits in crime are most lucrative. Business of the Mafia is what we term the commercial crimes that prey on man's human weaknesses, such as the illicit narcotics traffic, organized prostitution. counterfeiting, bootlegging, organized gambling, loan sharking and extortion. When the opportunity presents itself, the Mafia moves into legitimate business, selecting ventures where their strong-arm tactics and cash resources will quickly bring large profits.

Our extensive narcotic investigations of various members of Mafia fraternity during the past 18 years has repeatedly shown a pattern of either infiltration or complete dominance of several legitimate fields, including organized labor, with the follow-up labor-management ventures, the distribution of beer, liquor and soft drinks, the importation and distribution of Italian olive oil, cheese and tomato paste, control of the wholesale fruit and vegetable produce markets, the baking and distribution of Italian bread, pastry, the vending machine business of all types, including cigarette machines and juke boxes, the operation of night clubs, restaurants and bars. Their night club operations are frequently complemented through their interest in model and theatrical booking agencies and in musical recording companies.

Mafia members use "front people" who are completely trusted, as a means to own and operate these various legitimate interests. By doing this they overcome licensing and income tax problems. Although legally in our courts of law a "front man" or his ostensible owner of record could eliminate the actual owner from these businesses, one would never do so as this would bring certain death. This is never, or seldom, done, as these "front men" or owners of record are usually a Mafia brother of minor rank and ability, with no criminal record or unsavory reputation, or the members of the family of the actual owner.

To establish themselves in the community in order to further their legitimate enterprises and cloak their illicit operations, Mafia members conduct a well-planned program of ingratiating themselves with people of all walks of life. Their modus operandi calls for interest and activity in community and church affairs. They contribute outwardly and generously to charities and lead an ostensibly quiet family life. They are ever-ready to entertain and do favors for the right people.

The Mafia, as a secret society, has never been completely uncovered or exposed. However, down through the years there have been many published studies of the Mafia written by qualified persons and from those we learned that the cardinal virtue of the Mafia member is humility, prescribing an honorable, fearless criminal without braggadocio or truculence.

The following other duties are required of a Mafia member:

1. Reciprocal aid to all members in any case of need whatsoever.
2. Absolute obedience to the officers of the society.
3. An offense received by one of the members must be considered an offense to the entire society and must be avenged at any cost.
4. Never recur to governmental authorities under any circumstances for justice.
5. Never reveal the names of members or any other secret of the society.

It is difficult to say who is eligible to join the Mafia or who joins it today, whether there is a formal joining or whether members through family tradition are just born into the Mafia. However, it appears to us that one becomes a member only through family sponsorship, such as father sponsoring son, uncle sponsoring nephew, father-in-law sponsoring son-in-law and brother sponsoring brother. Also, by design, the Mafia fraternal ties are strengthened through intermarriage, which brings about an increase of loyalty to the society through the ensuing blood and family ties. . . .

With the coming of prohibition, no group was better qualified to assume a dominant role in the golden age of crime in America than the Mafia. During the prohibition era, Mafia members extended themselves to every part of the United States to carry out their traffic in illicit narcotics and liquor.

With the end of prohibition, we find the members of this fraternity continuing in their distribution of narcotics, increasing their activities in organized gambling, counterfeiting and prostitution. During World War II we find them engaged in the black marketing of sugar, meat, motor tires and in the counterfeiting of ration stamps.

Wherever the Mafia fraternity has gone, the members have developed working arrangements with other members of the particular country, or with mobs in this country of various national origins. Non-Mafia gangsters often prefer doing business with a Mafia man because of his known reliability. In almost every large city in the Western world, Mafia members are usually strong enough not to be pushed around or suppressed by rivals. However, our files indicate they prefer alliances and working agreements rather than open competition and the ensuing gang warfare. The organization Murder, Inc., is an excellent example wherein the Mafia allied itself with members of the Jewish underworld in the late 1930's to help carry out their crimes. During the prohibition era we find Mafia members working closely with the old Irish mobs of New York City's West Side and Greenwich Village in both bootlegging and narcotics. Today we find, particularly in New York and other parts of the country, Mafia members aligning themselves with Negroes and Puerto Ricans and many under-world elements, to further their narcotic, bootlegging and policy operations.

The Mafia, throughout the United States, Canada, Mexico, Cuba, Italy and France, is a fraternal organization divided into many different mobs, gangs, rings, syndicates or conspiracies. Members of the fraternity belong to one or more such groups which are often temporary in nature, organized usually to carry out one particular enterprise or venture, such as the importation and distribution of narcotics or the operation of a gambling casino.

Sicily is the ancient stronghold of the Mafia. Mafia mobsters still operate throughout Sicily, Italy, Europe and Africa in commercial crimes, specializing at the present time in the smuggling of narcotics and cigarettes, bootlegging and kidnapping. They, as recently as 1955, launched a reign of terror to control the produce market and the lucrative citrus fruit trade. There is a possibility that the titular head of the Mafia may reside in Sicily and that overall Mafia policy may still emanate from this aged stronghold.

We are informed that the Mafia society is divided into units of 10 men. The unit is supervised by a group chief and group chiefs, in turn, by an area chief. The area chief would, in all probability, be a member of the Grand Council. The meeting at Apalachin, New York, should be considered a meeting of the Grand Council, although all persons in attendance at Apalachin may not be members of the Grand Council.

Jack Dragna was a member of the Grand Council—as opposed to the board of directors of the Combination, which was made up of Sicilian and non-Sicilian mobsters of national im-

222

portance. Non-Sicilians like Meyer Lansky, Phil Kastel, Joe Stacher, Louis "Lepke" Buchalter, Bugsy Siegel, and Longie Zwillman were members of the board of directors along with Costello, Luciano, Moretti, Pisano, Adonis, Fischetti, Accardo, Marcello, and other *capi mafiosi.* In the Thirties and Forties, the board of directors was the highest court in organized crime. Today it is the Grand Council. The four biggest Jewish mobsters of recent years, Lepke, Siegel, Zwillman, and Kastel are dead—Lepke electrocuted at Sing Sing, Siegel executed in Beverly Hills, Zwillman a suicide by hanging in the basement of his twenty-room New Jersey mansion, and Kastel by natural causes. Slowly, but inexorably, the Mafia has assumed a position of supremacy that is total and absolute.

No doubt the fact that its antisocial ideology is rooted in seven centuries of pathological lawlessness has something to do with its present power position. No other criminal group in history has ever been as cohesive and paternal as the Mafia. Through the years it has become a criminal hierarchy, with blood ties spanning all the large cities of western civilization. Every *mafioso,* young or old, truly believes that he has an inalienable right to traffic in dope and prostitution, to plunder and murder. The laws of organized society do not bind him. He is bound only by the laws of *Omertà,* and those laws are as inexorable as the *Koran*'s.

Births, weddings, and funerals are important social events. Murder is something else again. That is business and demands the most serious consideration. Friends, cousins, and even brothers will be enlisted in the execution of a defector. And sentimentality never interferes with the business of crime.

The *dons,* or *capi mafiosi,* are the recognized leaders of the Mafia. Each *don,* according to his power, rules over a certain category of crime, or coordinates over a certain area. He may, as in the case of the late Joe Profaci, be the coordinator of

223

Brooklyn. As a *don,* he settles disputes and decrees punishment and reward in that area. But as a coordinator of such an area, he has to pay tribute to *dons* who control the various categories of crimes practiced in his area. Lucky Luciano collected tribute on prostitution and narcotics, Frank Costello collected on numbers and gambling games. Others collected on extortion, bootlegging, counterfeiting, vending machines, and countless other rackets and vices.

A *don* is never formally elected but, rather like a fungus, naturally grows into a position of importance. A *don*'s power is determined by his responsibility. A *don* of a large metropolitan area is more powerful than a *don* of a small city. The most powerful *dons* of all are the ones who have a slice of a national racket plus a large metropolitan area. They sit on the Grand Council, representing important rackets and areas and the Mafia itself.

Such a *don* today is John Rosselli, the *capo mafioso* who succeeded Jack Dragna in Las Vegas when the latter succumbed to a heart attack in 1957. Rosselli is definitely of the new school —sharp silk suits, diamond accessories, swanky apartment, busty show girls in full-length minks, big Cadillac, gourmet taste, sportsman, golfer—the best of everything in the best of all possible worlds.

Medium in height, slim, with iron-gray hair and sharp-features, Rosselli is also a quiet man in an ostentatious way. He owns no property, has no visible interests in any hotel–casino, and is unemployed. In fact, he has been unemployed since 1949. Rosselli's police record is long, but except for the "three years, seven months, and thirteen days" he served in the Bioff movie-extortion case, he has deftly managed to stay on this side of prison walls.

In his 1950 appearance before the Kefauver Committee, he took a leaf out of Georgetti's reform book. He sat there wide-eyed and innocent as he answered counsel Rudolph Halley's questions:

Q. Since 1947 what have you been doing? [1947 was the year he was released from prison.]

A. Since 1947 I have been in the picture business. I came home and worked as an assistant purchasing agent at Eagle Lion Studios. I later was assistant producer to Brian Foy [the head of the studio at that time] and associate producer with Robert T. Cain productions. . . .

Q. Associate producer? How did you get into that?

A. I have always had some knowledge of the picture business. When I came home on parole I went to work at Eagle Lion Studios. I knew I couldn't live long on any $60 a week without having to borrow money. Mr. Foy thought I had the ability to become a producer.

Q. Since when have you been unemployed?

A. It is a little better than a year.

Q. What are the circumstances of your being unemployed? Are you simply retired?

A. No. The circumstances, I think, is that 2 years ago when my parole was revoked [just momentarily] I was in the process of making these two pictures and they were later released. Since then I just haven't been able to get any employment anywhere since Mr. Foy went to Warner Bros.

Q. What was your occupation before you went to prison?

A. . . . I was with the Pat Casey Enterprise. I was in the insurance business. Pat Casey is a labor-relations man in the [motion picture] industry. . . .

Q. For how long were you with them? . . .

A. [Since] about 1933.

Q. Perhaps we might do best by working up from the other end. When and where were you born?

A. I was born in Chicago in 1905, June 4, 1905.

Q. Where did you have your first employment?

A. Well, it is hard to say. I did almost anything. I sold newspapers, shined shoes. I went out to California at the age of 15 or thereabouts, worked around as an extra in pictures and at various jobs, odds and ends. . . .

Q. Were you in the liquor business during prohibition?

A. Well, in some manner; yes.

Q. Would you state what manner?

A. Very, very, very small.

Q. Where were you?

A. In Los Angeles. . . .

Q. Then between 1928 and 1933, up to the repeal of prohibition, did you come back to Chicago often? . . .

A. On occasions, sporting events and so on.

Q. Did you ever visit the Hotel Lexington, headquarters of the Capone gang?

A. Yes, sir.

Q. You knew Al Capone?

A. I did know Al Capone.

Q. When did you first meet him?

A. During the Tunney–Dempsey fight.

Q. Who introduced you?

A. There must have been a thousand people in that place, at the Metropole Hotel. I guess everybody clamored to get up there.

Q. You must have been in the mob, so to speak at that time, to have gotten there and gotten in to see the big man.

A. No, sir. Al Jolson and quite a number of others.

Q. You weren't a celebrity, you were younger.

A. No. I was just taken there.

Q. Let's not just brush this off quickly, Mr. Rosselli.
It is all ancient history.

A. Surely, I know. To the best of my recollection, I
will tell you about it.

Q. Let's try to take it a little slower and not give it a
quick coat of varnish. . . .

But a quick coat of varnish was all the Senators got from
Rosselli. The reformed citizen did not feel like informing on
anybody, much less on himself. But, of course, having assumed
the image of reformation, he could not very well take cover
behind the Fifth Amendment. Instead he took cover behind a
faulty memory. On direct questions, linking him with top mobsters across the country, he admitted knowing just about everybody mentioned, but only casually, having run into them just
accidentally at sporting events and restaurants and hotels. Included in a long list were: Charlie Fischetti, Jack Dragna, Mo
Mo Adamo, Tony Accardo, Phil Kastel, Frank Costello, Gene
Normile, Mickey Cohen, Joe Sica, Bugsy Siegel, Joe Adonis,
Lil Augie Pisano, Joe Massei, Tony Gizzo, Frank Nitti, Sam
"Golf Bag" Hunt, Moe Sedway, Jack "Machine Gun" McGurn,
Paul "The Waiter" Ricca, Bones Remmer, Meyer Lansky, Louis
Campagna, Tony Cornero, Black Tony Parmagini, Frank Mi-
lano, Al Polizzi, Willie Moretti, Joe Profaci, Sam Maceo,
Lucky Luciano. With such friends, who needed a job?

Later in the testimony, Rosselli admitted working as a torpedo for Gene Normile, who operated the Nationwide wire
service for Moe Annenberg in Los Angeles in the middle
Thirties.

Q. . . . What were you going to do for your cut [2.5
to 10 per cent] in the business?

A. Get some customers for him.

227

Q. What customers did you get him?

A. To create good will. Bookmakers, I guess. . . .

Q. And what was your influence over these book-makers?

A. None at all.

Q. Was Nationwide competing with anybody else?

A. Not at all.

Q. He had no trouble selling wire service?

A. Yes, he would, I guess; maybe. Some could get along without him and others could not.

Q. Now, Mr. Rosselli, who could get along without it if they could get it? You know very well the wire service was something that every bookie wanted and really couldn't live without. If he couldn't get it he had to steal it some-where.

A. True enough. So they would be stealing it.

Q. So you didn't have to go around selling it?

A. So I would probably talk somebody into not steal-ing it.

Q. How did you persuade people to not steal it?

A. Just by discussing it with them.

Q. You had a lot of friends.

A. I had a lot of friends, yes. . . .

Q. You had a reputation for being perhaps a tough guy?

A. I probably did during prohibition.

Q. That reputation stayed with you, I suppose?

A. To my sorrow.

Q. It didn't hurt you much when you were trying to sell wire service; did it?

A. I don't like it today. . . .

John Rosselli is still trying to fob off the "reformed" image on anyone gullible enough to swallow it. Meanwhile, he lives the good life of a respected "elder." Don Giovanni, as he is known to the *mafiosi,* is soft-spoken and polite. The rough edges of the old torpedo days have been polished to a fine patina of masculine gentility. Gorgeous show girls—not top entertainers, but climbers—hover about him like pigeons waiting for a crumb of bread.

Rosselli spends his leisure hours (that is, all the waking hours of his day) at the Desert Inn Country Club. He has breakfast there in the morning, seated at a table overlooking the eighteenth green. Between golf rounds, meals, steam baths, shaves and trims, Twisting, romancing, and drinking, there is time for private little conferences at his favorite table with people seeking his counsel or friendship. It may be a newsman, a local politician, a casino owner, a prostitute, a famous entertainer, a deputy sheriff, a U.S. Senator, or the Governor of Nevada.

The only thing that has kept Nevada from plunging headlong into the depths of criminality has been pressure from the outside, the fear of national public opinion that would bring federal intervention into its local government. Nevertheless, in Nevada the hoodlum is admired not only by the society he has created in his own image but by the millions of tourists who look upon him as a jovial innkeeper and sportsman, a charming rogue in the tradition of the old Mississippi gambler. The hoodlum must be stripped of this glamour and "respectability" and exposed for the vermin that he is.

The Justice Department has assigned eighty-six investigators to Las Vegas since Robert F. Kennedy took over as Attorney General. The new attack is called "Operation Big Squeeze" and the idea is to make a systematic probe of the gambling town on four major points:

1. The extent to which it is being used as a meeting place for the heads of organized crime.

2. Whether a race wire service is being operated there for the benefit of bookmakers throughout the nation.
3. The background of some of the proprietors of state-licensed gambling casinos.
4. A check of the "counting room" operation at each casino to determine how much is slipping away tax-free into the underworld.

This is a giant and ambitious step, but so far it has not unduly alarmed the gambling fraternity. It is not the first time the federal government has promised an investigation of Las Vegas. Since the Kefauver probe it has been "systematically" investigated every single year with the same lack of results. Unfortunately, there has been too much quixotic windmilling along a forensic line, and too little realistic application of existing laws and federal executive powers.

If ever an enemy had a fifth column, it is organized crime. This fifth column is made up of naïve citizens and corrupt police officials, prosecutors, jurists, and politicians everywhere, from the lowly precinct to the nation's capital. In *The Enemy Within,* Robert F. Kennedy writes:

It seems to me imperative that we reinstill in ourselves the toughness and idealism that guided the nation in the past. The paramount interest in self, in material wealth, in security must be replaced by an actual, not just a vocal, interest in our country, by a spirit of adventure, a will to fight what is evil, and a desire to serve. It is up to us as citizens to take the initiative as it has been taken before in our history, to reach out boldly but with honesty to do the things that need to be done.

To meet the challenge of our times, so that we can later look back upon this era not as one of which we need be ashamed but as a turning point on the way to a better America, we must first defeat the enemy within.

It is time to wake up. This job belongs to all of us, not only to law-enforcement agencies, the courts, and elected officials. This is our fight. We, the citizens, must take the first step in the battle against "the enemy within." And the first step is to stop patronizing him. Remember, the power of the underworld is not a gun. It is money. Money in such overwhelming quantity that it staggers the imagination. Money that is used to corrupt and debase the very foundation of democracy. And that money is supplied by us: people who seek a little relaxation and don't see the harm in visiting a B-joint or brothel; or in placing a little bet with the corner bookie; or in buying some needed black-market item; or in accepting a little gratuity or bribe; or in voting for a candidate with hoodlum ties; or in allowing some punk to get away with blackmail; or in paying some other punk for the privilege of operating a constitutionally guaranteed business; or in traveling that crowded sucker route to Nevada.

Make no mistake about it, this is war; war against parasites and sycophants who feed and grow strong on human weaknesses. It is total war and there is no middle ground between combatants. We stand on opposite sides of a trench. It's either fight now or let the hoodlum horde dump us into that trench just in time for somebody else to come along and bury us. Remember, Rome succumbed to the barbarians only after it had succumbed to its own decadence.

APPENDIX

DUNES HOTEL

Licensees		Percentage
Wilbert Basinger	R.D. 1, Industry, Pa.	1.00
George Duckworth	812 Bracken, Las Vegas	6.00
Wendel S. Fletcher	1591 Virginia Ave., San Marino, Cal.	15.00
Louis M. Gengerella	1129 Beaver Ave., Midland, Pa.	1.00
Joseph Hersch	6622 St. Francis Ter., Hollywood, Cal.	1.00
Robert Rice	1311 South 5th Pl., Las Vegas	12.72
M. A. Riddle	812 Bracken, Las Vegas	37.28
Charles J. Rich	2622 W. Charleston, Las Vegas	12.00
Jerome Steinbaum	1109 Tower Rd., Beverly Hills, Cal.	2.00
Sidney Wyman	Dunes Hotel, Las Vegas	12.00

DESERT INN (Wilbur Clark's)

Licensees		Percentage
Wilbur Clark	313 Desert Inn Rd., Las Vegas	17.20
M. B. Dalitz	Desert Inn Hotel, Las Vegas	13.20
Cornelius J. Jones	Desert Inn Hotel, Las Vegas	2.00
Robert Kaye	Desert Inn Hotel, Las Vegas	5.00
Morris Kleinman	9861 E. Broadview Dr., Miami Beach, Fla.	13.20
Ruby Kolod	339 Desert Inn Rd., Las Vegas	13.10
Cornelius Krausnick	Desert Inn Hotel, Las Vegas	3.00
Martin Kutzen	Desert Inn Hotel, Las Vegas	1.00
Victor J. Mandotte	1208 Cashman Dr., Las Vegas	1.00
Thomas J. McGinty	142 Seaspray, West Palm Beach, Fla.	7.10
Allard Roen	355 Desert Inn Rd., Las Vegas	2.50
Bernard Rothkopf	341 Desert Inn Rd., Las Vegas	2.50
Cecil Simmons	37 Country Club Dr., East Las Vegas	1.00
Sam Solomon	1144 Westwood Dr., Las Vegas	1.00

Licensees		Percentage
Frank Soskin	1318 Houssells Ave., Las Vegas	1.00
Samuel A. Tucker	1437 88th St., Surfside, Fla.	13.20
Claude M. Webb	5236 Harris St., Las Vegas	1.00
Treasury		2.00

FLAMINGO HOTEL

Licensees		Percentage
Morris Baker	464 Desert Inn Rd., Las Vegas	1.00
Edward J. Barrick	1618 W. Charleston, Las Vegas	5.00
John R. Bean	186 N. Canon, Los Angeles	2.00
Samuel Cohen	2995 Flamingo Dr., Miami Beach, Fla.	42.75
John D. Gaughan	1131 Comstock Dr., Las Vegas	3.00
Morris S. Lansburgh	4887 Pine Tree, Miami Beach, Fla.	16.50
Daniel Lifter	2142 Sunset Isle #2, Miami Beach, Fla.	22.50
Sam Siegman	413 South 15th St., Omaha, Neb.	3.50
Chester Simms	1308 South 6th St., Las Vegas	3.75

FREMONT HOTEL

Licensees		Percentage
Edward J. Barrick	1618 W. Charleston, Las Vegas	3.00
Ben Bingham	1400 Santa Margarita, Arcadia, Cal.	1.50
Orville D. Bryant	920 W. Bonanza Rd., Las Vegas	.50
Bryant R. Burton	611 Wilshire Blvd., Los Angeles	5.00
Marvin Cole	9033 Wilshire Blvd., Beverly Hills, Cal.	9.00
Sam Delich	540 Oakey Blvd., Las Vegas	1.00
Louie Garfinkle	1818 Rexford, Apt. 4, Las Vegas	.75
James J. Hill	27 Country Club Lane, Las Vegas	.75
Connie Hurley	2231 W. Charleston, Las Vegas	5.00
Edward Levinson	3125 Ashby, Las Vegas	20.00
Richard E. Levinson	3708 Apache Lane, Las Vegas	3.00
Joseph M. Lyden	321 Pardway East, Las Vegas	1.00

Appendix

Licensees		Percentage
Wayne D. McAllister	206 Via DiJon, Newport Beach, Cal.	1.50
Lee McRitchie	1358 Polk St., Hollywood, Cal.	8.00
Jerome D. Mack	1501 South 6th, Las Vegas	12.00
Frank J. Mooney	205 Sunset Dr., Las Vegas	.50
Dixie E. Reese	116 South 10th, Las Vegas	.50
Lester Siegelbaum	4th Floor, DuPont Plaza Bldg., Miami, Fla.	3.00
Louis H. Stone	3478 S. Paradise Rd., Las Vegas	5.00
Edward Torres	Fremont Hotel, Las Vegas	6.00
Paul Weyerman	1912 Rexford, Apt. 3, Las Vegas	3.00
Sam Ziegman	103 South 52nd St., Omaha, Neb.	2.00

HACIENDA
(Owned by two separate groups)

Licensees (First Group)		Percentage
Warren Bayley	Hacienda Hotel, Las Vegas	80.50
Orville E. Chedester	Rt. 5, Box 381, Visalia, Cal.	4.50
Harold L. Curfew	7913 Melva St., Downey, Cal.	8.50
Emma E. Martell } LeRoy Martell	114 S. Locust, Visalia, Cal.	.50
Benjamin Seideman	1532 South 7th St., Las Vegas	3.00
Robert Seideman	1904 Rexford, Las Vegas	3.00

Licensees (Second Group)		Percentage
Warren Bayley	Hacienda Hotel, Las Vegas	26.65
James Boris	6333 West 3rd, Los Angeles	1.66
Orville E. Chedester	Rt. 5, Box 381, Visalia, Cal.	10.70
Shields B. Craft	10503 Mahoney Dr., Sunland, Cal.	4.16
Harold Curfew	7913 Melva St., Downey, Cal.	4.16
Louis Dessel	4502 Highland Place, Riverside, Cal.	3.33
R. C. Fuller	1616 Virginia Ave., Glendale, Cal.	2.50
R. E. S. Hesse	933 E. Cross St., Tulare, Cal.	2.30
Henry Hoeneman	315 N. Adams, Sierra Madre, Cal.	.30
Frank Hofues, Sr., Est.	9201 Wilshire Blvd., Beverly Hills, Cal.	1.66

Licensees (Second Group)

		Percentage
C. E. Jame	546 Grand Ave., Oakland, Cal.	1.66
Charlotte Jarratt	1655 East 65th St., Long Beach, Cal.	5.00
Elsa Koepke	5119 El Rio Ave., Los Angeles	2.26
LeRoy Martell Emma E. Martell }	114 S. Locust, Visalia, Cal.	2.80
Vincent Matthews	Box 436, Norfolk, Conn.	3.33
Hubert J. Miller	7953 Mt. Vernon St., Lemon Grove, Cal.	.60
Emerson Morgan	1230 Sunset Plaza Dr., Los Angeles	3.33
Florence Mulconnery	2131 West 37th St., San Pedro, Cal.	1.66
Wm. J. Mulconnery	2131 West 37th St., San Pedro, Cal.	4.66
J. H. Overholser	4530 Gable Dr., Encino, Cal.	4.10
John Rankaitis	7401 Naylor, Los Angles	1.00
Karl Reinhard	3706 Rosehedge Dr., Fullerton, Cal.	2.50
Benjamin Seideman	1532 South 7th St., Las Vegas	2.50
Robert M. Seideman	1904 Rexford, Las Vegas	2.50
Sophia Sexton	10017 Wiley Burke Ave., Downey, Cal.	1.66
Edward Terrazzi	1218 W. St. Andrews Pl., Santa Ana, Cal.	1.66

THE HORSESHOE CLUB

Licensees

		Percentage
Alvah O. Askin	239 Spencer St., Las Vegas	1.00
Fred Ayoub	2038 E. Charleston Blvd., Las Vegas	1.00
Robert E. Ayoub	2001 Franklin Ave., Las Vegas	1.00
Edward J. Barrick	1618 W. Charleston Blvd., Las Vegas	7.00
Jack Binion	2040 Bonanza Rd., Las Vegas	25.00
Bryant R. Burton	755 Hampton Rd., Arcadia, Cal.	2.00
Marvin R. Cole	9033 Wilshire Blvd., Beverly Hills, Cal.	2.00
Sam Delich	1700 Rexford Dr., Las Vegas	2.00
George Deverell	1711 Lewis St., Las Vegas	2.00
Leo Durr	3478 Paradise Rd., Las Vegas	6.00
Frank C. Falba	1725 Howard Ave., Las Vegas	1.00
Fritz Gerisch	1247 Douglas Dr., Las Vegas	1.00
John Grandi	1717 Cochran, Las Vegas	1.00
Connie Hurley	2231 W. Charleston, Las Vegas	6.00

Licensees		Percentage
Edward Levinson	3125 Ashby, Las Vegas	27.50
Jack Newman	1908 Rexford Dr., Las Vegas	2.00
Operating Co.		2.00
Oscar Rubinsky	601 Decatur Lane, Las Vegas	2.00
Paul E. Weyerman	1912 Rexford Pl., Apt. 3, Las Vegas	5.00
Harry E. Wrest	547 San Pablo, Las Vegas	1.00
Sam Ziegman	103 South 52nd St., Omaha, Neb.	2.50

THE MINT CASINO

Licensees		Shares
Dr. Montrose Bernstein	404 N. Roxbury Dr., Beverly Hills, Cal.	182
Sam Boyd	548 Griffith Ave., Las Vegas	68
Curtis Bryant	1611 Hastings Ave., Las Vegas	23
Herman Cassell	540 Oakey Blvd., Apt. 104, Las Vegas	23
Albert Garbian	% Lucky Strike Club, Las Vegas	45
Gil Gilbert	1700 Rexford, Apt. 205, Las Vegas	34
Harry A. Goldman	% Albert Parvin Co., 120 N. Robertson Blvd., Los Angeles	114
J. D. Hall	151 S. Rodeo Dr., Beverly Hills, Cal.	159
Vic Hall	2555 Sherwood St., Las Vegas	68
William Heath	Sahara Hotel, Las Vegas	114
John Hughes	750 Rancho Circle, Las Vegas	45
L. C. Jacobsen	Box 4066, Phoenix, Ariz.	114
Sidney Krystal	711 Roosevelt Bldg., 727 West 7th St., Los Angeles	23
Ed Mapel	709 Rancho Circle, Las Vegas	182
Kenneth Mapel	2209 Van Patten Pl., Las Vegas	11
Barney Morris	Sahara Hotel, Las Vegas	114
Edward R. Moss	1255 Arville, Las Vegas	23
Donald O'Connor	Blau, Miller & Shaw, 139 S. Beverly Hills Dr., Beverly Hills, Cal.	58
Robert E. Paradise	711 Roosevelt Bldg., 727 West 7th St., Los Angeles	23
Ralph Parker	Box 598, Tacoma, Wash.	23

237

Licensees		Shares
Milton Prell	Sahara Hotel, Las Vegas	227
Frank Schivo	565 E. St. Louis, Las Vegas	23
Alex Shoofey	Sahara Hotel, Las Vegas	23
Bernard Van der Steen	Box 3143, Beverly Hills, Cal.	56
A. F. Winter	Sahara Hotel, Las Vegas	227

NEW FRONTIER HOTEL

Licensees		Percentage
Warren Bayley	Las Vegas Hacienda, Las Vegas	90.00
Emma E. Martell ⎱ LeRoy Martell ⎰	2046 Sunset Dr., Visalia, Cal.	2.00
Karl Reinhard	3706 Rosehedge Dr., Fullerton, Cal.	8.00

RIVIERA HOTEL

Licensees		Percentage
Samuel Abrams	95 Wilshire Blvd., Beverly Hills, Cal.	1.00
Elias Atol	Riviera Hotel, Las Vegas	5.50
Frank J. Atol	1806 Rexford Dr., Las Vegas	1.50
Frederick J. Atol	1511 S. Main, Las Vegas	1.00
John M. Atol	2600 Greyslon Rd., Duluth, Minn.	1.00
Ernest W. Bates	413 South 4th St., Springfield, Ill.	2.00
Dave Berman Est.	Riviera Hotel, Las Vegas	4.50
Irving Briskin	10871 Chalon Rd., Bel Air, Los Angeles	2.50
Max Garth	826 S. Cloverdale, Los Angeles	1.25
Ben Goffstein	393 Desert Inn Rd., Las Vegas	2.50
J. Dee Goodman	2100 Kirkland Ave., Las Vegas	1.00
Gus Greenbaum Est.	Phoenix, Ariz.	12.50
Charles J. Harrison	126-3478 Paradise Rd., Las Vegas	2.00
Eugene Jordon	1206 Exchange Ave., Oklahoma City	3.00
Nathan S. Krems	1227 S. LaBrea Ave., Los Angeles	2.00

Licensees		Percentage
Tony Martin	1155 Shadowhill Way, Beverly Hills, Cal.	2.00
Edward Miller	2001 Santa Ynez Dr., Las Vegas	1.00
Ross Miller	28 Country Club Lane, Las Vegas	4.00
Bernard Nemerov	960 LaSenda Rd., Hillsborough, Cal.	4.00
Anthony I. Owens	1334 N. Beechwood Dr., Hollywood, Cal.	1.00
Treasury		43.75
Samuel Weiss	1126 San Julian, Los Angeles	1.00

SAHARA HOTEL

Licensees		Shares
Adolph Berman	907 S. Gramercy Pl., Los Angeles	192
Dr. Montrose Bernstein	404 N. Roxbury Dr., Beverly Hills, Cal.	191
Sam Boyd	400 South 16th, Las Vegas	96
Curtis Bryant	1611 Hastings, Las Vegas	96
Paul Camilli	% V. Silvestri, Sahara Hotel, Las Vegas	96
Lucille Cassell	540 Oakey Blvd., Las Vegas	96
Dr. Alexander Coblentz	717 North 5th St., Las Vegas	96
James Fleishman	623 Lumberman Bldg., Portland, Ore.	288
Robert Gordon	801 Park Paseo, Las Vegas	384
James Hannifin	2317 Canosa, Las Vegas	96
William H. Heath	Sahara Hotel, Las Vegas	496
Aaron Herman	569 E. St. Louis, Las Vegas	96
John P. Hoban	1619 Hastings, Las Vegas	96
John Hughes	750 Rancho Circle, Las Vegas	288
Milton Hyatt	Manchester Bldg., 311 S.W. 5th, Portland Ore.	190
L. C. Jacobson	Box 4066, Phoenix, Ariz.	1,920
Sidney Krystal	711 Roosevelt Bldg., 727 West 7th St., Los Angeles	96
Hermin Levin	2025 S.W. Vista, Portland, Ore.	96
Ed Mapel	709 Rancho Circle, Las Vegas	960
Kenneth Mapel	2208 Van Patten Pl., Las Vegas	96
Louis Miller	905 E. St. Louis, Las Vegas	96
E. D. Morgan	215 N. Broadway, Billings, Mont.	218
Barney Morris	Sahara Hotel, Las Vegas	532

Licensees		Percentage
Eddie Moss	1253 Arville, Las Vegas	384
Moe Moss	1829 E. St. Louis, Las Vegas	48
James W. Newman	1204 Arrowhead Ave., Las Vegas	48
Robert E. Paradise	727 West 7th St., Los Angeles	96
Ralph Parker	Sahara Hotel, Las Vegas	144
Milton Prell	Sahara Hotel, Las Vegas	674
Frank Schivo	565 E. St. Louis, Las Vegas	96
Alex Shoofey	1300 Cashman Dr., Las Vegas	144
Vincent Silvestri	Sahara Hotel, Las Vegas	192
Theodore Sutula	2416 E. McWilliams, Las Vegas	48
A. F. Winter	Sahara Hotel, Las Vegas	915

THE SANDS

Licensees		Percentage
Hyman Abrams	607 Boulevard, Revere, Mass.	9.00
L. R. Brooks	407 Lincoln Rd., Miami Beach, Fla.	4.00
Bryant R. Burton	611 Wilshire Blvd., Los Angeles	1.00
Carl Cohen	Sands Hotel, Las Vegas	9.50
Jack Entratter	720 E. Charleston Blvd., Las Vegas	12.00
Sadie S. Freeman	Sands Hotel, Las Vegas	10.00
Harry A. Goldman	% Albert Parvin & Co., 120 N. Robertson Blvd., Los Angeles	2.00
Charles Kandel	Sands Hotel, Las Vegas	3.00
Edward Levy	1804 S. Eighth Pl., Las Vegas	4.00
Dean Martin	601 Mountain Dr., Beverly Hills, Cal.	1.00
Albert Parvin	% Albert Parvin & Co., 120 N. Robertson Blvd., Los Angeles	2.00
Maxwell Rubin	% Albert Parvin & Co., 120 N. Robertson Blvd., Los Angeles	2.00
George F. Reese	Sands Hotel, Las Vegas	1.00
Jerry Ross	608 N. Rexford Dr., Beverly Hills, Cal.	2.50
Michael Shapiro	1253 Camden Dr., Beverly Hills, Cal.	2.50
Frank Sinatra	151 E. Camino Dr., Beverly Hills, Cal.	9.00
Treasury		21.00
Aaron Weisberg	Diplomat Apts., Paradise Rd., Las Vegas	4.50

SILVER SLIPPER

Licensees		Shares
Anthony T. Canino	1200 South 8th St., Las Vegas	2
Frank L. King	Box 1933, Texarkana, Tex.	8
Robert O. Schulze	3064 Kishner Dr., Las Vegas	120

STARDUST HOTEL

Licensees		Percentage
Wilbur Clark	303 Desert Inn Rd., Las Vegas	5.50
M. B. Dalitz	Desert Inn Hotel, Las Vegas	22.00
John F. Drew	333 Desert Inn Rd., Las Vegas	5.00
Milton Jaffe	Stardust Hotel, Las Vegas	2.00
Cornelius J. Jones	Desert Inn Hotel, Las Vegas	1.00
Robert Kaye	Desert Inn Hotel, Las Vegas	4.00
Morris Kleinman	12701 Shaker Blvd., Cleveland, Ohio	22.00
Ruby Kolod	339 Desert Inn Rd., Las Vegas	8.00
Thomas J. McGinty	3593 Washington Blvd., Cleveland Heights, Ohio	4.50
Allard Roen	355 Desert Inn Rd., Las Vegas	2.00
Bernard Rothkopf	341 Desert Inn Rd., Las Vegas	2.00
Samuel A. Tucker	1437 88th Dr., Surfside, Fla.	22.00

THUNDERBIRD HOTEL

Licensees		Shares
William Deer	Thunderbird Hotel, Las Vegas	7.2173
M. B. Hicks Est.	Thunderbird Hotel, Las Vegas	71.1308
Jack Lane	Los Angeles, Cal.	3.0072
James Schuyler	Thunderbird Hotel, Las Vegas	1.8043
Joe Wells	Thunderbird Hotel, Las Vegas	16.8404

TROPICANA HOTEL

Licensees		Shares
Paul Anderson	Box 602, Rancho Santa Fe, Cal.	4,835.2
Roger Clary	Box 70, Fort Walton Beach, Cal.	1,406.6
Edward J. Denvir	860 DeWitt Pl., Chicago, Ill.	200.0
Preston Feinberg	401 Parkway West, Las Vegas	2,059.3
Jackie Fields	1921 Ballard Dr., Las Vegas	300.0
W. D. Harrigan	Fulton, Alabama	8,547.4
J. K. Houssels, Sr.	1012 South 6th St., Las Vegas ⎫	
J. K. Houssels, Jr.	El Cortez Hotel, Las Vegas ⎭	8,583.2
Harold Johnson	738 Chicago St., Hammond, Ind.	1,900.6
Jack Kallis	1037 W. Congress Parkway, Chicago	918.8
Morton Kallis	1037 W. Congress Parkway, Chicago	218.6
Solomon B. Mirsky	3180 Lake Shore Drive, Chicago	2,189.3
Dr. Richard Muckerman Trustee Est. Richard C. Muckerman	63 Lake Forest St., St. Louis, Mo.	1,097.0
Sidney Saltz	412 S. Wells St., Chicago	1,976.0
Louis Urban	Rt. 1, Dundee, Ill.	425.0
Mrs. Grace Valentine	744 Broad St., Rm. 2001, Newark, N.J.	548.5
Harold Valentine	744 Broad St., Rm. 2001, Newark, N.J.	2,227.9